The Good Citizen

The Good Citizen

How a Younger Generation Is Reshaping American Politics

Revised Edition

Russell J. Dalton
University of California, Irvine

CQ PRESS

A Division of SAGE
Washington, D.C.

CQ Press
2300 N Street, NW, Suite 800
Washington, DC 20037

Phone: 202-729-1900; toll-free, 1-866-4CQ-PRESS (1-866-427-7737)

Web: www.cqpress.com

Cover design and illustration: Jeffrey Everett, El Jefe Design
Composition: BMWW

☺ The paper used in this publication exceeds the requirements of the American National Standard for Information Sciences—Permanence of Paper for Printed Library Materials, ANSI Z39.48-1992.

Printed and bound in the United States of America

12   11   10   09   08   1   2   3   4   5

Library of Congress Cataloging-in-Publication Data

Dalton, Russell J.
    The good citizen : how a younger generation is reshaping American politics / Russell J. Dalton. — Rev. ed.
        p. cm.
    Includes bibliographical references and index.
    ISBN 978-1-60426-556-9 (alk. paper)
        1. Citizenship—United States.   2. Voluntarism—United States.
3. Youth—United States—Political activity.   4. Political culture—United States.   5. United States—Politics and government—2001–   I. Title.

    JK1759.D179 2009
    324.0835'0973—dc22

                                                                    2008052009

To Jack Peltason
A colleague, then a mentor,
and now a friend

10 percent of this book's royalties go to aid programs for Darfur and other parts of Africa.

CONTENTS

TABLES AND FIGURES

PREFACE TO THE REVISED EDITION

wo years ago, this book made the argument that the academic chorus criticizing the American public—and young people in particular—had overlooked evidence to the contrary. Previous scholarship had produced a conventional wisdom that seemed to see only the negatives and overlook the positives. This conventional wisdom looked to the past with excessive admiration and to the future with guarded pessimism.

The catchphrase for the first edition was: "The good news is . . . the bad news is wrong" (or at least overstated). *The Good Citizen* argued that changing norms of citizenship were transforming American politics and society. The book described the positive and negative elements of this shift in citizenship norms and tried to provide a more balanced view of contemporary American democracy and its prospects for the future.

This study also had a strong generational theme. Like others, I saw much to admire in the "greatest generation" that lived through the Great Depression and World War II. But I also saw elements of greatness or potential greatness among American youth. So the first edition discussed the strengths and weaknesses of different generations and did not succumb to the idea that to praise senior Americans one must denigrate the young.

THE REVISED EDITION

The themes of *The Good Citizen* ran counter to the general tide in political science, which was pessimistic about the public and American youth. Books such as *The Dumbest Generation* castigated the young or skeptically asked *Is Voting for Young People?* Then came the 2008 U.S. presidential election. In a new epilogue, I discuss that election in the context of this book's central themes.

I think it is fair to say that conventional political science research implied that Barack Obama's campaign was doomed to failure. As one of the leading academic specialists on voting wrote on the eve of the Iowa caucuses: "Conventional wisdom has a name for candidates who rely on the youth vote: loser." His skepticism, and that of a score of other election specialists, proved incorrect. Obama amazed most observers by winning the Democratic Party's nomination. What was even more amazing is that Obama accomplished this with young voters as a major part of his coalition. And in November he won the election to become the forty-fourth president of the United States.

I view this as a transformational election in many ways—but one that is consistent with the themes in this book. A reader of *The Good Citizen* in 2007 would not be surprised either by Obama's successful appeal to young Americans or by their participation.

The epilogue to this revised edition focuses on the role of young people in the 2008 elections and their attraction to the Obama candidacy. The epilogue traces Obama's electoral success through the primaries and caucuses and explains the participation and support he received from young, engaged citizens. It also describes voting patterns in the general election and the appeal of Obama to various social and political groups. Finally, the epilogue discusses the potential long-term implications of Obama's mobilization of young Americans. What does 2008 say about the changing nature of American politics?

In addition, I added a brief statistical primer to help students understand the analyses of public opinion presented throughout the book, especially the interpretation of correlations and similar statistics. The primer appears as Appendix A.

The CQ Press Web site for this book now includes a *Statistical Package for the Social Sciences* (SPSS) subset of the 2004 General Social Survey that provided the main source of public opinion data for this book. This data file is available for free download for those who want to provide this research option to their students (see www.cqpress.com/cs/dalton).

ACKNOWLEDGMENTS

This project drew upon the support of many people. Part of the initiative came from the Citizenship, Involvement, and Democracy (CID) project at the Center for Democracy and Civil Society (CDACS) at Georgetown University. I thank Marc Howard and CDACS for this experience and for the use of the CID survey in this book. My thanks also go to the other members of the CID project: Sam Barnes, Jack Citrin, James Gibson, Greg Marcus, Eric Oliver, Kay Scholzman, Dietlind Stolle, Erik Uslaner, Mark Warren, and Cara Wong. The 2004 General Social Survey and the 2004 International Social Survey Program are the other major empirical resources for this study. I am indebted to the consortium of scholars who design and collect these extremely valuable resources for social sciences research.

Many colleagues have commented on various portions of this research as the project developed, and I thank them for their advice: Matt Beckmann, E.J. Dionne, Miki Caul Kittilson, Steve Weldon, and Christian Welzel. Pam Kelly shared the Bono quote at the end of the book, and Elizabeth Schiller provided valuable assistance. Students in some of my courses at UC Irvine read and commented on parts of this project, and they broadened my understanding of young Americans (I learned about Facebook from them). My UC Irvine colleague Martin Wattenberg was very helpful as I wrote this book, although his *Is Voting for Young People?* expresses a much different view. We did not change each other's minds, but the dialogue and the data Marty shared helped me develop my research. Finally, I want to acknowledge Ronald Inglehart. His studies of postmaterial/self-expressive values provide the intellectual base for much of this presentation, even though I present his logic in different terms.

My thanks also go to CQ Press, especially Charisse Kiino, David Rapp, and Carolyn Goldinger, for their support of this project. They are a wonderful team to work with and produced a book that I hope students and their instructors will read and debate.

Finally, I am honored to dedicate this book to Jack Peltason. Jack is part of the greatest generation, but he represents the freshness of new values to me. He took a leadership role in integrating the University of Illinois when he was chancellor; his scholarship focused on the role of the courts in expanding civil rights in America, and several generations of students learned about American politics from his textbook. He served as chancellor at UC Irvine and then as president of the University of California. Jack devoted his career to improving higher education in America and expanding the horizons of our young citizens. And he enriched my understanding of universities, American politics, and democracy.

Russell J. Dalton
Irvine, California

The Good Citizen

CITIZENSHIP AND THE TRANSFORMATION OF AMERICAN SOCIETY

> Every age since the ancient Greeks fashioned an
> image of being political [is] based upon citizenship
>
> Engin Isin, *Being Political*

What does it mean to be a "good citizen" in today's society? In an article on the 2005 annual UCLA survey of college freshmen, the *Los Angeles Times* presented an interview with a California university student who had spent his semester break as a volunteer helping to salvage homes flooded by Hurricane Katrina.[1] The young man had organized a group of student volunteers, who then gave up their break to do hard labor in the devastated region far from their campus. He said finding volunteers willing to work "was easier than I expected." Indeed, the gist of the article was that volunteering in 2005 was at its highest percentage in the 25 years of the college survey.

Later I spoke with another student who also had traveled to the Gulf Coast. Beyond the work on Katrina relief, he was active on a variety of social and political causes, from problems of development in Africa, to campus politics, to the war in Iraq. When I asked about his interest in political parties and elections, however, there was stark lack of interest. Like many of his fellow students, he had not voted in the last election. He had not participated at all in the 2004 campaign, which was his first opportunity to vote. This behavior seems paradoxical considering the effort involved; it's just a short walk from the campus to the nearest polling station, but almost a two thousand mile drive along Interstate 10 to New Orleans.

These stories illustrate some of the ways that the patterns of citizenship are changing. Many young people in America—and in other Western democracies as well—are concerned about their society and others in the world. And they are willing to contribute their time and effort to make a difference. They see a role for themselves and their government in improving the world in which we all live. At the same time, they relate to government and society in different ways than their elders. Research in the United States and other advanced industrial democracies shows that modern-day citizens are the most educated, most cosmopolitan, and most supportive of self-expressive values than any other public in the history of democracy.[2] So from both anecdotal and empirical perspectives, most of the social and political changes in the American public over the past half-century would seem to have strengthened the foundations of democracy.

Despite this positive and hopeful view of America, however, a very different story is being told today in political and academic circles. An emerging consensus among political analysts would have us believe that the foundations of citizenship and democracy are crumbling. Just recently, a new study cosponsored by the American Political Science Association and the Brookings Institution begins:

> *American democracy is at risk. The risk comes not from some external threat but from disturbing internal trends: an erosion of the activities and capacities of citizenship. Americans have turned away from politics and the public sphere in large numbers, leaving our civic life impoverished. Citizens participate in public affairs less frequently, with less knowledge and enthusiasm, in fewer venues, and less equally than is healthy for a vibrant democratic polity.*[3]

A host of political analysts now bemoans what is wrong with America and its citizens.[4] Too few of us are voting, we are disconnected from our fellow citizens and lacking in social capital, we are losing our national identity, we are losing faith in our government, and the nation is in social disarray. The *lack* of good citizenship is the phrase you hear most often to explain these disturbing trends.

What you also hear is that the young are the primary source of this decline. Authors from Robert Putman to former television news anchor Tom Brokaw extol the civic values and engagement of the older, "greatest generation" with great hyperbole.[5] Putnam holds that the slow, steady, and ineluctable replacement of older, civic-minded generations by the disaffected Generation X is the most important reason for the erosion of social capital in America.[6] Political analysts and politicians seemingly agree that young Americans are dropping out of politics, losing faith in government, and even becoming disenchanted with their personal lives.[7] Perhaps not since Aristotle held that "political science is not a proper study for the young" have youth been so roundly denounced by their elders.

Here we have two very different images of American society and politics. One perspective says American democracy is "at risk" in large part because of the changing values and participation patterns of the young. The other view points to new patterns of citizenship that have emerged among the young, the better educated, and other sectors of American society. These opposing views have generated sharp debates about the vitality of our democracy, and they are the subject of this book.

Perhaps the subtitle for this volume should be: "The good news is . . . the bad news is wrong." Indeed, something is changing in American society and politics. But is it logical to conclude, as many do, that if politics is not working as it did in the past, then our entire system of democracy is at risk? To understand what is changing, and its implications for American democracy, it is more helpful first to ask that simple but fundamental question:

What does it mean to be a good citizen in America today?

Take a moment to think of how you would answer. What are the criteria you would use? Voting? Paying taxes? Obeying the law? Volunteer work? Public protests? Being concerned for those in need? Membership in a political party? Trusting government officials?

This book examines how the American public answers this question— and the fact is, people answer it in different ways. This study will argue that the changing definition of what it means to be a good citizen—what I call the *norms of citizenship*—provides the key to understanding what is really going on.

Let's begin the analysis by examining the social restructuring of American society (Figure 1.1). Changing living standards, occupational

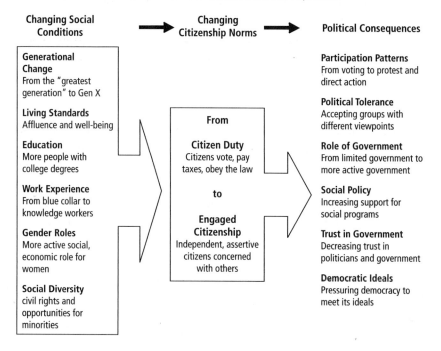

FIGURE 1.1   The Changing American Public

▶ *Changing social conditions reshape the norms of what it means to be a good citizen, and this affects how citizens act and think about politics.*

Changing Social Conditions	Changing Citizenship Norms	Political Consequences
Generational Change From the "greatest generation" to Gen X		**Participation Patterns** From voting to protest and direct action
Living Standards Affluence and well-being	**From**	**Political Tolerance** Accepting groups with different viewpoints
Education More people with college degrees	**Citizen Duty** Citizens vote, pay taxes, obey the law	**Role of Government** From limited government to more active government
Work Experience From blue collar to knowledge workers	**to**	**Social Policy** Increasing support for social programs
Gender Roles More active social, economic role for women	**Engaged Citizenship** Independent, assertive citizens concerned with others	**Trust in Government** Decreasing trust in politicians and government
Social Diversity civil rights and opportunities for minorities		**Democratic Ideals** Pressuring democracy to meet its ideals

experiences, generational change, the entry of women into the labor force, expanding civil rights, and other societal changes are producing two reinforcing effects. First, people possess new skills and resources that enable them to better manage the complexities of politics—people today are better educated, have more information available to them, and enjoy a higher standard of living. This removes some of the restrictions on democratic citizenship that might have existed in earlier historical periods when these skills and resources were less commonly available. Second, social forces are reshaping social and political values. Americans are more assertive and less deferential to authority, and they place more emphasis on participating in the decisions affecting their lives. The expansion of these self-expressive values has a host of political implications.[8]

These social changes have a direct effect on the norms of citizenship, if for no other reason than that citizenship norms are the encapsulation of the nation's political culture. They essentially define what people think is expected of them as participants in the political system, along with their expectations of government and the political process.

Most definitions of citizenship typically focus on the traditional norms of American citizenship—voting, paying taxes, belonging to a political party—and how these are changing. I call this **duty-based citizenship** because these norms reflect the formal obligations, responsibilities, and rights of citizenship as they have been defined in the past.

However, it is just as important to examine new norms that make up what I call **engaged citizenship.** These norms are emerging among the American public with increasing prominence. Engaged citizenship emphasizes a more assertive role for the citizen and a broader definition of the elements of citizenship to include social concerns and the welfare of others. As illustrated by the Katrina volunteers, many Americans believe they are fully engaged in society even if they do not vote or conform to traditional definitions of citizenship. Moreover, the social and political transformation of the United States over the past several decades has systematically shifted the balance between these different norms of citizenship. Duty-based norms are decreasing, especially among the young, but the norms of engaged citizenship are increasing.

Figure 1.1 illustrates the point that social and demographic changes affect citizenship norms, which in turn affect the political values and behavior of the public. For instance, duty-based norms of citizenship stimulate turnout in elections and a sense of patriotic allegiance to the elected government, while engaged citizenship may promote other forms of political action, ranging from volunteerism to public protest. These contrasting norms also shape other political values, such as tolerance of others and public policy priorities. Even respect for government itself is influenced by how individuals define their own norms of citizenship.

American politics and the citizenry are changing. Before anyone can deliver a generalized indictment of the American public, it is important to have a full understanding of how citizenship norms are changing and the effects of these changes. It is undeniable that the American public at the beginning of the twenty-first century is different from the American electorate in the mid-twentieth century. However, some of these differences actually can benefit American democracy, such as increased political tolerance and acceptance of diversity in society and politics. Other generational differences are just different—not a threat to American democracy unless these changes are ignored or resisted. A full examination of citizenship norms and their consequences will provide a more complex, and potentially more optimistic, picture of the challenges and opportunities facing American democracy today.

In addition, it is essential to place the American experience in a broader cross-national context. Many scholars who study American politics still study *only* American politics. This leads to an introspective, parochial view of what is presumably unique about the American experience and how patterns of citizenship may, or may not be, idiosyncratic to the United States. American politics is the last field of area-study research in which one nation is examined by itself. Many trends apparent in American norms of citizenship and political activity are common to other advanced industrial democracies. Other patterns may be distinctly American. Only by broadening the field of comparison can we ascertain the similarities and the differences.

The shift in the norms of citizenship does not mean that American democracy does not face challenges in response to new citizen demands and new patterns of action. Indeed, the vitality of democracy is that it must, and usually does, respond to such challenges, and this in turn strengthens the democratic process. But it is my contention that political reforms must reflect a true understanding of the American public and its values. By accurately recognizing the current challenges, and responding to them rather than making dire claims about political decay, American democracy can continue to evolve and develop. The fact remains, we cannot return to the politics of the 1950s, and we probably should not want to. But we can improve the democratic process if we first understand how Americans and their world are really changing.

THE SOCIAL TRANSFORMATION OF AMERICA

I recently took a cab ride from Ann Arbor, Michigan, to the Detroit airport, and the cab driver retold the story of the American dream as his life story. Now, driving a cab is not a fun job; it requires long hours, uncertainty, and typically brings in a modest income. The cab driver had grown up in the Detroit area. His relatives worked in the auto plants, and he drove a cab as a second job to make ends meet. We started talking about politics, and when he learned I was a university professor, he told me of his children. His son had graduated from the University of Michigan and had begun a successful business career. He was even prouder of his daughter, who was finishing law school. "All this on a cab driver's salary," he said with great pride in his children.

If you live in America, you have heard this story many times. It is the story of American society. The past five decades have seen this story repeated over and over again because this has been a period of exceptional social and political change.[9] There was a tremendous increase in the average standard of living as the American economy expanded. The postwar baby boom generation reaped these benefits, and, like the cab driver's children, were often the first in their family to attend college. The civil rights movement of the 1960s and 1970s ended centuries of official governmental recognition and acceptance of racial discrimination. The women's movement of the 1970s and 1980s transformed gender roles that had roots in social relations since the beginning of human history. (A generation ago, it was unlikely that the cab driver's daughter would have attended law school regardless of her abilities.) America also became a socially and ethnically diverse nation—even more so than its historic roots as an immigrant society had experienced in the past. Changes in the media environment and political process have transformed the nature of democratic politics in America, as citizens have more information about how their government is, or is not, working for them, and more means of expressing their opinions and acting out their views.

In *The Rise of the Creative Class*, Richard Florida has an evocative discussion of how a time traveler from 1950 would view life in the United States if he or she was transported to 1900, and then again to 2000.[10] Florida suggests that *technological* change would be greater between 1900 and 1950, as people moved from horse-and-buggy times all the way to the space age. But *cultural* change would be greater between 1950 and 2000, as America went from a closed social structure to one that gives nearly equal status to women, blacks, and other ethnic minorities. Similarly, I suspect that if Dwight D. Eisenhower and Adlai E. Stevenson returned to observe the next U.S. presidential election, they would not recognize it as the same electorate as the people they encountered in their 1952 and 1956 campaigns for the Oval Office.

In the same respect, many of our scholarly images of American public opinion and political behavior are shaped by an outdated view of our political system. The landmark studies of Angus Campbell, Philip Converse, Warren Miller, and Donald Stokes remain unrivaled in their theoretical and empirical richness in describing the American public.[11] However, they examined the electorate of the 1950s. At an intellectual level, we may be aware of how the American public and American politics have changed since 1952, but since these changes accumulate slowly over time, it is easy to overlook their total impact. The electorate of 1956, for instance, was only marginally different from the electorate of 1952; and the electorate of 2004 is only marginally different from that of 2000. As these gradual changes accumulated over fifty years, however, a fundamental transformation in the socio-economic conditions of the American public occurred, conditions that are directly related to citizenship norms.

None of these trends in and of themselves is likely to surprise the reader. But you may be struck by the size of the total change when compared across a long span of time.

Perhaps the clearest evidence of change, and the carrier of new experiences and new norms, is the generational turnover of the American public. The public of the 1950s largely came of age during the Great Depression or before, and had lived through one or both world wars—experiences that had a strong formative influence on images of citizenship and politics. We can see how rapidly the process of demographic change transforms the citizenry by following the results of the American National Election Studies, which have tracked American public opinions over the past half-century. Figure 1.2 charts the generational composition of the public. In the electorate of 1952, 85 percent of Americans had grown up before the outbreak of World War II (born before 1926). This includes the "greatest generation" (born between 1895 and 1926) heralded by Tom Brokaw and other recent authors. Each year, with mounting frequency, a few of this generation leave the electorate, to be replaced by new citizens. In 1968, in the midst of the flower-power decade of the 1960s, the "greatest generation" still composed 60 percent of the popu-

FIGURE 1.2	Generational Change

▶ *With the passage of time, the older "greatest generation" that experienced WWII is leaving the electorate to be replaced by baby boomers, the 1960s generation, and now Gen X and Gen Y.*

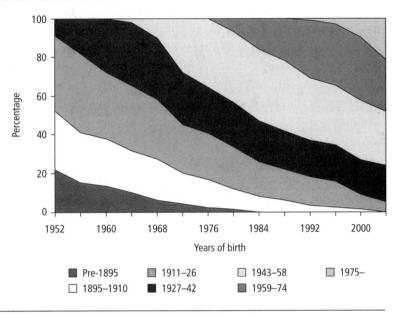

Years of birth

- ■ Pre-1895
- □ 1895–1910
- ■ 1911–26
- ■ 1927–42
- □ 1943–58
- ■ 1959–74
- □ 1975–

Source: American National Election Study (ANES) Cumulative File, 1952–2004.

lace. But by 2004, this generation accounts for barely 5 percent of the populace. In their place, a third of the contemporary public are post-World War II baby boomers, another third is the flower generation of the 1960s and early 1970s, and a full 20 percent are the Generation-Xers who have come of age since 1993 (born after 1975).

The steady march of generations across time has important implications for norms of citizenship. Anyone born before 1926 grew up and became socialized in a much different political context, where citizens were expected to be dutiful, parents taught their children to be obedient, political skills were limited, and social realities were dramatically different from contemporary life. These citizens carry the living memories of the Great Depression, four-term president Franklin Delano Roosevelt and

World War II and its aftermath—and so they also embody the norms of citizenship shaped by these experiences.

The baby boom generation experienced a very different kind of life as American social and economic stability was reestablished after the war. In further contrast, the 1960s generation experienced a nation in the midst of traumatic social change—the end of segregation, women's liberation, and the expansion of civil and human rights around the world. The curriculum of schools changed to reinforce these developments, and surveys show that parents also began emphasizing initiative and independence in rearing their children.[12] And most recently, Generation X and Generation Y are coming of age in an environment where individualism appears dominant, and both affluence and consumerism seem overdeveloped (even if unequally shared). If nothing else changed, we would expect that political norms would change in reaction to this new social context.

Citizenship norms also reflect the personal characteristics of the people. Over the past several decades, the politically relevant skills and resources of the average American have increased dramatically. One of the best indicators of this development is the public's educational achievement. Advanced industrial societies require more educated and technically sophisticated citizens, and modern affluence has expanded educational opportunities. University enrollments grew dramatically during the latter half of the twentieth century. By the 1990s, graduate degrees were almost as common as bachelor's degrees were in mid-century.

These trends have steadily raised the educational level of the American public (Figure 1.3). For instance, two-fifths of the American public in 1952 had a primary education or less, and another fifth had only some high school. In the presidential election that year, the Eisenhower and Stevenson campaigns faced a citizenry with limited formal education, modest income levels, and relatively modest sophistication to manage the complexities of politics. It might not be surprising that these individuals would have a limited definition of the appropriate role of a citizen. By 2004, the educational composition of the American public had changed dramatically. Less than a tenth have less than a high school degree, and more than half have at least some college education—and most of these have earned one or more degrees. The contemporary American public has a level of formal schooling that would have been unimaginable in 1952.

| FIGURE 1.3 | Educational Change |

▶ *Citizens with less than a high school education were a majority of the public in the 1950s; now a majority have attended college.*

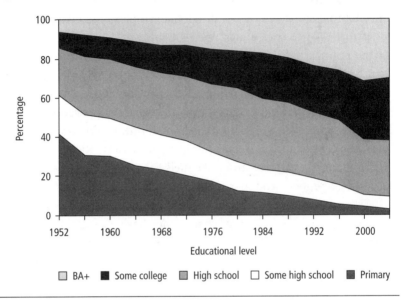

Educational level

☐ BA+ ■ Some college ▨ High school ☐ Some high school ■ Primary

Source: ANES Cumulative File, 1952–2004.

There is no direct, one-to-one relationship between years of schooling and political sophistication. Nonetheless, research regularly links education to a citizen's level of political knowledge, interest, and sophistication.[13] Educational levels affect the modes of political decision-making that people use, and rising educational levels increase the breadth of political interests.[14] A doubling of the public's educational level may not double the level of political sophistication and political engagement, but a significant increase should and does occur. The public today is the most educated in the history of American democracy, and this contributes toward a more expansive and engaged image of citizenship.

In addition, social modernization has transformed the structure of the economy from one based on industrial production and manufacturing (and farming), to one dominated by the services and the information sectors. Instead of the traditional blue-collar union worker, who manufactured goods and things, the paragon of today's workforce has shifted to the "knowledge worker" whose career is based on the creation, manipulation, and application of information.[15] Business managers, lawyers, accountants, teachers, computer programmers, designers, database managers, and media professionals represent different examples of knowledge workers.

If one takes a sociological view of the world, where life experiences shape political values, this shift in occupation patterns should affect citizenship norms. The traditional blue-collar employee works in a hierarchical organization where following orders, routine, and structure are guiding principles. Knowledge workers, in contrast, are supposed to be creative, adaptive, and technologically adept, which presumably produces a different image of what one's role should be in society. Richard Florida calls them the "creative class" and links their careers to values of individuality, diversity, openness, and meritocracy.[16]

These trends are a well-known aspect of American society, but we often overlook the amount of change they have fomented in politics over the past five decades. Figure 1.4 plots the broad employment patterns of American men from 1952 until 2004. (We'll track only males at this point to separate out the shift in the social position of women, which is examined below). In the 1950s, most of the labor force was employed in working class occupations, and another sixth had jobs in farming. The category of professionals and managers, which will stand here as a surrogate for knowledge workers (the actual number of knowledge workers is significantly larger), was small by comparison. Barely a quarter of the labor force held such jobs in the 1950s.

Slowly but steadily, labor patterns have shifted. By 2000–2004, blue-collar workers and knowledge workers are almost at parity, and the proportions of service and clerical workers have increased (some of whom should also be classified as knowledge workers). Florida uses a slightly more restrictive definition of the creative class, but similarly argues that their proportion of the labor force has doubled since 1950.[17] Again, if nothing else had changed, we would expect that the political outlook of the modern knowledge worker would be much different than in previous generations.

The social transformation of the American public has no better illustration than the new social status of women. At the time Angus Campbell

FIGURE 1.4 **Changing Occupations of Men**

▶ *Fewer American males are employed in the blue collar or agricultural occupations, while professional and service employment has increased.*

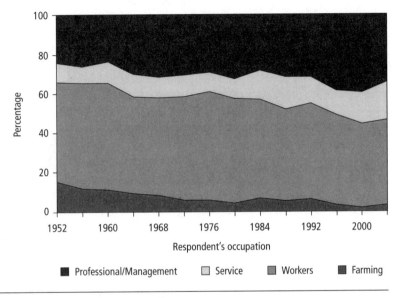

Source: ANES Cumulative File, 1952–2004; men only.

and colleagues published *The American Voter* in 1960, women exercised a very restricted role in society and politics. Women were homemakers and mothers—and it had always been so. One of the co-authors of *The American Voter* noted that their interviewers regularly encountered women who thought the interviewer should return when her husband was home to answer the survey questions, since politics was the man's domain.

The women's movement changed these social roles in a relatively brief span of time. Women steadily moved into the workplace, entered universities, and became more engaged in the political process. Employment patterns illustrate the changes. Figure 1.5 tracks the percentage of women who were housewives, in paid employment, or another status across the past five decades.[18] In 1952, two-thirds of women described themselves as housewives. The image of June Cleaver, the stay-at-home-mom on the popular TV show *Leave it to Beaver*, was not an inaccurate portrayal of

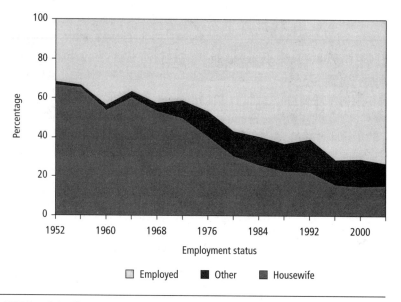

FIGURE 1.5 **Working Women**

▶ *The percentage of women who describe themselves as housewives has dropped sharply as most women have entered the active labor force.*

Source: ANES Cumulative File, 1952–2004; women only, retirees not included.

the middle class American woman of that era. By 2004, however, three-quarters of women were employed and only a sixth described themselves as housewives. The professional woman is now a staple of American society and culture. The freedom and anxieties of the upwardly mobile women in *Friends* and *Sex and the City* are more typical of the contemporary age.

The change in the social status of women also affects their citizenship traits. For instance, the educational levels of women have risen even more rapidly than men. By 2000, the educational attainment of young men and women were essentially equal. As women enter the workforce, this should stimulate political engagement; no longer is politics a male preserve. For instance, although women are still underrepresented in politics, the growth in the number of women officeholders during the last half of the twentieth century is quite dramatic.[19] Rather than being mere spectators or supporters of their husbands, women are now engaged on their own and create their own political identities. Though gender inequity and issues of upward professional mobility remain, this transformation in the social position of half the public has clear political implications.

Race is another major source of political transformation within the American electorate. In the 1950s, the American National Election Studies found that about two-thirds of African-Americans said they were not registered to vote, and few actually voted. By law or tradition, many of these Americans were excluded from the most basic rights of citizenship. The civil rights movement and the transformation of politics in the South finally incorporated African-Americans into the electorate.[20] In the presidential elections of 2000 and 2004, African-Americans voted at rates equal to or greater than white Americans. In other words, almost a tenth of the public was excluded from citizenship in the mid-twentieth century, and these individuals are now both included and more active. Moreover, Hispanic and Asia-Americans are also entering the electorate in increasing numbers, transforming the complexion of American politics. If Adlai Stevenson could witness the Democratic National Convention in 2008, he would barely recognize the party that nominated him for president in both 1952 and 1956.

Though historically seismic, these generational, educational, gender, and racial changes are not the only ingredients of the social transformation of the United States into an advanced industrial society.[21] The living standards of Americans have grown tremendously over this period as well, providing more resources and opportunities to become politically engaged. The great internal migration of Americans from farm to city during the mid-twentieth century stimulated changes in life expectations and lifestyles. The urbanization—and, more recently, the "suburbanization"—of American society has created a growing separation of the home from the workplace, a greater diversity of occupations and interests, an expanded range of career opportunities, and more geographic and social mobility. The growth of the mass media and now the Internet create an information environment that is radically different from the experience of the 1950s: information is now instantaneous, and it's available from a wide variety of sources. The expansion of transportation technologies has shrunk the size of the nation and the world, and increased the breadth of life experiences.[22]

These trends accompany changes in the forms of social organization and interaction. Structured forms of organization, such as political parties run by backroom "bosses" and tightly run political machines, have given way to voluntary associations and ad hoc advocacy groups, which in turn become less formal and more spontaneous in organization. Communities are becoming less bound by geographical proximity. Individuals are involved in increasingly complex and competing social networks that divide their loyalties. Institutional ties are becoming more fluid; hardly anyone expects to work a lifetime for one employer anymore.

None of these trends are surprising to analysts of America society, but too often we overlook the size of these changes and their cumulative impact over more than fifty years. In fact, these trends are altering the norms of citizenship and, in turn, the nature of American politics. They have taken place in a slow and relatively silent process over several decades, but they now reflect the new reality of political life.

THE PLOT OF THIS BOOK

This study uses public opinion surveys and other empirical research to analyze citizenship norms in America. Its goal is to make this information accessible to anyone interested in American politics who is not well versed in advanced statistics and research methodologies. The basic theme is quite straightforward: the modernization of American society has transformed the norms of citizenship, and this is affecting the political values and actions of the American public—often in positive ways that previous research has overlooked.

The book has three sections. The first section describes citizenship norms in theory and reality. Citizenship is an idea with a long history in political research, but an equally long list of meanings and uses. Chapter 2 summarizes the key principles of citizenship in contemporary political thought, then introduces a battery of citizenship norms developed through an international collaboration of scholars and citizen surveys. These questions appeared in the 2004 General Social Survey (GSS) of American citizens as well as surveys of other nations as part of the International Social Survey Program (ISSP)—the central evidence for our study.[23] In addition, the Center for Democracy and Civil Society (CDACS) at Georgetown University included a similar battery of questions in its 2005 Citizenship, Involvement, and Democracy Survey; this data replicates and extends the analyses from the GSS/ISSP.[24]

These surveys help us identify two clusters of citizenship norms—citizen duty and citizen engagement—that structure the analysis in this book. The first, citizen duty, reflects traditional norms of the citizen as loyal to, and supportive of, the traditional political order. The second cluster typifies the new, challenging values found among younger Americans.

The second section (Chapters 4–7) considers the potential consequences of changing norms of citizenship. We are limited to the topics included in the 2004 General Social Survey and the 2005 CDACS, but this fortunately provides evidence on an important range of political attitudes and activities. Chapter 4 challenges the idea that political participation is in broad decline, and it presents new evidence that Americans are engaged in different ways than in the past. Except for electoral participation, more Americans now participate in many forms of political action, especially direct, policy-focused, and individualized forms of activity, such as contacting politics, working with community groups, and protest activities. In fact, changing norms of citizenship affect the choice of political activities.

Chapter 5 examines the link between citizenship norms and political tolerance. Popular political discourse suggests that Americans have become polarized on ideological grounds, divided into "red" and "blue" states and comparable states of mind, and intolerant toward those who are different. In fact, various measures display a steady increase of political tolerance over the past several decades, and this tolerance is concentrated among the young and better educated. These findings provide a much more positive image of how the American public has changed its political values over the past several generations.

Chapter 6 examines the implications of citizenship norms on the making of public policy—how they translate into laws and regulations at both national and local levels. Long-term trends suggest that public expectations of government action have expanded over the past several decades, despite the efforts by some public officials to roll back the scope of government action. Moreover, citizenship norms are clearly linked to these expectations of government. The traditional image of citizen duty leads to a restrictive image of the government's policy role. Engaged citizens, meanwhile, see the need for greater government activity, and activity in distinct policy domains. Citizenship norms shape our expectations of government and what it should provide.

Some of the loudest voices in the crisis-of-democracy literature have focused on the decline of political support since the late 1960s as an ominous sign for our nation. Chapter 7 tracks these trends and analyzes the relationship between citizenship and political support. Again, it becomes clear that changing citizenship norms are related to these sentiments, but in complex ways. The engaged citizen is less trustful of politicians when compared to those who stress citizenship as a duty, but engaged citizens are also more supportive of democratic principles and democratic values. This suggests that changing citizenship norms are pressuring democracy to meet its ideals—and challenging politicians and institutions that fall short of these ideals.

While these analyses largely focus on the American experience, Chapter 8 places the U.S. findings in cross-national context. Using data from the International Social Survey Program, we can compare the consequences of citizenship norms between Americans and European publics. This enables us to detect what is distinct about the American experience, and what is part of a common process affecting other advanced industrial democracies.

The conclusion considers the implications of the findings for the democratic process in America. We cannot recreate the halcyon politics of a generation ago—nor should we necessarily want to. New patterns of citizenship call for new processes and new institutions that will reflect the values of the contemporary American public.

CONCLUSION

In many ways this book presents an unconventional view of the American public. Many of my colleagues in political science are skeptical of positive claims about the American public—and they are especially skeptical that any good can come from the young. Instead, they warn that democracy is at risk and that American youth are a primary reason.

I respect my colleagues' views and have benefited from their writings—*but, this book tells the rest of the story.* Politics in the United States and other advanced industrial societies is changing in ways that hold the potential for strengthening and broadening the democratic process. The old patterns are eroding—as in norms of duty-based voting and deference toward authority—but there are positive and negative implications of these trends if we look for both. The new norms of engaged citizenship come with their own potential advantages and problems. America has become more democratic since the mid-twentieth century, even if progress is still incomplete. Understanding the current state of American political consciousness is the purpose of this book. If we do not become preoccupied with the patterns of democracy in the past, but look toward the potential for our democracy in the future, we can better understand the American public and take advantage of the potential for further progress.

THE MEANING AND MEASUREMENT OF CITIZENSHIP

A t his inauguration in January 2001, with prompting from prominent political scientists, George W. Bush stated:

We are bound by ideals that move us beyond our backgrounds, lift us above our interests and teach us what it means to be citizens. Every child must be taught these ideals. Every citizen must uphold them.... I ask you to be citizens. Citizens, not spectators. Citizens, not subjects. Responsible citizens, building communities of service and a nation of character.

Citizenship is presumably a good thing, so more citizenship must be even better. But the exact meaning of citizenship is open to multiple interpretations. This idea has a history dating from the first democratic polity, and theorists—republicans, liberals, neo-liberals, communitarians, social democrats, and others—differ substantially in their definitions of citizenship. Moreover, which of these meanings applies in the United States, or any other single nation, is also a matter of much debate. Relatively little research directly examines how people actually perceive the norms of citizenship.

This chapter begins by summarizing previous writings on the meaning of citizenship. We will not discuss the full philosophical history of the concept because this would fill a volume, and many such studies are available.[1] Instead, this chapter seeks to identify the key elements of citizenship discussed in the contemporary debates. Then, we will shift our attention to a new study of citizenship norms among contemporary Americans, based on a module included in the 2004 General Social Survey. This survey determines how Americans themselves define what is important to being a good citizen.

CITIZENSHIP IN THEORY

Citizenship is a concept with a long history in political science, and its origins can be traced back to debates between Aristotle and Plato over how a citizen of Athens should act. Through the millennia, however, the term has acquired multiple meanings. This may, in part, reflect the importance of the idea of citizenship, so that scholars and political analysts compete to define its meaning.[2]

I begin with an open definition of citizenship: the term refers to what people feel is expected of them as "good" citizens. Typically, survey research examines the attitudes and values that individuals personally hold. Reflecting Almond and Verba's description of a political culture as a shared set of social norms,[3] this study defines citizenship as a shared set of expectations about the citizen's role in politics. A political culture contains a mix of attitudes and orientations, and I believe that images of the citizen's role are central parts of a nation's culture. They tell citizens what is expected of them and what they expect of themselves. As this book will show, these expectations shape other elements of the political process. Indeed, these norms of citizenship are the values that Tocqueville stressed as defining a democratic political culture.

This does not mean that individuals approve of these norms, or that their personal values are consistent with these norms. The interaction between these norms and behavior is, in fact, an important research question to consider. For instance, someone might say that tolerance is an important norm for a democratic citizen, but then not be tolerant in his or her own political beliefs. In short, we shall define citizenship as a set of norms of what people think they should do as a good citizen.

It is also important to identify what we are *not studying*. Sometimes citizenship is used to describe a legal status as a citizen of a nation. This book is not concerned with this specific legal definition of citizenship:

who is a citizen, how one becomes a citizen, the legal rights of citizenship. Similarly, a legal approach to citizenship sometimes examines the rights guaranteed to an individual as a function of citizenship. Again, this is an important topic, but it is not the topic of this study. Citizenship can also describe identity with a nation, feelings of patriotism and national pride; this is only partially related to our interests here. Citizenship can include the formal legal relationship between individuals and the state: the rights of citizenship or the legal protections of citizenship. These legal elements of citizenship are indirectly important to the topics examined here, but they are relevant to this discussion only to the extent that citizens define legal rights or responsibilities as part of their expectations of citizenship.

How, then, might citizenship be defined? An initial framework comes from Aristotle's observation that citizenship balances two contending roles: citizens are "all who share in the civic life *of ruling* and *being ruled in turn.*"[4] This simple, insightful observation underlies much of the theoretical literature about citizenship to the present.

First, **public participation** in politics is broadly considered a defining element of democratic citizenship.[5] The nation was founded based on citizen participation in political decision making, even if this participation was initially limited by the U.S. constitutional structure. The principle of citizen participation remains a defining element of American democracy, and Tocqueville argued that it was a distinctive element of the American political culture (see Chapter 4).

Because of this emphasis on participation, the current scholarly debate centers on the notion that political involvement is decreasing. On the one hand, some analysts argue that decreasing participation in elections and other forms of political activity are eroding the foundations of the democratic process.[6] Thus, citizenship norms themselves are weakening. Other analysts maintain that the social transformation of American society has increased the ability of the average citizen to be politically engaged.[7] This counter position maintains that Americans are turning to other forms of political engagement besides traditional electoral politics, and that this has the effect of expanding and empowering the public's influence.[8]

So a central issue for democratic citizenship involves the question of how much citizens believe they should participate. There is little consensus on how much participation, and in what forms, is beneficial for democracy. There is even less agreement on how much participation actually occurs today.

Often overlooked in discussions of citizenship is the other part of the Aristotelian equation: the acceptance of **the authority of the state.** Autocratic states emphasize the role of the loyal subject as the prime criteria of citizenship, and democracies also stress the importance of state sovereignty. Indeed, acceptance of the legitimacy of the state and the rule of law is often the implied first principle of citizenship, since without the rule of law meaningful political discourse and discussion cannot exist.

Political philosophy is replete with those who stress the acceptance of state sovereignty—from Bodin, to Hobbes, to Hamilton—even before the participatory elements of democracy. Similarly, this logic appears in how the U.S. government presents itself to its new citizens. A pamphlet prepared by the then-named Immigration and Nationalization Service for prospective citizens describes the Constitution's importance as first "everyone is protected by the law" and then "everyone must obey the law."[9] Then comes a discussion of the rights provided in the Constitution's Bill of Rights, which is paired with a discussion of the duties and responsibilities of citizenship: voting, serving in the army, and paying taxes.[10] The centrality of obedience is quite clear in what the United States tells its new citizens.

This fundamental dichotomy between ruling and being ruled is central to the definition of citizenship. Both are necessary in the modern democratic state, and the proper balance between these principles has been a central element of the philosophical literature on citizenship. One objective of this study is to learn how the American public views these principles.

Another element of citizenship involves our relation to others in the polity. T. H. Marshall described this as **social citizenship.**[11] The expansion of civil and political rights created a new category of social rights, such as social services, providing for those in need, and taking heed of the general welfare of others.[12] Citizenship thus includes an ethical and moral responsibility to others in the polity, and beyond. This idea of "distributive justice" provides a theoretical base for equality as a basis of citizenship. Unless individuals have sufficient resources to meet their basic social needs, this thinking goes, democratic principles of political equality and participation are meaningless. Although initially identified with the European welfare state and social democratic critiques of capitalism, this notion of social citizenship has been embraced by liberal interests in America.[13]

Social citizenship also potentially reaches beyond the nation state. Contemporary discussions of equality and distributive justice are often embedded in a framework of global human rights and responsibilities. Thus, a socially concerned citizen cares about those less fortunate at home, as well as issues of global inequality and the conditions of the global community. Many scholars now treat citizenship as part of a global community, with global interests and responsibilities.[14]

This study focuses on these three elements of citizenship—participation, state authority, and social rights—as central to defining citizenship. Democratic citizenship requires a mix of all three elements, and one can easily point to examples of the detrimental effects when one element—state authority, say—is given too much emphasis over the others. Yet, analysts continually assert that all three elements of citizenship are declining in contemporary America.[15] These claims of changing citizenship norms are what gives such urgency to the study of citizenship—and what prompted Bush to call for a renewal of citizenship in his 2001 Inaugural Address. If the norms of citizenship are what bind Americans to their polity and each other, then a broad decline will have fundamental implications for American society and politics.

The philosophical debate about contemporary citizenship is much richer and more extensive than I have briefly outlined here. Each theoretical tradition posits that a different mix of traits defines contemporary norms of citizenship, or a different mix of these norms is desirable. However, this debate has lacked one component: What do the citizens themselves think of citizenship? How do Americans weigh the various elements of citizenship? Let's consult the American public in the next section.

WHAT IS A "GOOD" CITIZEN?

How do Americans perceive the qualities of good citizenship? Building upon a recent series of studies,[16] the 2004 General Social Survey asked Americans to describe what it means to be a good citizen:[17]

There are different opinions as to what it takes to be a good citizen. As far as you are concerned personally, on a scale of 1 to 7, where 1 is not at all important and 7 is very important, how important is it to . . .

Respondents are asked how important various traits are to being a "good" citizen—the perceived norms of citizenship—rather than personal adherence to each behavior.[18] The 2005 "Citizens, Involvement and Democracy" survey conducted by the Center for Democracy and Civil Society at Georgetown University asked a similar question.[19] Both surveys asked about norms in four areas related to the categories that I identify in this section (Table 2.1).

Participation is a prime criterion for defining the democratic citizen and his or her role within the political process, and it is central to the philosophical literature on democracy. Both surveys thus ask about the importance of always voting in elections. In addition, these studies ask about the importance of participation beyond voting: being active in social or political organizations (participating in civil society), and choosing products for political, ethical, or environmental reasons even if they cost more. This does not include all the possible forms of political action (see Chapter 4), although it covers a range of opportunities. Moreover, the survey does not ask if the respondent participates in these activities— the questions ask whether they recognize such norms as existing in American society.

A second category, related to the idea of participation, taps what is called **Autonomy**.[20] Autonomy implies that good citizens should be sufficiently informed about government to exercise a participatory role. The good citizen should participate in democratic deliberation and discuss politics with other citizens, and ideally understand the views of others. Other researchers have described such items as representing critical and deliberative aspects of citizenship.[21] The GSS measures these orientations with a question on keeping watch on the government, and with another on understanding the reasoning of people with other opinions. CDACS asks about the importance of independently forming one's opinions.

Social Order represents the acceptance of state authority as part of citizenship. The GSS asks two items on obeying the law: never trying to

TABLE 2.1	Categories of Citizenship

▶ *The categories of citizenship and the questions in the General Social Survey (GSS) and Center for Democracy and Civil Society (CDACS) surveys that are used to measure each category.*

CATEGORY	GSS	CDACS
Participation	Always vote in elections	Vote in elections
	Be active in social or political associations	Be active in voluntary organizations
	Choose products for political, ethical or environmental reasons	Be active in politics
Autonomy	Try to understand reasoning of people with other opinions	Form opinion independently of others
	Keep watch on actions of government	
Social order	Always obey laws and regulations	Always obey the laws and regulations
	Never try to evade taxes	Serve on a jury if called
	Being willing to serve in the military in a time of need	Men serve in the military when the country is at war
		Report a crime that one may have witnessed
Solidarity	Support people in America who are worse off than oneself	Support people who are worse off than oneself
	Help people in rest of the world who are worse off than oneself	

Source: 2004 General Social Survey; 2005 CDACS Survey.

avoid taxes and always obeying laws and regulations. In addition, a willingness to serve in the military is another measure of allegiance. The CDACS survey includes a similar set of items, plus a question on willingness to report a crime.

Finally, **Solidarity** is a fourth category of citizenship norms that taps the idea of social citizenship. This idea represents the belief that good citizenship includes a concern for others. The GSS thus asks about the importance of helping others in America who are worse off, or helping people in the rest of the world who are worse off.

TABLE 2.2	Dimensions of Democratic Citizenship

▶ *Statistical analyses identify two dimensions of citizenship and the table displays the correlation of each survey question with both dimensions.*

	GSS			CDACS	
SURVEY QUESTION	Citizen Duty	Engaged Citizen	VARIABLE	Citizen Duty	Engaged Citizen
Vote in elections	.65	.17	Report a crime	.84	.12
Never evade taxes	.65	−.01	Always obey the law	.77	.09
Serve in military	.54	.07	Serve in the military	.64	.15
Obey the law	.51	.10	Serve on a jury	.63	.32
Keep watch on government	.51	.40	Vote in elections	.56	.43
Active in association	.39	.54	Form own opinions	.29	.47
Understand others	.28	.59	Support worse off	.16	.65
Choose products	.22	.59	Be active in politics	.15	.80
Help worse off in world	−.12	.77	Active in voluntary groups	.10	.84
Help worse off in America	.02	.77			
Eigenvalue	1.95	2.37		2.56	2.37
Percent variance	19.5	23.7		28.5	25.8

Source: 2004 GSS and 2005 CDACS; the order of the GSS dimensions has been reversed to simplify comparison across both surveys.

THE TWO FACES OF CITIZENSHIP

Although there is a distinct philosophical logic to these four separate categories of norms, the American public perceives citizenship in terms of a simpler framework. Two broad dimensions of citizenship structure their responses to these ten items.[23] Table 2.2 describes this clustering by presenting the correlations between each of the items and these two general citizenship dimensions.[24] The larger the correlation, the more the item taps the underlying dimension of citizenship.

One citizenship dimension is based on what we might describe as the principle of **Citizen Duty**. The responsibility to vote is strongly connected to this dimension in the GSS survey, closely followed by the three items on social order. Respondents in the CDACS survey also link voting turnout and social order. The fusion of these two different sets of norms suggests that some forms of participation—such as voting—are motivated by the same sense of duty that encourages individuals to be law abiding citizens. Citizen duty thus reflects traditional notions of citizenship as the responsibilities of a citizen-subject. The good citizen pays taxes, follows the legitimate laws of government, and contributes to the national need such as service in the military. In addition, previous research on voting turnout indicates that feelings of citizen duty are a strong stimulus of voting.[25] Allegiance to the state and voting are linked together. For instance, the U.S. Citizenship and Immigration Services (formerly the Immigration and Naturalization Service) begins its description of the duties and responsibilities of citizens as follows: "the right to vote is a duty as well as a privilege."[26] Thus, the clustering of participation and order norms into a single pattern of duty-based citizenship has a strong foundation in previous empirical research and democratic theory.

The other dimension, **Engaged Citizenship**, spans several elements of citizenship. It includes participation, but in non-electoral activities such as buying products for political reasons and being active in civil society groups. This dimension also incorporates the autonomy norm—that one should try to understand the opinions of others (in CDACS this dimension includes forming independent opinions). Engaged citizens also possess a moral or empathetic element of citizenship, and both solidarity items of helping others (at home and abroad) are strongly related to the underlying factor. This is significant, because analysts typically maintain that concern about the community is an element of traditional citizenship values; these surveys suggest just the opposite—that it falls most heavily in the engaged citizen cluster. Indeed, the clustering of items on the second dimension in the CDACS survey is strikingly similar to the GSS measure of engaged citizenship. This suggests a pattern of the socially engaged citizen: one who is aware of others, is willing to act on his or her principles, and is willing to challenge political elites.

The replication of these two basic dimensions in both the General Social Survey and the CDACS survey reinforces the validity of these patterns. These two dimensions of citizenship are not contradictory (since all items are positively related), but they reflect different emphases in the role of a democratic citizen. Both clusters involve a norm of participation, although in different styles of political action. Both define citizenship as a mixture of responsibilities and rights, but different responsibilities and different rights. Although both dimensions are linked to democratic theory, neither completely matches the mix of norms posited in previous philosophical models.

If citizen duty captures the traditional model of democratic citizenship, then it leads to a set of predictions about the causes and consequences of these norms. For instance, these are seemingly the citizenship norms of the "greatest generation" that analysts now see as waning in America. Previous research suggests that respect for authority and the rule of law is stronger among older Americans and weaker among the young.[27] Similarly, the emphasis on the voting may be strongest among older generations socialized during a period when this was considered a duty of citizenship.[28] One also expects that duty-based citizenship should promote distinct forms of political participation, policy preferences, images of government, and other attitudes and behavior; these themes are explored in more detail below.

In comparison, engaged citizenship partially overlaps with the liberal or communitarian models of citizenship. These norms stress the rights and social responsibilities of citizenship. But instead of seeing political participation primarily as a duty to vote, engaged citizenship prompts individuals to be involved in a wider repertoire of activities that give them direct voice in the decisions affecting their lives. This evokes the values implicit in Benjamin Barber's idea of "strong democracy."[29] Even more directly, engaged citizenship overlaps with the patterns of post-material or self-expressive values that Ronald Inglehart has described as a growing feature of advanced industrial societies.[30] Post-materialists emphasize participatory norms, elite-challenging behavior, and they are more interested in non-economic social issues. Engaged citizenship includes a responsibility to others in society. Such feelings of social responsibility have a long tradition in European social democratic and Christian social traditions, and they are present in American political norms.

This dichotomy in citizenship norms—duty-based citizenship versus engaged citizenship—provides the foundation for the analyses presented in this book. The recognition of these norms should be sufficient to shape citizen attitudes and behavior—if these are meaningful norms. Much of the rest of this book explains and then tests these distinctions.

THE DISTRIBUTION OF CITIZENSHIP NORMS

Having mapped the clustering of citizenship values that Americans see, let's now look at the support for each of these norms within the American public. Figure 2.1 presents the average importance score given to each

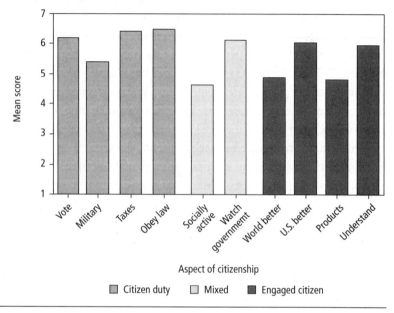

FIGURE 2.1 The Importance of Citizenship Norms

▶ *The importance Americans attach to each of the different aspects of citizenship;
the higher the bar the more important the item is.*

Citizen duty ☐ Mixed ☐ Engaged citizen

Note: Figure entries are the mean score of importance for each item on a seven-point scale for which 1 = not at all important and 7 = very important.

Source: 2004 General Social Survey.

norm based on the General Social Survey. Although I have emphasized the distinct clusters of citizenship norms, these data make it clear that most Americans accept all these norms. On the 7-point scale used in the GSS, all ten items score well above the midpoint of the scale (3.5), and several are heavily skewed with means above 6.0. So it's not that Americans accept one set of norms and reject others—rather, all these norms are recognized as important, with some more important to different individuals.

The items on the left of the figure are the norms most closely identified with duty-based citizenship. Nearly all Americans agree that these are important elements of citizenship. Obeying the law receives the highest importance rating of any of these ten items (mean = 6.5), closely followed by paying taxes (6.4), and always voting (6.2). The sense of duty is thus deeply embedded in Americans' notions of citizenship.

The three items on the far right of the figure are most closely linked to engaged citizenship. Although we have described these as new and emerging norms, most Americans also rank these as important. The solidarity norm of helping those worse off in America receives a relatively high rating (6.0), as does the norm of understanding others (5.8). The norms of engagement generally receive less attention from the public, but the differences in importance between both sets of norms are fairly modest.

These survey responses come from a single, recent time point, but other evidence points to an erosion of duty-based norms over time. For instance, the American National Election Study regularly asks whether it matters if one votes, which is widely interpreted as a measure of the civic duty to vote. Affirmative responses have slowly trailed downward over time, paralleling the decline in turnout. More generally, respect for authority has also decreased over the past several decades, also eroding the foundation of duty-based norms of citizenship.[31] In the same way, the evidence on the generational bases of citizen-duty and engaged citizenship, cited in this chapter and examined more directly in the next chapter, speak to the change in norms over time. Thus, norm shift is occurring within the public, a fact that has fundamental implications for how Americans define their role as citizens and relate to their government.

WHAT KIND OF CITIZENSHIP

If we return to President Bush's call for citizenship at the start of the chapter, how should we interpret it based on our findings? Rather than a single model of citizenship, Americans define citizenship in two distinctly different ways. **Duty-based citizenship** evokes traditional images of citizenship, with some variations. Duty-based citizenship first stresses the duties and responsibilities of citizenship, with a limited participatory role. This is a constrained model of citizenship, which reinforces the existing political order and existing authority patterns. It is consistent with what is generally described as an elitist model of democracy, which implies the limited role of the citizen. This is also close to the description of the subject-participant political culture that Almond and Verba described, which combined a propensity to obey the laws with a limited degree of political activity.[32]

Engaged citizenship, meanwhile, has a more expansive view of citizen norms. The engaged citizen also stresses participation, but this includes direct-action and elite challenging activities. Participation is not just an expression of allegiance and duty, but an attempt to express policy preferences. Significantly, engaged citizenship also includes a concern for the opinion of others, potentially an expression of support for a more deliberative style of political activity. In addition, these norms include a concern for others. Thus, engaged citizenship contains elements that are part of liberal and social traditions of citizenship.

These two elements of citizenship have a long tradition in American politics and political thought. More than five decades ago, for instance, Charles and Robert Merriam described citizenship in terms of dual principles that are very close to the empirical patterns described here:

> Certainly citizenship is something more than merely adding up a set of specific rights and duties or jobs to do, such as voting, paying taxes and obeying the laws. There is something beyond all that—something beyond the call of legal duties. We might expect of a good citizen, a distinctive if vaguely defined attitude—something akin to the idea of responsibility. Good citizenship properly embraces an acceptance of individual responsibility, moral as well as political, for the condition of the government and the general welfare of the community.[33]

Recognizing this duality of citizenship provides a means of understanding and explaining recent trends in American politics. In Chapter 1 I have suggested that the social transformation of society—rising educational levels, spreading cognitive mobilization, distinct generational experiences—is shifting the norms of citizenship within the contemporary public. Adherence to citizen duty is eroding as attachments to norms of engaged citizenship increase.

I suspect that President Bush (and many others) was thinking of duty-based citizenship when he called for the renewal of American citizenship. This form of citizenship would encourage Americans to vote, to obey the law, and respect their government. He would be surprised, and possibly concerned, to find that a new form of engaged citizenship has been increasing. This was probably not what he had in mind.

Instead, these two sets of norms may be shifting within the American public. Using norms as a guide, we can analyze the consequences of this shift for how Americans think and act. My reading of the literature suggests that many scholars, like President Bush, have focused only on the decline of duty-based norms and their consequences because these changes represent a shift in past patterns of behavior, and so they are more apparent. This stimulates the criticisms of the American public as described in Chapter 1. In contrast, the consequences—both positive and negative—of greater attention to engaged citizenship are often overlooked, or reported in research that is not linked to discussions about citizenship. Integrating both perspectives should produce a more accurate—and more positive—image of democracy in contemporary America.

FORMING CITIZENSHIP NORMS

Let's begin this chapter with a small thought experiment. In November of 2005, Senator Richard G. Lugar, a Republican from Indiana, had a private meeting with the actress and activist Angelina Jolie in his Senate office to discuss the United Nations' Millennium Development Goals. Now, both these individuals are "good citizens" to most people.[1] Senator Lugar had served in the U.S. Navy (1957–60) and entered politics soon after returning home. He was first elected to the Senate in 1976 and has been re-elected four times, serving as chairman of the Foreign Relations Committee and as a ranking member (and former chairman) of the Agriculture, Nutrition, and Forestry Committee. Ms. Jolie, besides her celebrity as an actress (and daughter of actor Jon Voight), has promoted humanitarian causes throughout the world and is noted for her work with refugees. She currently serves as goodwill ambassador for the Office of the United Nations' High Commissioner for Refugees (UNHCR).

The senator and the actress/activist had met a couple of times before when Ms. Jolie was in Washington. They obviously share an interest in foreign affairs and the plight of people in the developing world. And yet one might imagine that if they discussed the meaning of "good citizenship," they would emphasize very different points. We might assume that Lugar would place more emphasis on social order, and perhaps stress the need for more citizens to vote and participate in elections. For instance, his U.S. Senate biography begins with the statement: "Dick Lugar is an unwavering advocate of U.S. leadership in the world, strong national security, free-trade and economic growth." However, Jolie was there to discuss programs to benefit the needy in the developing world; thus we would expect her to stress solidarity and autonomy norms. And one hardly expects that social order is high on her priority list.

What causes these differences? There are many social contrasts between these two individuals that might explain their presumably different points of view: their early life experiences and family backgrounds (Lugar was born in 1932, grew up on a family farm, and his Wikipedia biography begins with his early Boy Scout accomplishments; Jolie was born in 1975, and her upbringing in Hollywood was much different), as well as their careers and peer networks, their genders, and their partisan orientations.

One really cannot generalize from these two individuals, no matter how intriguing it might be to entertain such speculations. However, the Lugar-Jolie encounter illustrates a significant point: although most Americans believe that all the elements of citizenship discussed in Chapter 2 are important, we expect that people differ systematically in the emphasis they place on these elements. Citizenship norms are not randomly distributed across the American public, but instead reflect the social and political forces shaping these norms. Building on the social trends described earlier, we expect that social groups differ in their views of citizenship. For instance, to what extent do norms differ by generation, social status, race, or partisanship?

Even more important, the social distribution of citizenship norms indicates the source of these norms and how they may have changed over time. Because we have survey data only for the current public, we cannot track the historical evolution of norms. However, if we project contemporary patterns over time, this provides indirect evidence. For example, to the extent that norms become fixed during early life socialization, then generational patterns suggest how norms have changed over time. Similarly, if there are strong educational differences in citizenship norms, then the expansion of education during the late twentieth century should have contributed to norm shift (see Chapter 1). This chapter examines how citizenship norms vary across a basic set of social characteristics—generation, education, social status, gender, ethnicity, religion, and partisanship—and the implications of the different norms of citizenship.

A GENERATIONAL GAP?

We can assume, first off, that the tremendous changes in the content and context of American politics since the mid-twentieth century have reshaped citizenship norms. The legacy of these changing historical experiences should appear in generational differences in norms. Older Americans—those of the pre-1945 generations—were raised in a different era, with different expectations and practices of citizenship. This is the "greatest generation" that Tom Brokaw wrote about, and who reflect the civic values that Robert Putnam praised.[2] Brokaw articulately summarized the experiences of this generation and the impact of these events on their political norms:[3]

> These men and women came of age in the Great Depression, when economic despair hovered over the land like a plague. They had watched their parents lose their businesses, their farms, their jobs, and their hopes. They had learned to accept a future that played out one day at a time. Then, just as there was a glimmer of economic recovery, war exploded across Europe and Asia. . . . When the war was over, the men and women who had been involved, in uniform and in civilian capacities, joined in joyous and short-lived celebrations, then immediately began the task of rebuilding their lives and the work they wanted. They were mature beyond their years, tempered by what they had been through, disciplined by their military training and sacrifices. . . . They stayed true to their values of personal responsibility, duty, honor, and faith.

Indeed, previous research suggests that feelings of citizen duty are more common among older Americans and older Europeans.[4]

In contrast, most contemporary writings on the citizenship of young Americans are much less flattering. The postwar baby boom generation was on the cusp of the old order, and some were the driving force for the social changes of the 1960s and 1970s. Since then, however, there is a nearly universal agreement that younger generations are what's wrong with contemporary American politics. To be sure, criticizing the politics of the young has a long tradition, but it has taken on a new intensity in the current discourse on citizenship. Compare the above description of the greatest generation with the following description of young Americans:

> *The Doofus Generation. That's what* The Washington Post *calls those of us in our twenties, who came of political age during the 1970s and 1980s. In the eyes of many observers, we are indifferent and ignorant—unworthy successors to the baby-boom generation that in the 1960s set the modern standard for political activism by the young. To an extent, they are right.*[5]

This is not an isolated example, and other journalists and political analysts express these same harsh views.[6] A recent blue-ribbon study of civic life in the United States spelled out what older Americans think about the political engagement of the young: "Each year, the grim reaper steals away one of the most civic slices of America—the last members of the 'Greatest Generation.' This is a cold generational calculus that we cannot reverse until younger Americans become as engaged as their grandparents."[7] What a cold-hearted description of American youth. But is it accurate?

I believe that these critical views of contemporary youth miss a larger reality. Older people typically castigate the young for not being like themselves—this has been true since the time of Aristotle—and they attribute negative political developments to the eroding values and poor behavior of the young. This is what old people do best: they complain. The fact that the young may not think of citizenship in the same duty-based norms as their elders is taken as evidence that the young lack good citizenship norms.

However, if feelings of citizen *duty* are eroding among the young, this may well be counterbalanced by new norms of *engaged* citizenship. Such a norm shift is consistent with evidence of the changing values priorities of youth. Ronald Inglehart's studies argue that young people in the United States and most other advanced industrial democracies more strongly favor self-expressive and participatory values and are more politically engaged.[8] Similarly, other work points to the strong values of social justice, equality, and tolerance among younger Americans.[9] These norms of engaged citizenship may have benefits for democracy that are missed by focusing on the decline in duty-based norms.

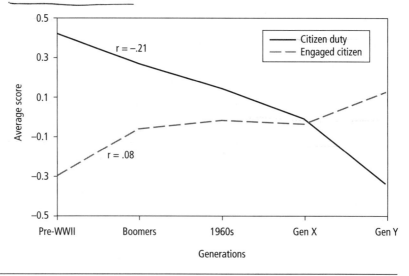

FIGURE 3.1   **Generations and Citizenship**

▶ *Citizen duty decreases among younger generations, and engaged citizenship increases among the young.*

Source: 2004 General Social Survey.

Figure 3.1 shows the pattern of duty-based citizenship and engaged citizenship across generations.[10] The value of zero on each citizenship dimension represents the average for the entire American public; positive values in the figure mean that a generation scores above the average. The generational shift in citizenship norms is quite clear. Older Americans who came of age (reached age 18) by the end of World War II and the postwar boomer generation score highest on citizen duty. These sentiments then steadily weaken among the 1960s generation, so-called GenX and GenY.[11] This is the pattern that analysts typically discuss, leading to negative comments on the declining citizenship of the young.

At the same time, the erosion of duty-based norms among the young is offset by increased support for engaged citizenship, which stresses alternative forms of political participation, concern for the less privileged, and attention to the views of others. A modest relationship between age and engaged citizenship runs opposite to the duty relationship. These are hardly undemocratic or un-American values, although few analysts write about the lack of such values among older Americans.

This figure displays a simple truth that we repeat throughout this study. Assertions about the decline in citizenship norms among younger Americans are incorrect. Rather, generations are changing in the types of citizenship norms they stress. Americans raised before and immediately after World War II generally define citizenship in terms of duties and obligations. Indeed, one might argue that these are the norms of a "loyal subject" (though not necessarily a good democratic participant).[12] In contrast, the young reflect a new political reality and stress alternative norms that encourage a more rights conscious public, a socially engaged public, and a more deliberative image of citizenship. Both norms have positive (and negative) implications for the practice of citizenship and the workings of the democratic process—implications that we examine in the later chapters of this book.

THE RISING TIDE OF SOCIAL STATUS

Chapter 1 put forth the idea that the tremendous socio-economic transformation of America during the last half of the twentieth century has reshaped citizenship norms. The expansion of educational levels, improvements in living conditions, increases in leisure time, and the restructuring of employment added to the politically relevant skills and resources of the average American. In addition, the shifting social context has exposed people to new experiences, new norms of social action, and thus also affects norms of democratic citizenship.

Many studies point to the power of education and other social status variables in shaping images of citizenship.[13] Nie, Junn, and Stehlik-Barry, for example, show that education is strongly related to political knowledge, political participation, and democratic norms such as tolerance.[14] These authors maintain that educational levels are strongly related to democratic participation and democratic enlightenment, although working in different ways. Research consistently finds that the better educated are more likely to vote more often, to be active in their community, to be more knowledgeable about politics, and to be more politically tolerant.

Better educated, higher income, and higher status Americans may be more likely to subscribe to duty-based norms of citizenship. The formal and informal civics training of the educational system presumably stresses these norms, and individuals from higher income and status groups typically are more supportive of the norms of the existing political order. These patterns are also consistent with the educational relationships for participatory norms in *The Civic Culture* study.[15]

Yet, once we realize that there is an alternative citizenship norm—engaged citizenship—the consequence of education becomes more ambiguous. If the skills and values produced by education are important in creating norms that one should vote, they should be even more important in stimulating participation in direct forms of engagement. Similarly, Nie, Junn, and Stehlik-Barry suggest that the cognitive skills linked to education should encourage engaged citizenship.[16] At least since the 1960s, furthermore, observers have maintained that the political ethos in higher education has shifted toward the norms of engaged citizenship—with increased stress on direct action, the critical role of the citizen, and social responsibility—partly as an alternative to traditional duty-based conceptions of citizenship.[17] In short, if education and higher social status are valuable in developing the norms of a good subject, they may be even more relevant to developing the norms of an engaged citizen.

Figure 3.2 presents the relationship between education and the two sets of citizenship norms. As expected, duty-based citizenship is higher among the better educated, but the increase is quite modest.[18] Individuals with graduate degrees are only a tenth of a point higher in citizen duty than those with only a high school diploma. Meanwhile, education is more strongly related to support for engaged citizenship. The gap between the high school educated and those with graduate degrees is almost four times greater than for duty-based norms.

The logic of educational patterns should extend to other social status measures. For instance, the respondent's occupational prestige is positively related to both duty-based and engaged norms (both with r = .08). Family income displays a positive relationship with citizen duty, consistent with the pattern for other social status variables. In contrast, income is negatively related to support for engaged citizenship. This reflects a distinct economic element of engaged citizenship: Lower income groups

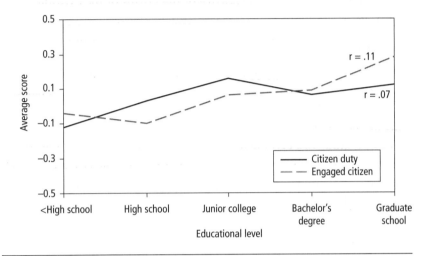

FIGURE 3.2   Education and Citizenship

▶ *Education slightly increases citizen duty and increases engaged citizenship even more.*

Source: 2004 General Social Survey.

attach greater importance to helping people who are worse off, un-doubtedly because they can more easily identify with those in need.[19]

Taken together, this evidence suggests that social modernization—rising educational levels and improving living standards—during the latter half of the twentieth century probably contributed to a shift in citizenship norms. These traits encourage a more engaged form of citizenship that goes beyond the deferential, subject-like role of duty-based citizenship. Participating in politics beyond voting and deliberating with others is more demanding than voting based only on a sense of duty. As more Americans possess these skills and resources, their norms of citizenship also change.

PATTERNS BY GENDER AND ETHNICITY

Another major social transformation in the late twentieth century involved the role of women in society: moving from positions of homemakers to active participants in the labor force. Putnam and others have linked this trend to the erosion of social capital and presumably to the erosion of political participation and other citizenship behaviors.[20]

However, past descriptions of gender patterns give only half the story. Gender research suggests that women traditionally were more conservative in their views and more concerned with a stable social environment when compared to men.[21] In part, this reflected the condition of most women as homemakers, where concern for family and the duties of motherhood were paramount. The entry of women into the workforce may have diminished gender differences in duty-based norms—because women became more like men in terms of employment and social experiences.[22]

The other half of the equation is the relationship between gender and the norms of engaged citizenship. There is little discussion in previous research of gender differences in citizenship, so the ideas offered here are speculative. We might expect that women are more socially conscious than men, and thus may express more concern for the welfare of others and the opinions of others—two elements of this mode of citizenship. Thus, as women have entered the workforce, participation in employment and exposure to these norms may have stimulated a more empowered self-image that encourages engaged citizenship.[23]

The gender differences in citizenship norms are quite small. Men and women are almost identical in their adherence to duty-based norms. Women are slightly more likely than men to score highly on engaged citizenship, and women who are employed are even more engaged than homemakers.[24] Although these gender differences are modest, the tremendous transformation in the social status of women over the past fifty years still implies significant aggregate effects. The entry of women into the labor force has probably eroded support for duty-based norms and increased support for engaged citizenship.

Race and ethnicity present another instance where the relationship to citizenship norms is potentially complex. If education or social status drives citizenship norms, then we might expect minority groups to display lower support for both citizenship dimensions since minorities have lower social status positions. However, the specific racial component of citizenship may function in a different manner. For instance, given the history of racial policies (explicit and implicit) in America, African

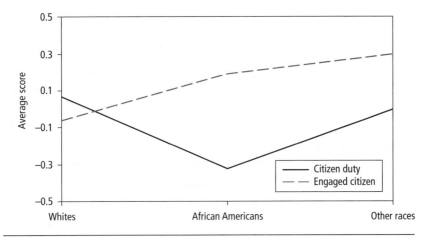

FIGURE 3.3   Race and Citizenship

▶ *Whites emphasize citizen duty; African Americans and other races give more importance to engaged citizenship.*

Source: 2004 General Social Survey.

ethnicity

Americans and other minorities may be more restrained in their sense of citizen duty. In addition, the emphasis on empowerment and engagement that accompanied the civil rights movement and other rights campaigns may stimulate norms of engaged citizenship.

Figure 3.3 presents the citizenship norms of white Americans, African Americans, and a combined category of the other racial groups. African Americans score distinctly lower than the average on duty-based norms (−.32), and above average on engaged citizenship (+.19). Similarly, the "other races" category is even higher on engagement (+.30). In contrast, white Americans are the one group that score higher on citizen duty than engaged citizenship. This suggests that historical experiences and racial identifies also shape citizenship norms.

CITIZENSHIP AND RELIGION

As noted earlier, the historical discussion of American citizenship was often embedded in religious values and the imagery of religious fundamentalists (of various denominations) who played a prominent role in American history. Americans saw themselves as creating a new nation, and a nation that differed from all others. More generally, religion instills norms of behavior that may carry over to the political domain because they define expectations about power relationships and appropriate social behaviors.[25]

Is there still a connection between religion and citizenship? For instance, it is typically argued that Catholicism increases acceptance of hierarchy and authority because of the structure of the Roman Catholic Church and its teachings. This might translate into duty-based norms of citizenship. The variations among Protestant denominations make it more difficult to offer clear predictions. Reformation Protestants (Lutherans, Episcopalians, etc.) might be less likely to view citizenship in duty-based terms, but Calvinists (Presbyterians, among others) might be more duty oriented; Baptists probably divide by race.

The difficulty, however, is that in a single survey the number of respondents in discrete denominations is too small to examine these patterns in detail. Therefore, we must compare Protestants, Catholics, Jews, and other religions and those with no religious affiliation. This uncovers only modest differences in citizenship norms: none of the three major religious groups differed substantially from the national average.[26]

Rather than interdenominational differences, the largest contrast is between religious and nonreligious Americans. Therefore, let's focus on religiosity using a question that asked about the strength of religious feelings.[27] Figure 3.4 shows that the strength of religious attachments is positively related to adherence in duty-based citizenship. The range from the strongly religious to those with no religion spans almost half a scale point on the citizen duty dimension.[28] Engaged citizenship displays a more complex pattern: those high in religiosity are the only group that scores significantly above average on this dimension, presumably because their religious commitment stimulates a concern with others. However, the second highest score comes from those without a religious attachment, perhaps because of a humanist concern for the same set of values.

Like the other findings, the religious distribution of citizenship norms suggests that these political identities at least partially evolve from social experiences and identities. Identifying citizenship with duty-based norms

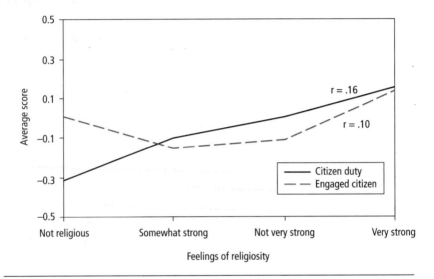

FIGURE 3.4   Religiosity and Citizenship

▶ *Religious feelings steadily increase citizen duty, but engaged citizenship is most important among the most and least religious.*

Source: 2004 General Social Survey.

tends to overlap with strong feelings of religiosity. This implies that the gradual secularization of American society during the late twentieth century may be another factor contributing to the erosion of duty-based norms and the increased attention to engaged citizenship.

PARTISAN DIFFERENCES IN CITIZENSHIP

Partisan loyalties to the Democrats or Republicans may also influence citizenship norms. On the one hand, the adherence to good citizenship norms should span all the political parties in a well-functioning democracy. Support for democracy and the principles of good government and good citizenship should not be the domain of only one party. But the theoretical discussions of citizenship suggest that adherents of different parties may vary in the conceptions of citizenship. That is, democracy functions best when Republicans and Democrats both believe it is important to obey the law and to keep a watchful eye on government, but one party may place more emphasis on the former and the other on the latter.

The philosophical discussion of citizenship also suggests that there is an ideological or partisan component to specific norms. Liberal, neo-liberal, communitarian, and social-democratic images of citizenship are often linked to specific partisan or ideological orientations.[29] Especially in the current political environment, the Republican Party seems closely identified with an emphasis on the duty-based elements of citizenship. When President George Bush calls for a strengthening of citizenship, he is probably not thinking in terms of autonomy and solidarity. Ironically, the party that is most likely to favor smaller government and greater individual autonomy is also more likely to stress the need for greater respect for the authority of the state and its agents (especially during a Republican administration). Conversely, the contemporary Democratic Party is more likely to emphasize the social dimension of citizenship: the protection of those in need and the rights of individuals to challenge the state. It is not that Republicans (or Democrats) favor one aspect of citizenship to the exclusion of the other—they share both sets of norms but with a different emphasis.

These contrasts seem apparent in the current party alignments, but they may reflect more enduring images of citizenship rooted in party history and ideology. For instance, Merriam's description of the Republican administrations of the late 1800s and early 1900s sounds surprisingly similar to descriptions of the current Republican Party:[30]

> *Thus, the political mores of the leading group was divided against itself. On the one hand, it preached patriotism, devotion to the state in international affairs, and in internal affairs respect for law and order as often as it became necessary to call upon the government for protection of persons and property in industrial disputes; but on the other hand the broader social interests of the state, the majesty of the public purpose, the supremacy of the common interests against the special, could not be too vigorously emphasized.*

Figure 3.5 shows that the partisan ties of Americans are clearly connected to norms of duty-based and engaged citizenship. Republican

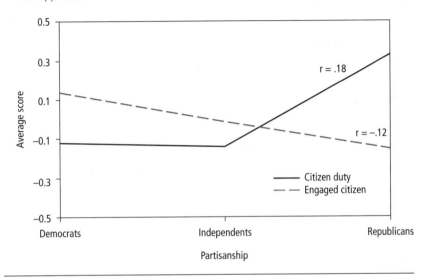

FIGURE 3.5 **Partisan Differences in Citizenship Norms**

▶ *Democrats emphasize engaged citizenship over citizen duty, and Republicans are the opposite.*

Source: 2004 General Social Survey.

Party identifiers score substantially above average (+.33) on citizen duty, and below average (–.15) on engaged citizenship; if we isolate strong Republican identifiers, they are even more distinct on both dimensions. Conversely, Democratic Party identifiers score below average on citizen duty (–.12), but higher than average on engaged citizenship (+.14). Although the figure does not present this evidence, those who voted for Ralph Nader in 2000 were among the lowest on citizen duty of any of the social groups examined (–.46), while scoring far above average on engaged citizenship (+.27).

These partisan differences in citizenship norms explain what might be described as a contemporary "dialogue of the deaf" on this topic. Both Democratic and Republican politicians, and a host of academics, argue that we need to strengthen citizenship through civic education programs, public service programs, and other political reforms.[31] Even if there are bipartisan calls for improving citizenship, these views are inevitably linked to different definitions of what values of citizenship are lacking. George W. Bush and Ralph Nader are both strong believers in good citizenship and advocates for more democracy—but they have dramatically different ideas about how the values of Americans should be changed and what civic education should stress. These different citizenship emphases are reflected among party identifiers in the public at large.

BRINGING THE PIECES TOGETHER

Now that we have identified the social and political correlates of citizenship norms, let's integrate these separate discussions. As a first step, we shall map the norms of key social groups identified in the above analyses so we can compare and contrast the various groups.

Figure 3.6 plots a group's score along the duty-based dimension on the horizontal axis, and the group's position on engaged citizenship along on the vertical axis. For the sake of readability, I do not plot all groups; for instance, only the oldest and youngest age cohorts are shown here. However, this figure provides a good mapping of the overall patterns described above. The first apparent pattern is the contrast between alternative models of citizenship. The lower right quadrant identifies groups that are high in citizen duty but low in engaged citizenship: The clearest examples are older Americans (the pre-World War II generation) and Republican Party identifiers. Conversely, the upper left quadrant displays groups that are high in engaged citizenship but below average in duty-based norms. Young Americans, African Americans, and Democratic Party identifiers (and especially Nader voters in 2000) are the clearest examples of this pattern. This diagonal axis thus represents a political cleavage within the American public, between those who think of citizenship first in terms of duties, and those who think of citizenship in terms of rights and engagement. It is no wonder that Democrats and Republicans (or young people and senior citizens) talk past one another when they discuss the abstract goal of good citizenship. They have different conceptions of citizenship.

The other broad pattern in the figure is the relationship between education and citizenship norms. The most educated (with a graduate degree) score high on both dimensions; these are the individuals who have a full definition of citizenship spanning both duties and rights. The least

FIGURE 3.6	Social Groups on Two Dimensions of Citizenship

▶ *The position of each group in this space represents its score on citizen duty and engaged citizenship.*

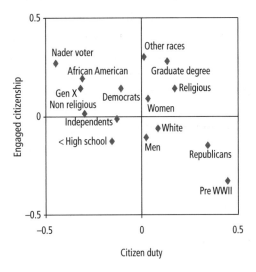

Source: 2004 General Social Survey.

educated (with less than a high school degree) score below the mean on both dimensions. By projecting this cross-sectional relationship to the changes over time, we can infer that increasing education levels of Americans may strengthen support for both modes of citizenship (holding other factors constant).

What complicates the separate comparisons of social groups is that many of these characteristics overlap. Sometimes these effects may be reinforcing, and sometimes they may encourage different patterns of citizenship. For instance, are the contrasts across age groups a result of their distinct socialization experiences, or because the generations differ substantially in their educational level and other life conditions? Race, class, and education are also closely intertwined within the American public.

Therefore, we combine all of the above social characteristics into a statistical analysis of citizenship norms.[32] This analysis produces statistical estimates of the effect of each item while holding constant the effects of all the other items in the model. In other words, this provides a pure measure of each characteristic's effect separate from all the others. These results are presented in Figure 3.7.

The upper model in the figure presents the predictors of citizen duty. Age displays a strong positive relationship with feelings of citizen duty (ß=.19). A Republican Party identification, strong religious attachments, and a high income are also strongly linked to duty-based citizenship. In comparison, the lower panel displays the factors influencing engaged citizenship. Education is one of the strongest predictors of engaged citizenship, while having little impact on citizen duty. Several characteristics also have contrasting effects. While the old favor duty-based norms, they are less likely to endorse engaged citizenship (ß=–.06) even after considering how age groups differ on all the other traits in this list. A Republican Party identification weakens feelings of engaged citizenship. African Americans are lower in citizen duty, but higher in engaged citizenship. And while high income stimulates duty-based norms, it diminishes support for engaged citizenship. Thus, most of the patterns we examined for single social characteristics also persist when we look at all these variables combined.

THE SOCIAL ROOTS OF CITIZENSHIP

We have seen that the definition of "good citizenship" varies across different subgroups of the American public. Older Americans are much more likely to stress duty-based norms, while younger generations tend to emphasize engaged citizenship. Republicans and Democrats display a similar polarization, as do racial groups and religious/secular Americans. The generalizations from the meeting of Senator Lugar and Angelina Jolie at the start of this chapter may be hypothetical, but they do reflect many of the social patterns in citizenship norms demonstrated here.

Moreover, the social bases of citizenship norms follow patterns consistent with the themes of social change presented in Chapter 1. The social transformation of the American public has at least partially contributed to a change in the meanings of citizenship. The age contrasts are especially significant. Some of the age differences might be life cycle effects, where

FIGURE 3.7   Predictors of Citizenship Norms

Citizen Duty

▶ *Age, income, religious attachments, and a Republican party identification significantly increase citizen duty, but duty is lower among African Americans.*

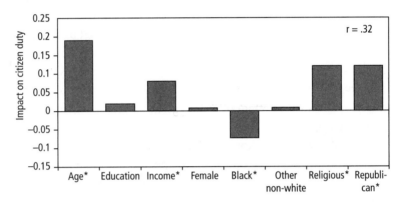

Engaged Citizenship

▶ *Education, racial minority, and religious attachments significantly increase engaged citizenship; but age, income, and Republican party identification lower engaged citizenship.*

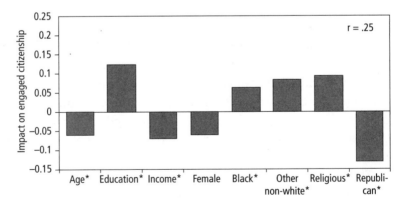

*Statistically significant effects (exceeding .05).

Note: Table entries are standardized coefficients from a multiple regression analysis; each bar represents whether the predictor has a positive or negative effect on citizenship norms.

Source: 2004 General Social Survey.

individuals place more stress on authority and order as they age. But there appears to be a strong generational element to these patterns, reflecting early political socialization and the changing context of American politics over the past half-century or more. If this interpretation is correct, it suggests that the slow, steady shift in citizenship norms will continue. As demographic change decreases the number of older Americans who subscribe to duty-based norms of citizenship, these trends also add new Generation Y and "Millennials" who are less motivated by a sense of duty and more motivated by norms of engaged citizenship. Moreover, such changes seem consistent with broader and deeper patterns that are transforming citizen values in America and other advanced industrial democracies.[33] There is little evidence to suggest that younger generations can be persuaded to begin thinking like their grandparents. If this demography is our destiny, then we should begin a more serious discussion of how the shifting norms of citizenship will reshape democratic politics.

The one contrasting pattern occurs for educational differences. Better educated Americans place greater emphasis on both sets of citizenship norms, while the less educated are lower than average on both. This suggests that rising educational levels have reinforced both set of norms, but the impact on engaged citizenship is proportionally greater. So even in this instance, social change increased the relative attention to engaged citizenship.

The larger lesson is the need to fully understand the nature of citizenship norms. Political commentators have often stressed the erosion of duty-based citizenship, praising those social groups that adhere to these norms and criticizing groups that are less duty-oriented. Calls for renewing American citizenship are often equated with this dimension of citizenship. The social patterns in this chapter underscore the point that groups who are lower in citizen duty typically do not lack citizenship norms, they just emphasize different norms of engaged citizenship.

The remainder of this book examines the effects of both sets of citizenship norms. Both have positive implications for the functioning of the political process and the behavior of the American public—and both also carry limitations. Rather than lamenting the loss of duty-based citizenship, we should first understand the consequences of the changing emphases of citizenship.

BOWLING ALONE OR PROTESTING WITH A GROUP

A participatory public has been a defining feature of American politics and a strength of the U.S. political system. Tocqueville, for example, was impressed by the participatory tendencies of Americans when he toured the nation in the 1830s:

> The political activity that pervades the United States must be seen to be understood. No sooner do you set foot upon American ground than you are stunned by a kind of tumult; . . . here the people of one quarter of a town are meeting to decide upon the building of a church; there the election of a representative is going on; a little farther, the delegates of a district are hastening to the town in order to consult upon some local improvements; in another place, the laborers of a village quit their plows to deliberate upon a project of a road or a public school. . . . To take a hand in the regulation of society and to discuss it is [the] biggest concern and, so to speak, the only pleasure an American knows.[1]

Thomas Jefferson emphasized the importance of participation to the functioning of the democratic process. Social scientists maintain that political participation "is at the heart of democratic theory and at the heart of the democratic political formula in the United States."[2] Without public involvement in the process, democracy lacks both its legitimacy and its guiding force.

Studies of political participation in the 1960s and 1970s stressed the public's high activity levels. The political culture encouraged people to participate: Americans were active in voluntary associations, engaged in political discussion, and involved political affairs.[3] Tocqueville's description of America apparently still applied in the mid-twentieth century.

And yet, a considerable body of contemporary research argues that political participation is declining among the public. Although education levels, socio-economic status, and access to political information and the other resources of democratic citizenship have increased substantially over the past several decades (as described in Chapter 1), this has apparently not stimulated participation. Fewer Americans seem engaged in elections, and other evidence points to a drop in campaign activity.[4] William J. Bennett, the former Education Secretary under President Ronald Reagan, and former Senator Sam Nunn, Democrat of Georgia, observed that "too many of us lack confidence in our capacity to make basic moral and civic judgments, to join with our neighbors to do the work of community, to make a difference. Never have we had so many opportunities for participation, yet rarely have we felt so powerless."[5] In his influential book that provides the title for this chapter, *Bowling Alone,* Robert Putnam similarly concludes: "declining electoral participation is merely the most visible symptom of a broader disengagement from community life. Like a fever, electoral abstention is even more important as a sign of deeper trouble in the body politic than as a malady itself. It is not just from the voting booth that Americans are increasingly AWOL."[6]

Moreover, most analysts view the young as a primary source of this decline. Authors from Tom Brokaw to Robert Putnam extol the civic values and engagement of the older, "greatest generation" with great hyperbole. At the same time, the young are described as the "Doofus generation" or the "invisible generation," even by sympathetic journalists who are members of Generation X. Political analysts and politicians seemingly agree that young Americans are dropping out of politics, producing the erosion of political activity.[7]

Is the situation really so dire? Other evidence points to increases in several forms of political action, especially among the young.[8] Ronald Inglehart, for example, described a much more optimistic image of contemporary citizen engagement: "One frequently hears references to growing

apathy on the part of the public . . . These allegations of apathy are mis-
leading: mass publics *are* deserting the old-line, oligarchical political organizations that mobilized them in the modernization era—but they are
becoming more active in a wide range of elite-challenging forms of political action."[9] This is starkly different from the decline in civic engagement
literature.

Many political causes still motivate the young, such as helping the less
fortunate in America, addressing poverty in Africa (and America), or improving the global (and American) environment. So there is at least some
countervailing evidence that Americans are changing their style of political action rather than dropping out from politics entirely. And these
trends are most apparent among the young. From this perspective, America is witnessing a change in the nature of citizenship and political participation that is leading to a renaissance of democratic participation—
rather than a general decline in participation.

We suggest that the norms of citizenship may provide the key to resolv-
ing this debate. Duty-based norms of citizenship can stimulate political
engagement, especially turnout in elections. The decline of these norms
thus may contribute to the erosion of electoral participation. In contrast,
engaged citizens apparently are not so drawn to elections, but prefer more
direct forms of political action, such as working with public interest
groups, boycotts, or contentious actions. Let's first examine how political
participation patterns are changing over time. Then, we can find out how
the modes of citizenship are linked to the patterns of participation.

WHAT COULD YOU DO TO INFLUENCE THE GOVERNMENT?

Instead of starting with the common assumption that participation is
synonymous with voting in elections, let's begin with a citizen-centered
view of participation. How do people think of their participation options? If one wants to influence politics, how should this be done? Answers to these questions reflect a combination of the tools an individual
thinks will be effective and what he or she feels prepared to do. To tap
these opinions, we use a standardized survey question that asks about
participation options:

> *Suppose a regulation was being considered by (your local com-*
> *munity) which you considered very unjust or harmful; what do*

TABLE 4.1	How One Can Try to Influence the Government

▶ *Americans increasingly perceive more ways to influence the government, and direct contact and protests have increased the most.*

	Local Government		National Government	
WAYS TO INFLUENCE GOVERNMENT	1959	1981	1959	1981
Work with informal, unorganized group	60	48	30	25
Work with formal group	4	6	4	8
Contact politicians, officials	23	55	60	84
Voting, party contact	16	15	8	14
Protest, demonstrate, petition	1	33	<1	16
Other means	3	10	1	3
Can do nothing	18	17	22	14
Total	124%	183%	125%	165%

Note: Each column totals more than 100 percent because up to three responses were possible in each survey.

Sources: Civic Culture Study (1959), Political Action II Study (1981).

you think you could do? Suppose a law was being considered by Congress which you considered to be very unjust or harmful: what do you think you could do?

This question was first asked in 1959 as part of the cross-national *Civic Culture* study. Table 4.1 shows that most Americans felt relatively efficacious; only 18 percent said they could do nothing about a bad local regulation and only 22 percent said they could do nothing about a bad national law. When this question was repeated in the 1980s, the level of efficacy held stable for local politics, and increased for national politics. This is a first suggestion that political engagement is not decreasing in America.

The expanding repertoire of political action is even more apparent in responses to how people would be politically active. Many people say they would work through informal groups, neighbors, or friends to influence policy, especially at the local level where the possibility of face-to-face cooperation is greater. This is the type of collective action that represents Tocqueville's image of participation in America. Although responses are slightly less frequent in 1981, this remains a common form of proposed political action.[10]

By the second time point, however, participation means more avenues of influence. In 1959, protests, demonstrations, petitions, and other examples of contentious politics barely were apparent in Americans' thinking about politics; they were mentioned by 1 percent or less of the public. In 1981, 33 percent mention some direct action related to local government and 16 percent for national government. Most of these responses (26 percent and 12 percent respectively) involve circulation of petitions, but this still means that a substantial percentage cite protests, demonstrations, and boycotts as a primary means of political influence.

The tendency to think of political influence as direct contact has grown even more over this time span. Both contacting a local government official and a national government official have increased by more than 20 percent across these two decades. Direct contacting becomes the most frequently proposed method of political action for local government (55 percent) and national government (84 percent). This trend reflects two reinforcing patterns. First, people today are less deferential to elites and more likely to assert their own political views. Second, people possess the resources and skills to take direct, individual action, such as writing a letter to an official or calling his or her office. And even these data are relatively old; in the modern context of e-mail and faxes, direct contacting has become even simpler for the individual.[11]

Table 4.1 also illustrates the role of voting in the participation repertoire. In 1959, voting or working with a party in some other way was the third most frequently cited means of influence for both local and national government. The percentages citing elections and parties did not change dramatically in the next two decades—but other forms of action expanded. Voting is important, but citizens are now much more likely to say they would turn to other methods when trying to influence government.

In other words, people see expanding options for how they can influence government. Moreover, the growth in the participation repertoire has come primarily in forms of direct action—such as contacting and protest—that typify a style of participation that is much different from the institutionalized and infrequent means of electoral participation of prior years. If more recent data were available, we expect these trends would be even stronger.

THE MYTH OF THE DISENGAGED AMERICAN

American citizens see new avenues of political action available to them—but do they use these opportunities? Surprisingly, comprehensive data on the participation patterns of Americans are relatively rare.[12] For instance, the American National Election Study has a rich battery of items on campaign activity that extends back to the 1950s, but the study does not regularly monitor non-electoral participation. The Political Action/World Values Surveys regularly ask about protest activities, but not about voting, campaign activity, contacting, or other activities. Even when a survey includes a large battery of participation items, the wording of questions changes in ways that make time comparisons suspect.[13] Several recent studies have presented trends from the Roper and DDB surveys, but these are lower quality commercial polls with changing methodology over time. Unfortunately, there is no definitive source for data on American participation patterns over the last several decades, and so we must combine a variety of sources to track activity patterns.

It's important to start the analyses as early as possible in order to describe patterns before the inflection point of the early 1970s, when some researchers maintain that participation began to erode. With a long time span, we also can better see the long term consequences of social change in the American public, effectively weeding out types of engagement that stem from the ebb and flow of specific events or specific election campaigns.

The first comprehensive assessment of participation in the United States was Sidney Verba's and Norman Nie's classic, *Participation in America*. They surveyed Americans in 1967 and asked about their involvement in a range of political activities. This study identified four distinct **modes of political action** that citizens use: voting, campaign activity, communal activity (working with an informal group in the community), and contacting officials. They found that people tend to specialize in activities that match their motivations and goals. Those who are involved in campaigns, for example, perform a variety of campaign activities; those who are active in community groups are more likely to engage in other community activities. A host of subsequent studies has built upon this framework.

In 1987 Verba, Schlozman, and Brady replicated the 1967 participation battery, also asking a different set of participation questions.[14] Let's begin with these 1967–87 surveys, then extend the series with more recent data from the 2000 Social Capital Survey and the 2004 Comparative Study of Electoral Systems survey (CSES).[15] The questions in these recent surveys are not always identical to the Verba-Nie questions, but they are the most comparable set of current participation measures. We can also supplement these data with other surveys to provide more evidence of trends.

Table 4.2 describes participation patterns over time. As a starting point, the 1967 Verba-Nie survey asked about general interest in politics. Two-thirds of the public said they were very or somewhat interested in politics.[16] Indeed, in the midst of the Vietnam War and the civil rights controversies of the 1960s, this should have been a time of broad political interest. Twenty years later, however, rather than a subsequent drop in interest, political interest held steady in 1987, and it remained at this higher level when the question was repeated in 2000.[17] Meanwhile, the Gallup Poll/Pew Center find a slight increase in political interest between 1952 and 2000.[18] This evidence is an indication that Americans have not become politically disengaged.

As one would expect, voting in elections was common in the 1967 survey; two-thirds of the respondents said they regularly voted in presidential elections, and half said they always voted in local elections. However, both statistics had dropped significantly when these questions were repeated in 1987. Other research generally describes a decrease in turnout since the early 1960s among the voting age public (VAP).[19] However, new studies show that when turnout statistics are recalculated to adjust for the growing proportion of the American public that is not eligible to vote, the decline in turnout is more modest among this voting eligible public (VEP).[20] Figure 4.1 presents both the VAP and VEP trends over time. Still, initiatives such as simplified registration requirements (such as voter registration while getting a drivers license) and mail voting have not fundamentally altered the downward slide in turnout.

Participation in campaigns extends electoral participation beyond voting. Fewer people are routinely active in campaigns because campaign work requires more initiative, more time, and arguably more political sophistication. Along with the additional effort, however, campaign activity

| TABLE 4.2 | Trends in Political Participation, 1967–2004 |

▶ *Participation in elections and voting has decreased, but most other activities have increased or held fairly constant.*

QUESTION	1967	1987	2000	2004
Are you interested in politics and national affairs?	66	66	66	—
Voting				
Report voting in the last presidential election	66	58	—	—
Official vote statistics in last presidential election (voting age public)	62	53	47	49
What about local elections—do you always vote in those?	47	35	—	—
Campaign Activity				
Do you *ever* try to show (2004: convince) people why they should vote for one of the parties or candidates?	28	32	—	44
Have you done (other) work for one of the parties or candidates?	26	27	—	—
In the *past three or four years,* have you attended any political meetings or rallies? (2000: last year)	19	19	16	—
In the *past three or four years,* have you contributed money to a political party or candidate or to any other political cause?	13	23	—	—
Contacting				
Have you *ever* personally gone to see, or spoken to, or written to some member of local government or some other person of influence in the community about some needs or problems?	21	34	—	28[a]
Contact state/national government	20	31		
Community Action				
Have you *ever* (2000: last year; 2004: past five years) worked with others in this community to try to solve some community problems?	30	34	38	36
Protest				
Have you participated in any demonstrations, protests, boycotts, or marches *in past two years* (2004: past five years)?	—	6	7	7

[a] Over the past five years or so, have you done any of the following things to express your views about something the government should or should not be doing: contacted a politician or government official either in person, or in writing, or some other way?

Sources: 1967 *Participation in America* Study; 1987 NORC General Social Survey; 2000 Social Capital Survey; 2004 Comparative Study of Electoral Systems survey; IDEA Turnout database.

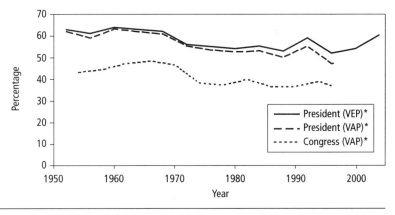

FIGURE 4.1 **Levels of Voter Turnout**

▶ *Turnout in presidential and congressional elections has been trending slightly downward since the 1960s.*

Voting-age public (VAP) includes all adults in the potential electorate; voting-eligible public (VEP) excludes non-citizens, felons, and others without the right to vote.

Source: U.S. Election Project at George Mason University (http://elections.gmu.edu/voter_turnout.htm).

can provide more political influence to the individual citizen and convey more information than voting. Campaign activities are important to parties and candidates, and candidates generally are more sensitive to, and aware of, the policy interests of their activists. Several analysts argue that campaign activity has also followed a downward spiral.[21]

The Verba-Nie survey asked several questions on campaign activity. In 1967, about a quarter of the public had tried to influence the vote of others or worked for a party; somewhat smaller numbers attended a campaign rally or contributed to a campaign. By 1987, campaign activity had actually increased slightly for most of these indicators, despite the decreasing numbers who said they voted.[22] The 2000 Social Capital Survey asked about attending a rally or political meeting in the past 12 months (the survey was done in August/September before the election); yet participation is almost equal to the less restrictively worded question from the 1967/87 surveys. The 2004 CSES questions are not phrased in identical terms, but they suggest that campaign activity has at least held constant.

The American National Election Study (ANES) has more extensive time trends on campaign activity (Table 4.3). The ANES asks about working for a party, going to a meeting, giving money, displaying campaign material, and persuading others how to vote. Between 1952 and 2004, there are ebbs and flows in campaign involvement related to specific campaigns, with a slight downward drift except for the 2004 election.[23] Displaying a campaign button or a bumper sticker was more popular in the 1950s, but today personal discussion about the campaign is actually more common. (One suspects that in contemporary elections more people forward election related e-mails and Web sites than place placards on their lawns.) Except for the upward bounce in 2004, a marked trend does not appear over this fifty-two-year period. Although there is some conflict between different survey trends, the ANES and Verba-Nie comparisons suggest a relatively flat level of campaign activity over time.[24] Even if fewer people vote, election campaigns still engage a significant share of the American public.

A third mode of political action is personally contacting a politician, government official, or media person about a political issue. This is a fairly demanding form of action, requiring an individual to identify a political target and formulate a statement of his or her own policy preferences. Table 4.2 shows that in 1967 a fifth of the public had contacted a member of the local government or a member of the state/national government. By 1987 both questions show that a third of the public had contacted politicians at both levels. Indeed, other evidence suggests that more and more people use this method of individualized participation, which allows them to select the issue agenda, the timing and means of communication, and the content of the message to policy makers.[25] The CSES did not contain an identically worded question, but still finds high levels of individual contacting.[26] A century ago, active citizens marched en masse to the polls with their ballots held high over the heads and voted as their ward captain or union leader told them. Today, they sit in the comfort of their home and write politicians about the issues of the community and the nation.

A fourth mode of action is working with others to address political issues—communal activity. Communal participation can take many forms. It often involves group efforts to deal with social or community problems, ranging from issues of schools or roads to protecting the local

TABLE 4.3

Trends in American Campaign Activity

▲ *Campaign activity has fluctuated over time without a clear consistent trend, and participation in 2004 was unusually high.*

ACTIVITY	1952	1956	1960	1964	1968	1972	1976	1980	1984	1988	1992	1996	2000	2004
Work for a party or candidate	3	3	6	5	6	5	4	4	4	3	3	2	3	3
Go to a meeting	7	7	8	8	9	9	6	8	8	7	8	5	5	8
Give money	4	10	12	11	9	10	16	8	8	9	7	7	6	10
Wear a button or have a bumper sticker	—	16	21	17	15	14	8	7	9	9	11	10	10	21
Persuade others how to vote	28	28	34	31	33	32	37	36	32	29	38	27	34	49
Participate in two or more activities	—	16	21	17	16	17	16	12	12	12	14	11	11	30

Source: American National Election Study, 1952–2004.

environment. From the PTA to local neighborhood committees, this is democracy in action. The existence of such autonomous group action defines the character of a civil society that theorists from Jefferson and Tocqueville to the present have considered a foundation of the democratic process. Today, participation in citizen groups can include involvement in public interest groups with broad policy concerns, such as environmental interest groups, women's groups, or consumer protection.

Group based participation has long been cited as a distinctive aspect of the American political culture, but it is difficult to measure without representative survey data. Verba and Nie asked if individuals had ever worked with others in their community to solve some local problem; 30 percent were active in 1967. By 1987, participation in community groups had increased to 34 percent. The 2000 Social Capital Survey found that 38 percent had participated on a community project, even though the time frame was now restricted to the previous twelve months.[27] The CSES survey asked the question with a longer time frame that is closer to the 1967/87 surveys, and found that 36 percent of Americans said they had worked on a community project. This question is perhaps the closest to the Tocquevillian image of grassroots democracy in America, so it is very significant that informal collective action has become more common among Americans.

Protest is another form of participation. Protest not only expands the repertoire of political participation, but it is a style of action that differs markedly from electoral politics. Protest can focus on specific issues or policy goals—from protecting whales to protesting the policies of a local government—and can convey a high level of political information with real political force. Voting and campaign work seldom focus on a single issue because parties represent a package of policies. Sustained and effective protest is a demanding activity that requires initiative, political skills, and cooperation with others. Thus, the advocates of protest argue that citizens can increase their political influence by adopting a strategy of direct action.

Although protest and similar activities are part of democratic politics, early participation surveys did not ask these items. This partially reflected the low level of protest in the 1950s and early 1960s, as well as the contentious nature of these activities. The 1967 survey, for instance, did not include a question on protest even though the survey occurred in the

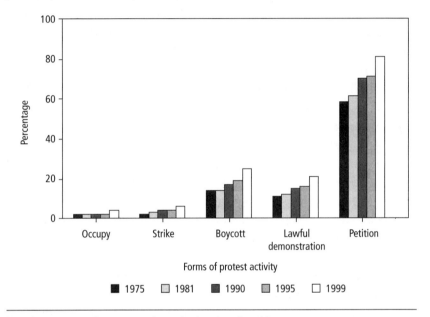

FIGURE 4.2   Protest Activity

▶ *Participation in various forms of protest activity are increasing.*

Note: Figure entries are the percentage who say they have done the activity.

Sources: 1975 Political Action Study; 1981, 1990, 1995, and 1999 World Values Survey.

midst of one of the most turbulent periods of recent American history. In the 1987 survey, 6 percent said they had participated in a demonstration, protest or boycott in the past two years. More than a decade later, 7 percent said they had participated in a protest in 2000 Social Capital Survey (in past year) and in the 2004 CSES survey (in past five years). If we expanded the definition of protest to include political consumerism, internet activism, and other new forms of action, the increase in contentious politics would be even more dramatic.[28]

The Political Action/World Values Survey (WVS) asked about participation in several types of contentious action (Figure 4.2).[29] In the mid-1970s about half of Americans said they had signed a petition; now this is over four-fifths of the public. Participation in demonstrations, boycotts, and unofficial strikes has roughly doubled over this time span. This WVS series may exaggerate the trend in protest because it asks if the respondent had ever participated in these activities, instead of asking about participation over a discrete time span. However, if we could extend our time series back to the quieter times of the 1950s and early 1960s, the growth of protest activity would undoubtedly be dramatic. Protest has become so common that it is now the extension of conventional political action by other means.

Finally, the Internet is creating a form of political activism that did not previously exist. The Internet provides a new way for people to connect to others, to gather and share information, and to attempt to influence the political process.[30] For instance, congressional reports state that e-mails are now the most common form of communications from constituents, and they are growing most rapidly.[31] Moveon.org became a vital tool to connect like-minded individuals during the 2004 Democratic primaries, and its methods have broadened into a new practice of political communication and mobilization. While Web sites were unheard of in the 1992 campaign (except, perhaps, to Al Gore), they are now a standard feature of electoral politics. The potential of the Internet is illustrated on the Facebook.com Web site, where young adults communicate and can link themselves to affinity groups that reflect their values as a way to meet other like-minded individuals. In Fall 2006 the top ten advocacy groups on Facebook included nearly half a million members in total.[32] The Web is the medium of the young—and often an unknown world to their grandparents.

Because it is so new, the Internet was not part of the classic studies of American participation during the latter part of the twentieth century. The 2005 CDACS survey found that 17 percent of Americans had visited a political Web site in the previous year, 13 percent had forwarded a political e-mail, and 7 percent had participated in other political activities over the Internet. The 2004 GSS found that just over 5 percent say they participated in an Internet political forum. Those in the CDACS who had done any of these activities exceeded the percentage of those who had donated money to any political group, worked for a party or candidate, or displayed campaign materials over the same time period. The numbers are still modest, and the uses are still growing, but the Internet is adding to the tools of political activism, especially among the young.

OLD REPERTOIRES AND NEW REPERTOIRES

Why have the participation patterns of Americans changed? There is no single answer because several factors shape the decision whether to participate, and then the choice of how to participate. However, something in this network of factors has changed.

Political activity makes time and cognitive demands upon the citizen. To be fully informed about the candidates and issues of an election is a challenging task, even if the act of voting is relatively simple. The demands increase substantially for other types of political activity, especially individualized, direct forms of action. For instance, to write a letter to a member of Congress or to speak at a city council meeting typically requires an even deeper knowledge of politics, more personal initiative, and a significant time commitment.

Participation research thus stresses the importance of social status as a predictor of political activity. Better education, upper status occupations, and higher incomes provide the resources of time and money that facilitate political action. In addition, these social traits normally indicate a set of cognitive abilities and organizational skills that facilitate activity. Thus, the participation literature commonly describes social status as the "standard model" to explain political participation.[33] This reality still holds true today; the various surveys used in this volume generally display a positive correlation between social status and various forms of action.

Consequently, the increase in social status and other political resources discussed in Chapter 1 should stimulate political engagement. In large part, this has occurred—especially for individualized and direct forms of action, such as protests and direct contacting. However, this has not happened for voting and participation in electoral campaigns. Fewer people are following elections and casting a ballot, and the drop-off in voting is proportionately greater among the young.[34] The voting decline literature thus misses a larger reality because it focuses only on elections and campaigns. Similarly, arguments that complexity is pushing voters away from voting conflicts with evidence that more people are participating in forms of activity that require more initiative, skills, and resources than voting.

Rather, Americans are changing the ways they choose to participate. Voting is a form of action for those with limited skills, resources and motivations—the simplicity of voting explains why more people vote than any other single political activity. As political skills and resources expand, citizens realize the limits of voting as a means of political influence (see Table 4.1) and participate through individualized, direct, and more policy-focused methods. In addition, the growth of self-expressive values encourages participation in activities that are citizen initiated, less constrained, directly linked to government, and more policy oriented. In short, changing skills and norms encourage Americans to engage in more demanding and more assertive means of political action.

Age also influences participation patterns. As a baseline model, we should expect increasing political involvement with age, as individuals assume more family and career responsibilities and become integrated into their political communities. This is generally known as the "life cycle model" of participation.[35]

In addition, participation patterns may shift across generations. Several scholars have argued that the young are dropping out of politics. For instance, William Damon states: "Young people across the world have been disengaging from civic and political activities to a degree unimaginable a mere generation ago. The lack of interest is greatest in mature democracies, but it is evident even in many emerging or troubled ones. Today there are no leaders, no causes, no legacy of past trials or accomplishments that inspire much more than apathy or cynicism from the young."[36]

Are the young really this bad? Although many young people seem disengaged with voting, and alienated from electoral politics—so too are many older Americans. Volunteerism and other forms of direct action seem especially common among younger Americans.[37] When life cycle and generational effects are reinforcing, older Americans are more likely to participate in voting or belonging to a political party or related group.[38] However, in other instances a generational shift toward non-electoral forms of participation is so strong that it may reverse the normal life cycle pattern. Cliff Zukin and his colleagues recently examined the full repertoire of political action among the young, and they rejected the general claim of youth disengagement: "First and foremost, simple claims that today's youth . . . are apathetic and disengaged from civic live are simply wrong."[39]

Therefore, both social modernization and generational change may be reshaping the participation patterns of Americans. To display the interaction of both factors, I defined six "generational units" in terms of age and educational level. I divided the General Social Survey sample into two equally sized groups according to educational level. I also divided the sample into three equally sized age cohorts (aged 18–34, 35–51, 51 and over).[40]

Figure 4.3 presents the patterns of voting and party activity for these six generational units. For example, the top panel in the figure displays the percentage of each generational unit who said they voted in 2000—this defines the center point for each of the six "bubbles" in the figure. The width of the bubble for each group is proportionate to its share of the overall public. For instance, the better educated group among the oldest cohort is smaller than the lesser educated group; and this pattern is reversed for the youngest cohort.[41] The bubble graph displays both the relative participation levels of different generational units and differences in the size of these units.

Figure 4.3 shows that turnout is significantly lower among the young, whatever their educational level. However, rising educational levels mean that the better educated (who participate more) constitute a growing percentage of younger cohorts. The increase in educational levels among the young has not reversed the general decline in turnout, but it moderates this downward trend.[42] Another way to visualize this effect is that the greater mass of the lesser educated among the older voters pulls down the average participation of the oldest generation, and the greater mass of the better educated among the youngest cohort pulls up the participation rates of the young overall. The same pattern appears for working with political parties. In fact, the movement away from party involvement among the young is greatest among the better educated, as they shift their focus to other forms of political action.

Figure 4.4 shows examples of the new participation tools of the young—and they follow a much different pattern. The top panel displays the percentage of each generational unit that has boycotted a product for political reasons in the past year. This activity is more common among the young and among the better educated—so these two effects reinforce each other. For instance, only 12 percent of the oldest, less-educated cohort has engaged in these activities, compared with 33 percent among the better educated youth. If one simply compared all the young (26 percent who had boycotted) to all the old (21 percent), the reinforcing effect of generational change and educational change would not be so apparent.

FIGURE 4.3   Voting and Party Work by Generation

Voted in 2000 Election

▶ *Voting is more common among older age groups and the better educated within each age group.*

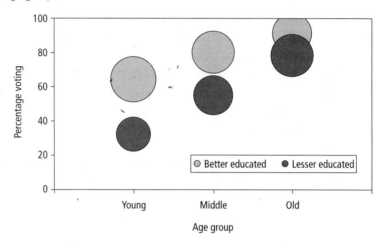

Political Parties

▶ *Party membership increases with age, especially among better educated.*

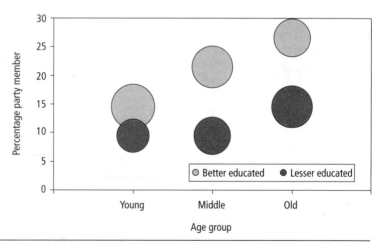

Note: The width of the circles represents the proportion of the sample in each group. The center of each bubble is the percentage who have done the activity for each generational unit.

Source: 2004 General Social Survey.

FIGURE 4.4   **Boycotts and Demonstrations by Generation**

Boycotted a Product

▶ *Boycotting is more common among the young and by the better educated in each age group.*

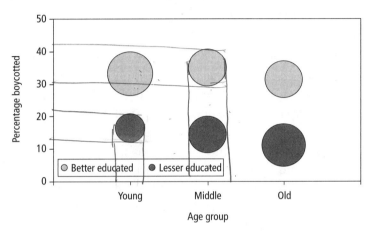

Attended a Demonstration

▶ *Demonstrating rises among the young and is much more common among the better educated.*

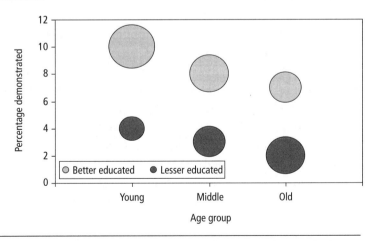

Note: The width of each bubble represents the proportion of the sample in each group. The center of each bubble is the percentage who have done the activity for each generational unit.

Source: 2004 General Social Survey.

The lower panel in the figure displays protest participation. Again, the simple differences between young and old are fairly small, but when age differences are reinforced by increasing educational levels that encourage contentious action, the overall contrast is much greater.[43]

CITIZENSHIP NORMS AND PARTICIPATION

Educational and generational patterns show how social change is reshaping political action. In addition, these social characteristics change the norms of citizenship that lead people to different styles of participation.[44]

Duty-based norms should reinforce traditional forms of political activity, such as voting and party activity, especially since citizen-duty includes as one of its elements the duty to vote. Wolfinger and Rosenstone, for example, stressed the role of duty in describing why people vote: "the most important benefit of voting [is] a feeling that one has done one's duty to society . . . and to oneself."[45] Andre Blais saw images of duty-based voting in even stronger terms: "To use a religious analogy, not voting can be construed as a venial sin: it is a wrong, one that weak human beings should be urged not to commit but may be forgiven for if they indulge in it."[46]

In contrast, engaged citizenship taps participatory norms that are broader than electoral politics. The engaged citizen is more likely to participate in boycotts, "buycotts," demonstrations, and other forms of contentious action.

I combined the two dimensions of citizenship with age and education into a multivariate analyses to explain each of the participation items in the 2004 GSS, including these variables and a measure of cognitive skills (a vocabulary test asked in the GSS) (Table 4.4).[47] Education and cognitive skills are strongly related to electoral participation, as is age. In addition, the norms of citizen-duty, which combines norms to vote and obey the laws, are significantly related to electoral participation. In contrast, engaged citizenship is unrelated to electoral participation. I also repeated the basic analyses with the CDACS survey and find comparable results.[48] Citizen duty in the CDACS survey has its strongest relationship with voter turnout. (The full set of correlations between citizenship norms and participation in the GSS and CDACS surveys is presented in Table 4.5.)

Participation in contentious action presents a different pattern. For the three items on the right side of Table 4.4—boycotts, attending a demon-

TABLE 4.4   Predicting Participation

▲ The table describes the impact of citizenship norms and other predictors in explaining participation in each activity; activities that are more dependent on citizen duty are on the left of the table and activities more dependent on engaged citizenship are on the right.

PREDICTOR	Vote	Party member	Contact official	Sign petition	Attend rally	Donate money	Boycott	Internet forum	Attend demonstration
Citizen duty	.17*	.09*	.13*	.07*	.06*	.08*	.02	-.02	-.05
Engaged citizenship	-.04	.05	.11*	.07*	.17*	.18*	.14*	.13*	.21*
Age	.26*	.10*	.15*	.03	.03	.03	-.09*	-.11*	-.11*
Education	.21*	.19*	.20*	.11*	.20*	.15*	.17*	.08*	.11*
Cognitive level	.14*	.18*	.23*	.30*	.17*	.20*	.28*	.14*	.15*
Multiple R	.46	.36	.45	.39	.38	.38	.44	.27	.34

Note: Table entries are standardized regression coefficients (β); each coefficient represents whether the predictor has a positive or negative effect on each political activity independent of the other predictors. Statistically significant effects (more than .05) are noted by an asterisk.

Source: 2004 General Social Survey.

| TABLE 4.5 | The Correlations between Citizenship Norms and Participation |

▶ *The table describes how citizen duty and engaged citizenship are related to different forms of political activity.*

| | GSS Survey | | CDACS Survey | |
ACTIVITIES	Citizen duty	Engaged citizen	Citizen duty	Engaged citizen
Voting/Elections				
Voted in election	.25	−.04	.11	.06
Worked for party	.13	.07	−.03	.17
Worked for campaign	—	—	.01	.14
Donated money (GSS: any political group)	.10	.20	.03	.18
Contacting				
Contacted politician	.18	.12	.02	.20
Contacted media	.02	.08	—	—
Contentious Actions				
Signed petition	.09	.09	−.01	.23
Lawful demonstration	−.07	.23	−.15	.09
Illegal demonstration	—	—	−.17	.09
Consumer Action				
Boycott product	.02	.18	−.05	.19
Bought product	—	—	−.04	.18
Internet Action				
Visited Web site	—	—	−.02	.21
Forward political email	—	—	−.02	.14
Web activity	−.03	.16	−.06	.17

Note: Table entries are Pearson correlations (r); each coefficent represents whether citizen duty or engaged citizenship increases or decreases participation in each political activity.

Source: 2004 General Social Survey; 2005 CDACS Survey.

stration, or participating in an Internet forum—the young are more active than older Americans. Furthermore, engaged citizenship stimulates participation in these areas, while traditional norms of citizen-duty have no impact (see Table 4.5). The CDACS survey yields similar patterns: engaged citizenship stimulates contentious action, while duty-based citizenship dissuades participating in these activities.

Finally, the five participation examples in the middle of the table represent forms of political action driven by a mix of forces. Each of these activities is strongly related to education and cognitive skills, but age differences are often modest (three age coefficients are not statistically significant). Moreover, the normative basis of these activities is also diverse. Contributing money and attending rallies, for instance, is related to both traditional notions of citizen-duty and social activism—perhaps because individuals motivated by these two norms are contributing to different types of groups and attending different types of rallies. These individualized forms of participation appear driven by multiple motivations, which implies that social change within the American electorate will not have clear implications for participation in these activities.

In summary, the contrast in the normative basis of participation in electoral politics versus contentious politics highlights how different images of citizenship, combined with rising skill levels of the better educated public, are transforming the patterns of political action in America. Given the causal forces behind these participation patterns, this shift may be a continuing feature of democratic politics.

ENGAGED DEMOCRATS

I first presented the evidence from this chapter to a group of government officials at a lunch talk hosted by the Carnegie Endowment in Washington, D.C. I began by sharing the academic argument that Americans are disengaging from the political process, which may undermine the bases of American democracy. Hibbing and Theiss-Morse, for example, assert that Americans prefer to be politically disengaged: "The last thing people want is to be more involved in political decision making: They do not want to make political decisions themselves; they do not want to provide much input to those who are assigned to make these decisions; and they would rather not know all the details of the decision-making process."[49] Similarly, this chapter cited other recent academic studies insisting that civic life is becoming extinct in America.[50]

To the audience of government officials and administrators, I asked how many of them worried that too few Americans were contacting their offices for advice or in attempts to influence government policy—how many worried that citizens were too passive. No one raised a hand. As you might imagine, just asking this question generated laughter about the unrealistic claim. Few members of Congress, for instance, complain that they receive less input from their constituents than in the past; few administrators yearn for a lobbyist to break the dullness of their daily routine. Instead, they see individual citizens, lobby organizations, and public interest groups as part of an expanding network of activism that had developed in Washington over the previous generation. As stated in the introduction: the good news is . . . the bad news is wrong. America remains a participatory society.

Election turnout has declined, but this is not typical of all political activity. The repertoire of action has actually expanded, and people are now more engaged in more forms of political participation. Participation in election campaigns is still common. People are working with informal groups in their community to address local problems—and this has grown over time. More people today make the effort to directly contact their elected representative or other government officials. The repertoire of political action now includes a variety of protest activities. When one adds political consumerism and Internet activism, the forms of action are even more diverse.

The new faces of democratic citizenship among the young can be seen in two examples from a recent *USA Today* series on changing patterns of political engagement.[51] Alex is an eighteen year old who lives in northern California. She switched shampoos over animal testing and will not buy clothes produced by child labor. She yells at those who do not recycle, and last year in high school she helped organize a protest over the genocide in the Sudan, raising $13,000 for Darfur relief. All this was before she was even eligible to vote. Jaime is a high school student in Maryland who learned about Darfur from one of her courses. She created a teen group to encourage high school students to become socially involved. And when she created a Web page for the group on Facebook, membership boomed. These two examples are not representative of all young people, but they illustrate the new focuses and forms of political activism that exist beyond elections, and that can enrich our democratic process if we understand these new forms of political action.

Thus, there are three major lessons from our findings. First, turnout rates in elections provide a poor indicator of the overall political involvement of Americans. It is the most easily available statistic for local, state, and national politics—and it extends back in time. However, there is more to democracy than elections. Other non-electoral modes of individualized or direct political action have increased over time. Ironically,

Putnam's 2000 Social Capital Survey replicated four questions from the Verba-Nie participation series: general interest, attending a rally, working with a community group, and protest. Despite the *Bowling Alone* thesis of decreasing political engagement, none of these four questions displays a statistically significant decrease from the Verba-Nie participation levels of 1967 and 1989. Rather than disengagement, the repertoire of political action has broadened.

Changes in political participation are analogous to changes in the contemporary media environment. Compared to a generation ago, Americans are consuming much more information about politics, society, and other topics. People are also consuming information from a greater diversity of media sources, some of which did not exist a generation ago. If one only tracked the viewership of the news programs on the major television networks, however, the statistics would show a downward trend in viewership over time. The declining viewership for ABC, CBS, and NBC is not because people are watching less television—they are watching more hours per day—but because they have more alternatives today. This is the same with participation: people are more active in more varied forms of action.

Certainly we should not dismiss the decrease in voting turnout. Elections are important because they select political elites, provide a source of democratic legitimacy, and engage the mass public in the democratic process. If large proportions of young (and older) Americans do not vote, this lessens their representation in the political process (and may change election outcomes). It is not healthy for democracy when half or more of the public voluntarily abstains from electing government officials. This is especially problematic when the elected government does not represent all the people—and makes decisions that a full majority of Americans do not support. For instance, given these differential turnout rates, it is not surprising that the government devotes increasing resources to programs benefiting seniors while providing proportionately less support for the young. This realization has stimulated efforts to re-engage young people in elections.[52] However, the goal of participation reforms should not be only to encourage young people to act like their grandparents (and vote out of a sense of duty), but also to show them how engaged citizenship should lead to voting as well as new forms of participation.

Second, changes in citizenship norms and the social composition of the American public are shifting the nature of political action. Turning out to vote requires little initiative since this activity is institutionalized and often mobilized by social or political groups. The clearest examples are the "get out the vote" drives that are a common part of American elections. At the midpoint of the twentieth century, when most Americans had only limited formal education, modest living standards, and limited access to political information beyond the local newspapers, voting and campaigns were the primary focus of political action—and norms of duty-based citizenship encouraged individuals to participate.

As the political skills and resources of the public have increased, this alters the calculus of participation. More people today can engage in more demanding forms of political action, such as individualized activity and direct action. Writing letters to a government official, for example, is less likely when three-fifths of the public has less than a high school education (the electorate of 1952), than when three-fifths have some college education (the electorate of 2004).

In addition, changing norms reinforce a new style of political action. Engaged citizenship stimulates people to be active, especially in methods that give them more direct say and influence. Engaged citizens will still vote because of the importance of elections to the democratic process. However, their participation repertoire includes more direct and individualized forms of action. The engaged citizen is more active on referendums than elections, and direct action over campaign work; volunteering is preferred to party activity.[53]

Third, the changing mix of participation activities has implications for the nature and quality of citizen influence. Verba and Nie, for example, describe voting as a high pressure activity because government officials are being chosen, but there is limited specific policy information or influence because elections involve a diverse range of issues.[54] Therefore, the infrequent opportunity to cast a vote for a prepackaged party is a limited tool of political influence. This influence may increase when elections extend to a wide range of political offices and include referendums, as in state and local governments. Still, it is difficult to treat elections as mandates on specific policies because they assess relative support for broad programs and not specific policies. Even a sophisticated, policy-oriented electorate cannot be certain that its policy interests are represented in an election or that the government will follow these policies once elected into office. Consequently, many people vote because of a sense of civic duty, involvement in a campaign, or as an expression of political or partisan support, rather than as a major means to influence policy. Indeed, the importance of citizen-duty as a predictor of voting turnout and party work illustrates how these citizenship norms motivate turnout.

In contrast, direct action methods allow citizens to focus on their own issue interests, select the means of influencing policymakers, and choose the timing of influence. The issue might be as broad as nuclear disarmament or as narrow as the policies of the local school district—citizens, not elites, decide. Control over the framework of participation means that people can convey more information and exert more political pressure than they can merely through election campaigns. Political institutions are also adapting to accept and encourage these new forms of citizen access.[55] In short, the control of political activism is shifting to the public and thereby increasing the quantity and quality of democratic influence.

5

TOLERATING OTHERS

L istening to the pundits on the TV news and political talk shows, one might conclude that America is an intolerant and divided nation—and getting worse. These loud voices clamor that the public is polarized into red and blue states, with liberals and conservatives continually at odds, and that intolerance toward those different from us (however defined) seemingly abounds. Indeed, these debates have intensified following the terrorist attacks of September 11, 2001. The Patriot Act and other government anti-terrorism actions and immigration legislation continue to stimulate intense debate on the balance between security and civil liberties in a democracy. It appears that political debate is deteriorating to the point that anyone who disagrees with the talk show host is not just wrong or mistaken, but is a liar, conspirator, dupe, or even a traitor.

Are the talk shows portraying an accurate picture of America? Political analysts imply that political tolerance is decreasing and that America is becoming a more divided nation. There are vague images of a more tranquil and tolerant America of the past. But let's do a reality check. Starting with the Red-Blue "culture war" election of 2004, turn the clock back fifty years to consider the levels of political tolerance in America in 1954. This is an auspicious year to select, because it was marked by Sen. Joseph McCarthy's notorious Army-McCarthy hearings. Following the lead of the earlier House Un-American Activities Committee, McCarthy brought a series of military, political, and social figures before his Senate subcommittee investigating Communist Party influence in America.[1] Intertwined

with the Red Scare was the Lavender Scare, as Congress also targeted homosexuals as potential security risks.[2] By the end of 1954, approximately
2,200 individuals had been removed from the federal workforce as security risks because of their political views or sexuality. The Senate eventually censured McCarthy for his outrageous behavior, but only after he
threatened and intimidated a long series of witnesses, compiled millions
of words of testimony, and broadcast the hearings on live television.

McCarthy was not an isolated case. In mid-1954, the Supreme Court
upheld the constitutionality of the Internal Security Act, thus making
membership in the Communist Party sufficient grounds for the deporta-
tion of aliens. A full nineteen states had legislation banning communists
from public service or politics.[3] Thousands had been removed or encouraged to leave positions in state and local governments, and loyalty oaths
were prerequisites for employment in many workplaces. Earlier in that
year the U.S. Information Agency, which ran America House libraries
around the world, banned Henry David Thoreau's *Walden* because of its
socialist orientation. In 1954 a system of "voluntary" censorship still existed in the movie industry.[4] To link religion to patriotism, President
Dwight D. Eisenhower signed legislation to add "under God" to the Pledge
of Allegiance. The Supreme Court handed down the landmark *Brown v.
Board of Education* ruling on racial desegregation of schools in 1954, but
this was only necessary because 17 states mandated segregated education.
Anti-Semitism remained common in America, and nearly all of the Ivy
League universities discriminated against Jewish students, minorities, and
women in their admission processes.[5] I could continue—1954 was a very
busy year for intolerance.

Coincidentally, the first surveys of Americans' political tolerance were
also conducted in 1954, and they painted a clear image of public prejudice.
Jim Gibson notes that nearly five thousand people were surveyed in
Samuel Stouffer's seminal study of tolerance, and barely 2 percent were
willing to give communists the right to free speech, assembly, and employment as a schoolteacher.[6] Socialists and atheists fared only slightly better.
Racial prejudice was still widespread—and one can just imagine what the
average American would say about gay rights in 1954. Despite the rhetoric
of American politics and the promises of the U.S. Constitution and Bill of

Rights, America in the 1950s was not a society of broad political and social tolerance.

The extent of political tolerance is vitally important to the functioning of democracy. The Bill of Rights begins by enumerating the freedom of religion, speech, press, assembly, and petitioning the government to underscore the importance of these rights. A study of tolerance in the mid-1970s began by noting, "The founding fathers of this country prescribed tolerance in the marketplace of freely flowing ideas as the key to the democratic process and the necessary condition for orderly change and innovation in a democratic society."[7] A more recent book states that "support for the freedom of expression of unpopular views represents an understanding of the meaning of an open and democratic polity. To a substantial extent, tolerance is the cornerstone of a democratically enlightened citizenry."[8]

Clearly, political tolerance is a key feature in judging the vitality of American democracy. And, in contrast to the alarmist claims of some pundits, opinion surveys over the past half-century generally describe spreading tolerance among the American public.[9] Furthermore, the growth of political tolerance is often linked to the processes of social modernization described in Chapter 1, such as rising educational levels, generational change, and the empowerment of minorities. That's why it is important to examine how changes in citizenship norms may have contributed to increasing political tolerance among the public.

Let's begin by reviewing the prior public opinion research on political tolerance in America and the measurement controversy intertwined with this research. Then we'll turn to the changing levels of political tolerance over time, followed by an examination of the relationship between citizenship norms and political tolerance.

HOW TO MEASURE POLITICAL TOLERANCE

Analyses of political tolerance have a long—and controversial—history in American public opinion research. The first study by Samuel Stouffer examined tolerance for socialists, atheists, and communists by assessing Americans' willingness to allow each group to give a public speech in the community, to teach in a college, and to have books on their views included in the public library among other activities.[10] Stouffer concluded that tolerance of these specific groups was limited, despite public support for abstract democratic principles of free speech and minority rights. Stouffer's research occurred in a context where the increasing tensions of the Cold War overlapped with a society that had not accepted principles such as racial and gender equality. However, Stouffer believed that tolerance would gradually increase among Americans because of rising education levels and generational change.

Further research in the 1970s and early 1980s seemingly justified Stouffer's optimistic projection of tolerance trends. Replicating Stouffer's core measures of tolerance for atheists, communists, and socialists, James Davis found that tolerant responses had increased by 23 percent by 1972.[11] Another project in 1973 found a broad increase in tolerance; most Americans (55 percent) scored high on their overall scale of tolerance (up from 31 percent since 1954).[12] Similar patterns occurred for tolerance of other non-conformist activities, such as protesting the Vietnam War, showing pornographic movies, or teaching sex education in the schools. The study concluded that "this is a critical shift [in American public opinion] since the existence of a tolerant majority greatly enhances the prospect that expansion of support for civil liberties will be accelerated."[13]

The evidence of increasing tolerance was soon challenged on methodological grounds.[14] Several scholars argued that Americans had not simply become more tolerant; rather, the perceived threat attached to the anti-system groups of the 1950s—communists, socialists, and atheists—had waned by the 1970s, and so people expressed more tolerance of these three groups. These researchers argued for a "content-controlled" assessment of tolerance; one should first identify the specific groups an individual dislikes, and then measure tolerance for these groups. Consequently, when these scholars asked about the contentious groups in the 1970s—such as anti-war protesters—this yielded a less positive view of political tolerance. In addition, the Stouffer items were criticized for focusing only on extreme groups on the left, so that ideological closeness to these groups could bias the results.

The debate over the measurement of political tolerance has continued to the present. One step forward was the expansion of the tolerance battery to include extreme groups on both the left and right, which lessens the ideological bias of a tolerance scale. However, research found that tolerance is often generalized and applied to extremist groups on both the left and right,[15] which undermines the argument of the content-controlled approach. Other studies showed that the correlates of tolerance were quite similar for both the balanced Stouffer items and the content-controlled measures, again suggesting that both methods tapped a common reality.[16]

Tracking levels of tolerance over time is admittedly difficult, because the groups that test the tolerance of a nation will change. For instance, until September 11, 2001, few survey researchers in the United States thought that Muslim fundamentalists were a major test of political tolerance.[17] And questions about tolerance of communists now seem quaint antiques as the memory of the Soviet Union fades into history. But by including a balance of groups, and using alternative methodologies, I believe we can monitor the broad contours of political tolerance in America and see how these feelings are linked to norms of citizenship.

THE UNCONVENTIONAL EVIDENCE: RISING POLITICAL TOLERANCE

As just noted, measuring tolerance is not a simple task. Since 1976 the General Social Survey has included questions that measure tolerance toward five social groups: communists, atheists (anti-religion), homosexuals, militarists, and racists. This methodology tries to avoid the content of tolerance problem by including groups on the right and left. In retrospect, this is difficult to do over a long time, because the political context changes so much over three decades. When the battery began in 1976, one could not foresee the collapse of communism in 1989–91. The political efforts of the gay/lesbian movement have also changed the public impressions of this group over time. The survey series spans the period from the end of American involvement in Vietnam to the invasion of Iraq and the ongoing sectarian violence in that country and the continuing war on terrorism at home and abroad, which might affect attitudes toward militarism. We thus might expect that Americans have a highly variable image of different potential extremist groups over time, so that tolerance waxes and wanes.

The GSS asked if members of each group:

- Should be allowed to speak in the respondent's community
- Should be allowed to teach in a college or university
- Should have books by this group removed from the local library

TABLE 5.1	Tolerance of Challenging Political Groups

▶ *Americans are more tolerant toward all five groups over the past three decades.*

TARGET GROUP	Action	1976	1988	1994	2004	Change
Communist	Allow to speak	53	62	68	70	+17
	Allow to teach	40	50	57	66	+26
	Don't remove book from library	55	61	68	71	+16
Atheist	Allow to speak	62	71	73	77	+15
	Allow to teach	39	47	54	66	+27
	Don't remove book from library	58	65	71	73	+15
Homosexual	Allow to speak	62	73	81	83	+19
	Allow to teach	52	60	72	80	+28
	Don't remove book from library	56	63	70	70	+14
Militarist	Allow to speak	53	58	64	67	+14
	Allow to teach	35	39	47	54	+19
	Don't remove book from library	55	59	65	69	+14
Racist	Allow to speak	60	63	62	62	+2
	Allow to teach	41	43	44	47	+6
	Don't remove book from library	60	64	68	66	+6
Average		**52**	**59**	**64**	**68**	

Source: General Social Survey, (1976–2004).

Table 5.1 displays the percentage giving tolerant responses on each of the three activities for each of the five groups. Four time points show the general patterns: 1976, which begins the survey series; 1988, before the tumultuous political upheavals in Eastern Europe of 1989–91; 1994, early in the Clinton administration; and the most recent survey point in 2004.

Americans' tolerance toward all five groups has gradually broadened over the past three decades. Averaging together the three activities, tolerance of leftist groups has steadily increased: communists (+20 percent), atheists (+19 percent) and homosexuals (+20). Similarly, there is increased tolerance of militarists (+16 percent) and racists (+5 percent). Allowing a representative of these groups to teach at a university was originally the least tolerated activity for each group, but this increases the most over time—and all three activities show increases.

Most striking is the consistent shift toward tolerance across all five groups. One might assume that the demise of communism altered images of communists, for example, but much of the change occurred by 1988, before the Berlin Wall collapsed. The increased tolerance of communists since 1988 seems like a continuance of this trend. One might expect that the U.S. involvement in Iraq could have shifted opinions toward militarists in the most recent survey, but 2004 marks a continuation of the trend found in earlier time points. These trends could also reflect different patterns within subgroups of the population: liberals becoming

more tolerant of liberal groups while conservatives grow more tolerant of conservative groups—with both remaining intolerant of their opposites. This is not the case, however—the trends in tolerance are broadly comparable for self-identified liberals, centrists, and conservatives.[18] Indeed, this evidence speaks to a slow, broad increase in political tolerance of all groups over this three-decade span.

The shift in tolerance is even more apparent in Figure 5.1. This figure charts the average number of tolerant responses by year, with a maximum of fifteen different items asked in each year (three activities for five groups). Again, the steady increase in tolerance over time is striking; it is a relatively continuous trend rather than showing abrupt shifts in reaction to political events or changes in political context. In the mid-1970s, the average American gave less than eight tolerant responses out of fifteen; in 2004 there are more than ten tolerant responses. These tolerance trends would be even more dramatic if we could extend these series back to the 1960s or 1950s.

Other research broadly documents the growth of political tolerance in other areas. There is growing racial tolerance and support for gender equality over time.[19] Robert Putnam tracked increasing support for racial integration, civil liberties, and gender equality among the American public. He concluded that "behind each of these statistical trends stands a category of Americans increasingly liberated from stigma and oppression."[20] On most dimensions, Americans are more tolerant today than at the mid-twentieth century.

Certainly intolerant aspects of the American political culture still exist, so we should be cautious about an overly optimistic reading of these trends. There are still too many examples of intolerance toward others be-

FIGURE 5.1   **Rising Political Tolerance**

▶ *Americans' tolerance of the activities of challenging political groups has increased over time.*

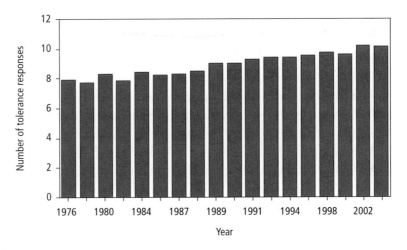

Note: The figure presents the average number of tolerant responses across the 15 items in table 5.1.

Source: General Social Survey (1976–2004).

cause of their political beliefs, religion, or lifestyle choices. Some Americans are still unwilling to grant the rights assured by the Constitution to those with whom they disagree. Racial, ethnic, religious, and political divisions remain part of the American experience. In addition, expressions of tolerance are also distinct from actual behavior. The literature is replete with examples of people doing unreasonable things to their fellow citizens—and too many people watch this happen and remain silent.

Still, while the media and the political pundits would have us think that the situation is getting worse, the evidence from public opinion argues just the opposite.[21] People were once openly hostile to those they disagreed with, ready to withhold freedom of speech, freedom to publish, or the ability to teach. Today, such expressions of intolerance are much less common. Americans have moved closer to the Jeffersonian ideal that the democratic response to extreme political beliefs is to engage in discussion and debate.

WHO IS TOLERANT AND WHO IS NOT

Researchers generally agree on the factors correlated with feelings of tolerance; they disagree on the interpretation of these influences. Education is strongly and consistently related to tolerance for extremist groups at either end of the political spectrum. Some scholars argue that education increases cognitive sophistication, and that this stimulates tolerance.[22] Others maintain that education leads to critical and moral reasoning, and thus support for tolerance.[23] This educational effect is likely reinforced by the apparently increasing attention to tolerance and diversity in the educational system. Consequently, the absolute increases in educational levels over the past several decades should have systematically increased tolerance levels.

It is also possible that educational differences in tolerance represent the social stratification of society. Upper status individuals have more social resources and privileges, which may make them less sensitive to extremist threats or diminish their concern about extremist groups. Thus, education might identify this social ranking rather than having independent effects. Such a stratifying effect would diminish the impact of rising educational levels on tolerance because the top strata would simply be identified by a higher education level (the bachelor's degree of the 1960s is equivalent to the master's degree of today). Stratification can be a constant effect over time, just measured by different cutting points (the same with income). We can evaluate this idea in our analyses.

Another standard predictor of tolerance is age, or more precisely, generation. Typically, younger generations are more tolerant than older generations.[24] Generation is a surrogate for the different socialization experiences of age cohorts. While there is much that is positive about American society in the 1950s, it was not a period noted for its tolerant political environment. It is still shocking to remember that older Americans raised before the mid-1960s grew up in a nation that tolerated and institutionalized racism and consciously restricted the role of women. McCarthyism was an extreme example of political intolerance under the guise of national security, but anti-communism was official doctrine.

In contrast, the efforts of the civil rights movement and women's movement transformed public opinion in these two instances, and exemplified a general process of increasing political tolerance and greater consciousness of basic human rights. Successive generations have been raised in environments that were progressively more tolerant in both their social norms and legal protections. Accordingly, age group differences in tolerance increased between 1954 and 1973.[25] Presumably, different socialization experiences left their imprint on the values of each generation.

However, some analysts question the existence of a generational trend in tolerance. Robert Putnam, for instance, argued that Generation Xers are no more tolerant than the early Boomers, and he felt the cohort born around 1940–45 (pre-baby boom) represented the high point of tolerance.[26] In addition, a portion of generational differences may be a result of rising educational levels rather than generational experiences per se. For Putnam, the biggest generational gains in tolerance were already behind us, and the erosion of social capital held negative implications for political tolerance. (It should be noted, however, that we now have another 10 years of survey data, and the tolerance trend continues.)

Previous research thus suggests that growing tolerance partially depends on the public's increasing education and a process of generational change. To illustrate the effects of each factor, I use a bubble graph as in Chapter 4. The 2004 GSS sample is divided into two equally sized groups according to educational level; it's divided into three equally sized age cohorts (18–34, 35–50, 51 and over). Combining both factors produces six "generational units" defined by their age and educational level; the width of each bubble depends on the size of each group. For each of these groups we calculated the mean number of tolerant responses on the fifteen items—this defines the center point for each of the six bubbles in Figure 5.2. The bubble graph thus describes both the relative tolerance levels of generational units, and differences in the size of these units.

Figure 5.2 shows strong educational differences in tolerance. Within each of the three age groups, the better educated are significantly more tolerant. There is a four-item gap in the number of tolerant responses between the education groups in the oldest cohort, for example. In addition, even independent of educational level, tolerance increases among the younger generations. Moreover, these data show little evidence that tolerance peaked among the pre-Boomers, since the generational shift toward tolerance is continuing even among the youngest Americans.[27]

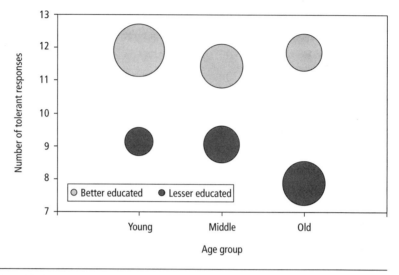

FIGURE 5.2   Tolerance by Generation

▶ *Overall political tolerance is greater among the better educated in each generation, and increases as education rises among younger generations.*

Note: The width of each bubble represents the proportion of the sample in each group. The center of each bubble is the number of tolerant responses by the generational unit to the five groups in table 5.1.

Source: 2004 General Social Survey.

When one compares the contrasting modal groups in Figure 5.2, the cumulative impact of age and educational change are substantial. The older, less-educated group gave 7.9 tolerant responses, compared to 11.9 among the younger, best-educated group.

CITIZENSHIP AND TOLERANCE

Education and generation help to map the social distribution of tolerance, but political tolerance should also be embedded in definitions of citizenship. Democratic citizens should be socialized into tolerant beliefs, but this may vary across different norms of what citizenship means.

On the one hand, respect for the majority, social order, and the rule of law are essential elements of the democratic contract. But too strong an emphasis on these values may discourage dissent and promote intolerance of unconventional political and social views. For those who value duty and social order, tolerance of political dissidents may be seen as threatening this order, and consequently undesirable. Although Tocqueville admired Americans' emphasis on participation and equality, he also believed that the majoritarian elements of the American political culture created pressures for conformity and limited tolerance of minority beliefs.[28] Other studies similarly demonstrate that perceptions of the soundness and stability of the values that underlie the social order are strongly related to tolerance.[29] So those who follow a duty-based definition of citizenship may be less tolerant of unconventional or anti-system political groups.

Meanwhile, those who adhere to norms of engaged citizenship may be more supportive of political tolerance. A concern for social rights and the protection of the disadvantaged is embedded in this conception of citizenship, and these orientations should promote tolerance. The ability to sympathize with others and the acceptance of unconventionality in interpersonal relations is linked to political tolerance.[30] Libertarian/postmaterial values are similarly linked to engaged citizenship as well as political tolerance.[31] Tolerance also makes more cognitive demands on the citizen to balance out conflicting political values and accept the rights of others, which also requires a more expansive definition of citizenship. In this way, norms of engaged citizenship may contribute to the spread of political tolerance.

Figure 5.3 shows the relationship between citizenship norms and tolerance (using a different scale included in the GSS citizenship module).[32] Attachment to engaged citizenship increases political tolerance; there is roughly a half-point difference in tolerance as a function of these norms. Conversely, high levels of citizen-duty decrease political tolerance, although by a modest amount. Combining these two effects, the shift in citizenship norms provides a strong stimulant for increasing political tolerance in America over the past several decades.

Age, education, and citizenship are all interrelated, and so it is initially difficult to know if citizenship differences are separate effects from these other influences. For this reason, I also conducted analyses to estimate statistically the independent effects of citizenship norms, age, and education. I included a measure of cognitive skills (based on a vocabulary test)

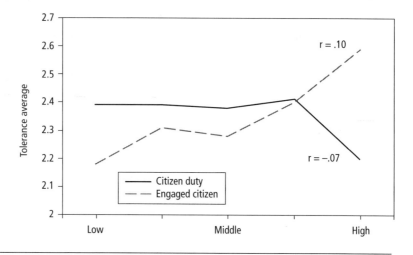

FIGURE 5.3   **Citizenship and Tolerances of Three Groups**

▶ *High citizen duty lowers overall political tolerance, but high engaged citizenship raises tolerance levels.*

Note: The figure plots the average score on an index that combines tolerance of religious extremists, those who wish to overthrow the government, and racists; 1=low tolerance, and 4=high tolerance.

Source: 2004 General Social Survey.

to separate cognitive skills from formal education. In addition, to control for political position, I also include party identification in the analyses.

Table 5.2 presents these statistical analyses predicting a summary index of overall tolerance, plus each of the specific items in the index. The coefficients in the table indicate the relative importance of each predictor, while statistically adjusting for the effect of the other predictors. Education and cognitive skills are strongly related to tolerance in each of the four models, which reaffirms the importance of both social learning and cognition in promoting political tolerance. This implies that rising education levels have contributed to increases in tolerance, even beyond the public's cognitive skills. In addition, party identification does not significantly affect their overall tolerance once these other factors are excluded.

Citizenship norms also shape feelings of political tolerance even when these other factors are weeded out. Engaged citizens are more tolerant on

TABLE 5.2   **Predicting Tolerance**

▶ *Citizen duty consistently decreases tolerance, while engaged citizenship, higher education, and cognitive sophistication increase tolerance.*

PREDICTOR	Tolerance Index	Religious Extremist	Overthrow Government	Racist
Citizen duty	−.09	−.06	−.11	−.06
Engaged citizenship	.08	.12	.05	.02
Age	−.01	.01	−.08	.07
Education	.15	.13	.09	.16
Cognitive skills	.16	.12	.07	.16
Party identification (R)	.03	.07	−.04	.04
Multiple R	.30	.29	.22	.28

Note: Table entries are standardized coefficients from a multiple regression analysis; each coefficient represents whether the predictor has a positive or negative effect on tolerance. Statistically significant effects (more than .05) are noted by shaded boxes.

Source: 2004 General Social Survey.

all four measures, which range across groups with quite different political orientations (although one coefficient is not statistically significant). Part of the political orientation of engaged citizenship is to support the rights of challenging groups, even those with whom you may disagree. In contrast, those who emphasize a duty-based image of citizenship are less tolerant. Despite the values of a challenging group, citizen-duty has a negative effect.

These different norms of citizenship also shape other aspects of tolerance and inclusion in America. For instance, the General Social Survey included a short battery on attitudes toward immigrants. Engaged citizens are more favorable toward immigrants, with relationships even stronger than for the Stouffer tolerance questions.[33] Engaged citizens are more likely to feel that immigration improves American society, that the government does not spend too much on immigrants, and that citizenship should be extended to immigrants. The effect of citizenship norms is often substantial; for instance, among those lowest in engaged citizenship, 79 percent say the government spends too much on immigrants, versus only 32 percent among those highest in engaged citizenship. Conversely, duty-based norms of citizenship encourage the opposite policy positions. So how a person defines what it means to be a citizen shapes how he or she applies the rights of citizenship to others.

Citizenship and Tolerance: A Second Look

The sources of political division today look far different from those that preoccupied Stouffer and his initial successors. The collapse of the Soviet empire and the end of the Cold War made communism an example of another era. Problems such as racial intolerance and gender discrimination remain, although in dramatically different forms than a half-century ago. Homosexuals have moved from the dark shadows of society toward broader social acceptance. And in a post-September 11th world, the threats of religious fundamentalism and international terrorism loom large.

Tolerance measures should reflect these changing realities. The 2005 CDACS survey included just such a content-controlled question. The survey first asked respondents to identify their least-liked group from a list provided by the interviewer.[34] The groups identified as the least-liked differ across the two dimensions of citizenship. Those high in citizen duty mention groups that span the political spectrum: the Ku Klux Klan (34 percent), radical Muslims (19 percent), people who are against churches and religions (12 percent), and American Nazis (9 percent). Those high in citizen engagement list their least-liked groups as: the Ku Klux Klan (52 percent), American Nazis (11 percent), radical Muslims (8 percent), and those against churches and religions (7 percent). Several of the groups in the Stouffer battery no longer seem to concern many Americans: 6 percent of the full sample mention militarists, 4 percent mention communists, and only 3 percent mention gay rights activists.

After identifying the least liked group, the CDACS survey asked whether this group should be allowed to make a speech in the community, be banned from running for public office, or be allowed to hold rallies in the community. This content-controlled measure should be a more rigorous sign of political tolerance because individuals are first asked which group they dislike the most—and then tolerance is based on this most-disliked group. It is easy to imagine being tolerant of groups that one is ambivalent toward; the real test of tolerance comes when one's values conflict with an opponent.

Figure 5.4 presents the relationship between citizenship norms and this content-controlled measure of tolerance. Engaged citizenship is pos-

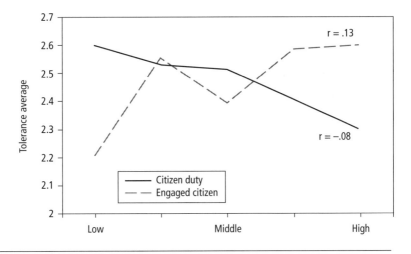

FIGURE 5.4   Citizenship and Tolerance of Least-Liked Group

▶ *High citizen duty lowers political tolerance toward the least-liked group, but high engaged citizenship raises tolerance levels.*

Note: The figure plots the average score toward the least-liked political group by both citizenship dimensions; 1=low tolerance, and 5=high tolerance.

Source: 2005 CDATS Survey.

itively related to tolerance. Conversely, feelings of citizen duty slightly decrease political tolerance. These two comparisons are based on different groups—but they are the groups that are most disliked by each person. So this analysis yields similar conclusions: the norms of citizenship shape how we apply the rights of citizenship to others, even those we dislike the most.

Citizenship and Tolerance: A Third Look

In the post-September 11th world, there is a lively and important debate on how America can balance its commitment to freedom and civil liberties while protecting its citizens.[35] The public deliberations on the terms of the Patriot Act and its renewal illustrate this conflict. The treatment of prisoners at Guantánamo Bay, the CIA secret prisons, and domestic surveillance programs raise the specter of the United States abandoning its democratic legal commitments to gain vital national security information.

Similarly, those involved in the drafting of the Patriot Act and related government policies argued that we are living in a new age where past rules of privacy and civil rights no longer fit reality. In late 2005, the Bush administration acknowledged directing the National Security Agency to conduct a domestic spying operation that avoided judicial approval, and this created new debates on the balance between liberty and security. These are the new crucibles of tolerance and civil liberties in contemporary America.

The CDACS survey asked Americans about their support for civil liberties when the political system was challenged. One set of questions focused on domestic dissent, such as the government investigating protestors, requiring that high school teachers support government policies, and expanding the government's investigative powers.[36] Other items focused explicitly on terrorist threats: making it illegal to belong to a group that supports terrorism and making it legal for the government to detain non-citizens indefinitely if they are suspected of belonging to a terrorist organization.

Loyal and patriotic Americans can honestly debate these issues and disagree on the answers, but it is clear that citizenship norms at least partially shape how people feel toward these issues. The first set of items in Figure 5.5 deals with civil liberty issues generally involving dissent (or at least separate from a terrorist connection). The strength of the correlation is represented by the length of the bars in the figure, and the direction of the relationship. For each of these items, feelings of citizen duty encourage individuals to support a policy restricting civil liberties. In contrast, engaged citizenship has essentially no relationship or even a negative relationship with these policy choices. The lower part of the table presents two items that explicitly involve a potential terrorist threat. Citizen duty has an even stronger effect, prompting individuals to support policies that would restrict potential terrorists, even if these policies raise basic civil liberty questions. Again, engaged citizenship is essentially unrelated to these policy choices.

For instance, only 28 percent of those low in citizen duty strongly approve of a law that would make it illegal to belong to or contribute money to a group that supports international terrorism, but this percentage rises to more than 50 percent among those high in citizen duty. On first blush,

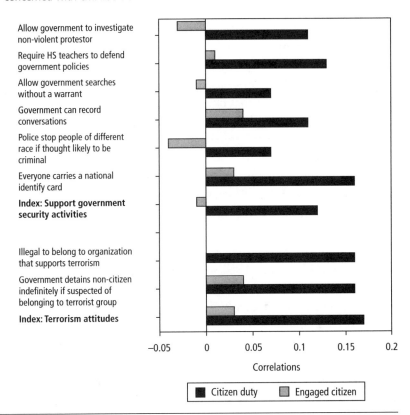

FIGURE 5.5   Citizenship and Civil Liberties

▶ *Citizen duty prompts support for stronger government action to promote security, while engaged citizens are less supportive of government action and more concerned with civil liberties.*

Allow government to investigate non-violent protestor

Require HS teachers to defend government policies

Allow government searches without a warrant

Government can record conversations

Police stop people of different race if thought likely to be criminal

Everyone carries a national identify card

Index: Support government security activities

Illegal to belong to organization that supports terrorism

Government detains non-citizen indefinitely if suspected of belonging to terrorist group

Index: Terrorism attitudes

−0.05   0   0.05   0.1   0.15   0.2

Correlations

■ Citizen duty   ▨ Engaged citizen

Note: Figure entries are correlation coefficients (Pearson r) that measure the relationship between citizenship norms and these civil liberties questions.

Source: 2005 CDACS survey.

we might say that such a law is needed in today's uncertain and insecure world. But life is more complex, and in reality one might belong to a group without knowing about all of its activities. Americans also disagree on what is a terrorist act and what is a defensible use of violence. This is not to argue that people should be free to support terrorism, only that this is a complex issue, subject to different interpretations, and so caution is warranted before accepting a blanket statement.

One can legitimately debate each of these policy options. It is easy to understand that in the present world many Americans feel that stronger actions must be taken to limit crime and the terrorist threat. At the same time, people are sensitive to the potential loss of civil liberties engendered by these actions. Some analysts might decry the limited support for strict measures to ensure public order among those low in citizen duty—but others might insist that duty-based citizenship too easily sacrifices liberty for security. The point is that citizenship norms shape these policy positions, and thus partially define the two sides of this debate.

IMPLICATIONS OF CITIZENSHIP AND TOLERANCE

The recent motion picture, *Flags of our Fathers*, directed by Clint Eastwood, has a subplot that illustrates some of the contrasts from contemporary norms of citizenship in America. One of the heroes of the flag raising on Iwo Jima in World War II was a U.S. Marine who was also a Native American. Even while he is on a government tour across America to celebrate this event and sell war bonds, he runs into repeated acts of prejudice. In one scene he is battling police and his Navy buddy shows up. When the friend asks why he is so angry, the Marine points to a nearby bartender and says that he was refused service because he was an Indian. The bartender shrugs and says he was only following the rules. This was common in America of the 1940s and 1950s.

Such intolerant acts still happen in America, but less often than in previous decades. Increasing public support for political tolerance runs counter to much of the contemporary punditry about the current political culture. While politicians and public figures decry the intolerance and polarization of Americans, the evidence from public opinion surveys describes a slow, steady increase in tolerance toward a range of contentious groups over the past several decades.

Given the recent history of American politics, it would be surprising if feelings of tolerance had not changed. The civil rights movement dramatically altered the landscape of American politics, and a wealth of survey data document the fundamental transformation of public opinion on racial discrimination. Today, in fact, one measures tolerance not by acceptance of African Americans, but by acceptance of racists. The women's movement similarly transformed attitudes toward gender equality, and it helped to reinforce the rights revolution in America. Some may look back to the 1950s as a golden age of American politics—but this was not so for persons of color, women, other minorities, and those concerned about social equality.

Furthermore, these political changes are linked to shifting norms of citizenship, from duty-based norms that are less accepting of difference to norms of engaged citizenship that encourage tolerance. This places the core support for political tolerance among young, better-educated Americans—with the least support among older and less educated citizens. Thus, the expansion of citizen rights and tolerance for others during the second half of the twentieth century is one of the major historic achievements of American democracy—and changing citizenship norms contributed to these processes.

Why, then, have these trends been missed by politicians and pundits who insist that Americans are becoming less tolerant of others? In part, the explanation may simply be that as a nation becomes more tolerant, it is less accepting of remaining intolerance. The "political correctness" emphasis that is so common on university campuses and liberal parts of society arises because most Americans believe we should be tolerant of others, and some take this goal to an unreasonable degree. However, the political correctness in the 1950s would have worked in the opposite direction, to discourage differences. In much the same way, the rights revolution creates a new set of forces that heighten claims that one's rights have been violated—sentiments that people would not have expressed several decades ago. In short, as tolerance becomes more common, this increases pressure on remaining examples of intolerance.

This positive image of the political culture also conflicts with a mindset that social analysts should be critics. Treatises on the crisis of American democracy or the imminent collapse of American society draw more attention than a book announcing that the sky is *not* falling. That is why few of the recent books on the crisis of the American spirit note the spread of political tolerance.[37] Even Putnam, when summarizing the evidence of increasing political tolerance, discounts the significance of these trends, and the positive evidence is even presented in a chapter titled "The Dark Side of Social Capital."[38] Any description of the "greatest generation" as politically intolerant does not fit the image of this cohort as the font of social capital.

At the same time, some critical reflection is warranted   if it builds on the facts. Although expressions of tolerance have grown over the past several decades, we know that there is a gap between statements and behavior. The change in public sentiments has not been fully matched by the reality of public actions or public policy. The reality of life is improving, but it is lagging behind the even larger shift in public opinion. In short, more must yet be done to make America a tolerant society.

In addition, although we might embrace tolerance as an ideal, we should recognize the need to balance social needs and individual freedom. America (and other Western democracies) is now struggling to balance tolerance of diversity and multiculturalism with real worries about the terrorist threats and actions of political and religious extremists. Some challenges to the status quo are presenting ideas we might dislike, yet which should be tolerated. Other contemporary challenges present real threats that test democracy's ability to balance social needs against individual rights. The difficulty is to identify the nature of the challenge and the appropriate response. The evidence of the rising political tolerance and broadening views of citizenship by Americans suggests, to me, that the nation is now better suited to address these questions than in earlier periods of American history, when intolerance was tolerated.

IS GOVERNMENT THE PROBLEM
OR THE SOLUTION?

A few years ago, I gave a talk about citizen attitudes at the Leisure World retirement community a few miles away from my university. The audience was attentive and informed; they asked lively questions and challenged my ideas—perhaps even more than in a typical university class. In informal discussions after the talk, I met many residents who had fought in World War II, and some had worked on postwar reconstruction in Japan or Germany. They followed politics, and they voted. The turnout of registered voters in the community was 78 percent in 2004 (the national turnout for 18–24 year olds was 58 percent of registered voters). As I left the community center, I noticed the range of other lectures, social groups, and activities scheduled during this week. More than 200 informal groups are listed on the community's homepage with a range of social, cultural, and political themes. This was, clearly, a sample of the generation that Brokaw and Putnam admired, and this group of seniors displayed many of the positive political traits identified with this generation.

Much of the current discussion about citizenship focuses on such examples of political engagement and the individual's expected role within the political system, as discussed in the previous chapters. However, citizenship norms also shape images of the role of government and its public policies. The political culture includes both expectations toward political inputs and political outputs.

For instance, the residents of Leisure World held fairly conservative political views, as might be expected of a community where the average

age was 78 years. They disproportionately supported George Bush and Arnold Schwarzenegger in the last national and state elections, while we expect their grandchildren to lean more toward the Democrats. In discussing politics after the lecture, these seniors favored lower taxes, and they remembered and preferred an earlier era when government was less active—of course, they made exceptions for Social Security and Medicare. Some of these people were interested in new issues such as environmental quality or foreign aid, but these were not priorities. The typical senior felt that the government was doing too much, or doing it wrong.

When a politician calls for a return to traditional images of citizenship, this implicitly includes expectations about the appropriate role of government and even specific government policies. For instance, when George W. Bush called for a renewal of citizenship in his 2001 Inaugural Address, he presumably expected that this would include a more limited role of government. And when Ralph Nader lectures on the need for greater civic engagement, it is connected to a specific, but very different, policy agenda.

How are citizenship norms linked to Americans' policy preferences? This chapter examines the potential impact of citizenship norms at three levels. First, how do citizenship norms shape an individual's view of the overall scope of government activity? Although the size of government grew during the latter half of the twentieth century, debate over its appropriate size continues. Second, what specific policy areas should receive more or less government spending? For instance, should government spend more on social programs or focus its priorities on its guardian role in providing security and basic public services? Embedded in the two models of citizenship are different expectations about what policies should be the priority of government and which policies should receive less attention. Third, what is the relationship between citizenship norms and a range of domestic and foreign policy issues? The evidence now available provides a better understanding of the range of political values linked to contemporary norms of citizenship.

WHAT SHOULD GOVERNMENT DO?

Theories of citizenship typically focus on the individual's role in the political process. The implications of citizenship norms for attitudes toward the role of government are not always clear, but we can extract a set of ideas from previous writings. For instance, several theoretical models of citizenship (for example, neo-liberalism) imply that these norms should favor limited government. Neo-liberalism holds that an expanding role of government means that "individualism is sacrificed to equality; privacy, to bureaucracy; and furthermore, security is bought at the price of stigma and the loss of that very dignity of citizenship it was designed to enhance." [1] Many neo-liberals see more personal freedom emanating from a smaller government that requires less of its citizens (and provides less in return). Even when social rights are recognized, this perspective would limit the government's responsibilities by stressing the individual obligations of citizens. [2] To an extent, we expect that these orientations are linked to duty-based citizenship, similar to those articulated by many Leisure World residents. Duty-based citizenship should prompt individuals to favor a smaller role for government.

This image of limited government is ingrained in an American political culture that emphasizes individual freedom and skepticism of a powerful government. The Republican Party has actively advocated these goals. In his first inaugural address in 1981, Ronald Reagan stated: [3]

> *Our government has no power except that granted it by the people. It is time to check and reverse the growth of government which shows signs of having grown beyond the consent of the governed.*
>
> *It is my intention to curb the size and influence of the Federal establishment and to demand recognition of the distinction between the powers granted to the Federal Government and those reserved to the states or the people.*

Even if less effectively than Reagan probably hoped, this mantra guided his presidency as well as succeeding Republican administrations of George H. W. Bush and now George W. Bush.

In contrast, the idea of social citizenship implies a more expansive view of the role of government. A top priority of engaged citizenship is social rights, and it primarily falls upon the government to provide these rights. [4] In much the same way, the traditional social-democratic perspective stresses the potential economic and social hardships that face the disadvantaged, and thus the need for government to redress these conditions. Engaged citizenship presumably represents a more proactive view of government as a means to address social needs. Part of this no doubt stems from a concern for others, a sentiment that prevails among engaged citizens (see Chapter 2).

In this way, duty-based citizenship and engaged citizenship should affect specific policy preferences. An emphasis on duty and individual responsibility should restrict support for social programs, redistributive policies, and the "big government" initiatives normally identified with the New Deal and Great Society. Engaged citizenship, on the other hand, should lead to almost diametrically opposed policy priorities: support for an activist government that provides for the needy, develops social service programs, and is a guarantor of basic civil rights.

The clearest contrast in the policy implications of citizenship norms may come in the foreign policy domain. Citizen duty should encourage support for defense spending as an extension of a commitment to national security. In contrast, the norms of citizen engagement would encourage support for foreign aid and a more cooperative foreign policy style. Expressed in the vernacular of Washington, norms of citizen duty are most apparent in support for the Department of Defense, while norms of engaged citizenship may lean toward support for the Department of State.

Admittedly, the theoretical literature on citizenship includes contradictions to the positions just described, with various political philosophers providing contrasting statements on the appropriate scope of government. Our questions on citizenship norms focus on the role of the individual and his/her responsibilities as a citizen, and the questions do not explicitly ask about specific public policies or the overall scope of government. However, by examining the relationship between citizenship norms and policy attitudes, we can illustrate how these norms are affecting the agenda for government action.

WE WANT GOVERNMENT TO BE A BIG SPENDER

One of the broadest policy attitudes involves support for the overall role of government—should government be large and active, or small and

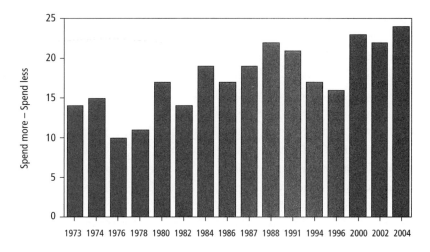

FIGURE 6.1 **Increasing Support for Government Spending**

▶ Americans' average preferences for spending in eleven policy areas has increased over time.

Note: Figure entries are the percentages saying "too little" is being spent on the problem minus the percentage saying "too much," averaged across 11 separate policy areas.

Source: General Social Surveys (1973–2004).

limited in its goals? Surveys use a variety of ways to measure public opinion on the role of government.[5] One approach examines support for taxes and the input side of government. We will not investigate those opinions here, in part because of limited evidence in the available surveys.[6]

Instead, we will consider whether Americans believe their government should increase or decrease public spending. This focus is partially based on theoretical concerns because it broadly describes what people expect of their government. I also chose this focus because the General Social Survey includes questions tapping these preferences.

The GSS asked whether the government should spend more or less in a variety of policy areas.[7] Figure 6.1 presents the overall trend in spending preferences over the past three decades—and the results are a surprising contrast to the conventional wisdom. Across eleven different policy domains (see Table 6.1), we can count the percentage that thought government should be spending more, and subtract the percentage that thought government should spend less. In every year, those who want more government spending exceed those who want less spending by a significant amount. Despite the neo-conservative policies of the Reagan/Bush administrations—or perhaps because of these policies—public support for greater spending has generally trended upward during this time span. The ironic legacy of the twelve years of the Reagan/Bush administration was that federal government was larger when they left, perhaps because public demands for policy outputs restrained the rhetoric of the Republican Party. Even while the George W. Bush administration declared its desire to cut government spending, Americans' preference for more government spending increased in the 2000s.

These patterns are not unique to the General Social Survey. Other opinion surveys find that most people expect the government to do more in most policy areas, even while complaining that taxes are too high or government must be more efficient.[8] Moreover, even when spending is paired with the costs of these programs, such as in higher taxes, more people support an active government. Bennett and Bennett concluded that when faced with the alternatives of limited government and a larger role of government, Americans "have made a choice, and it is in favor of big government"—Americans have grown comfortable living with the leviathan.[9]

Averaged within these overall statistics are preferences on specific policy goals. Table 6.1 displays the difference between the percentage of Americans who favor more government spending in a policy area minus those who want to spend less for a few illustrative time points. These statistics describe a long-term consensus for increased government spending on crime prevention, education, health care, preventing drug addiction, environmental protection, and solving the problems of urban America. Only welfare, the space program, and foreign aid are consistently viewed as candidates for budget cuts.[10]

Americans' priorities for spending on specific programs do, however, respond to changes in the federal budget and the political context.[11] For instance, the perceived military weakness of the Carter administration stimulated calls for greater defense spending; 56 percent of Americans

TABLE 6.1 **Budget Priorities of the American Public**

▲ This table tracks the changes in public spending priorities over time.

PRIORITY	1973	1976	1980	1984	1988	1991	1996	2000	2002	2004
Halting rising crime rate	64	61	65	62	64	59	61	55	50	52
Protecting the nation's health	58	57	49	53	65	66	60	69	71	75
Dealing with drug addiction	64	55	56	57	64	50	48	53	49	45
Protecting the environment	57	47	35	54	60	63	50	55	53	58
Improving the educational system	42	42	44	59	60	62	65	67	69	69
Solving problems of big cities	41	26	21	31	36	35	45	40	30	29
Improving the condition of blacks	12	2	0	19	19	20	13	21	15	20
The military and defense	-28	-2	48	-21	-22	-13	-15	-2	9	9
Welfare	-33	-49	-45	-16	-19	-15	-43	-19	-20	-17
Space exploration program	-53	-51	-21	-27	-16	-26	-32	-29	-26	-24
Foreign aid	-70	-75	-69	-65	-63	-68	-69	-52	-59	-53
Average	14	10	17	19	22	21	16	23	22	24

Note: Table entries are the percentages saying "too little" is being spent on the problem minus the percentage saying "too much." A positive value means people want to spend more; a negative value means they want to spend less. Missing data has been excluded from the calculation of percentages.

Source: General Social Survey (1973–2004).

thought the government was spending too little on defense in the spring of 1980. This feeling supported the large defense expenditures of the early Reagan administration. Then, as examples of Pentagon waste became commonplace (news accounts of $500 hammers and $7,000 coffeepots), popular opinion shifted to preferring the status quo or even cutting in defense budgets. Similarly, limitations on social spending enacted by the Reagan administration exceeded the wishes of many Americans. During Ronald Reagan's presidency, support increased for *more spending* in the areas of health care, environmental protection, education, urban problems, and minority aid.

These patterns may be surprising to those unfamiliar with these public opinion trends, since the political rhetoric of the Republican Party for the past two decades has called for less government spending—and it has seemed to be a generally successful electoral strategy. In fact, the Republican appeal to voters has had a different focus—cutting taxes—while being less than forthcoming on how this will impact spending. The public's endorsement of increased spending on specific policy areas is typically paired with criticism of taxation levels as too high (and general cynicism about government). These contrasting orientations, I will argue, are embedded in the norms of citizenship.

Our Spending Priorities

How do the norms of citizenship shape the public's specific policy preferences? Duty-based citizen norms seem more consistent with conservative and neo-liberal images of the role of government, which would limit support for overall government spending and favor a narrow definition of the role of government. In contrast, engaged citizenship should prompt a more encompassing view of the scope of government. These norms should lead individuals to accept a larger government role across a range of policy areas, especially those that address social needs.

We can link citizenship norms to support for more government spending across the full range of policy areas in the GSS. We simply count the number of policy areas where an individual favored more spending minus the number of policies where he or she favored less spending.

Figure 6.2 plots this balance of spending preferences by citizenship norms. As expected, duty-based norms generally lower support for government spending. Those scoring highest in citizen duty see total gov-

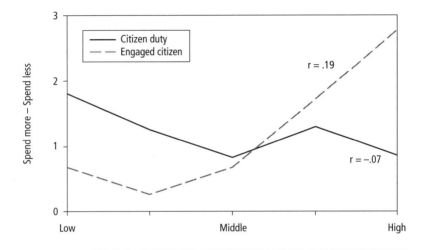

FIGURE 6.2   **Citizenship and Government Spending**

▶ *Citizen duty slightly lowers support for government spending, while engaged citizenship increases support for spending.*

Note: Figure entries are the average number of areas where respondents favored more spending minus the number of areas where they favored less spending.

Source: 2004 General Social Survey.

ernment spending as about what they would prefer (preferences for more spending in some areas are balanced by less spending in other areas, so the net opinion is for spending to increase in less than one policy area). In contrast, engaged citizenship strongly stimulates support for greater government spending. There is more than a fourfold increase in support for greater spending across the range of engaged citizenship. To address the social interests of engaged citizenship, these individuals feel, the government should be larger.

Beyond general attitudes toward government spending, citizenship norms should also affect support for spending in specific policy areas. Duty-based norms may encourage a Reagan-like preference to focus spending on defense spending, infrastructure, transportation, and similar programs. These are the policy preferences one most closely identifies with the residents in our Leisure World example. In contrast, engaged citizens—perhaps the grandchildren of the Leisure World residents—

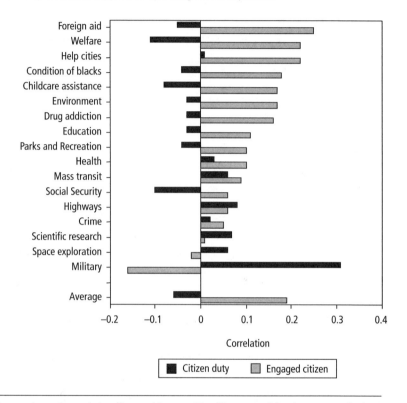

FIGURE 6.3 Citizenship and Spending Priorities

▶ *Engaged citizenship increases support for spending more on most policies, while citizen duty decreases support for spending on most policies.*

Note: Figure entries are the correlations (Pearson *r*) between citizenship norms and favoring more spending in each policy area. A positive correlation means the norm is related to a preference for more spending; a negative correlation means the norm is related to less spending.

Source: 2004 General Social Survey.

should favor more spending on government programs that provide social services and protect the needy. Thus, the different definitions of citizenship should translate into contrasting public policy priorities.

In addition to the eleven time series questions described above, the 2004 General Social Survey tapped spending preferences for six additional policy areas. Figure 6.3 presents the correlations between citizenship norms and spending for each of these areas (positive correlations show a preference for more spending). The table is arranged by the policy priorities of engaged citizens; their strongest positive correlations are toward the top of the figure. The social dimension of engaged citizenship yields support for greater spending on welfare, support for programs to aid cities, support for blacks, childcare, and drug addiction programs. These are all examples of how the solidarity norms of engaged citizenship stimulate concern for the underprivileged. Each area displays a strong positive relationship with engaged citizenship (and a weak or negative relationship with duty-based norms).

Citizen duty encourages much different spending priorities. People guided by this norm generally favor less spending on social programs and more spending on defense and the military—the only area where engaged citizenship is significantly linked to cuts in spending. In addition, duty-based norms promote support for more spending on infrastructure programs: highways, mass transit, space exploration, and scientific research.

Combining Predictors

The citizenship patterns in policy priorities are striking, but they may reflect the influence of other attitudes. For instance, there is a strong ideological or partisan element in attitudes toward government spending, and this may underlie the patterns I have just described.[12] Democrats typically support greater government spending, especially on the social programs emphasized by engaged citizens. Republicans are more likely to hold the line on total government spending, and focus spending on other priorities such as national security. Similarly, policy priorities may reflect different generational or educational experiences that are related to citizenship norms.

To determine if citizenship norms exert an influence on spending attitudes independent of other characteristics, we can conduct a statistical analysis to include partisanship, age, and education along with the two dimensions of citizenship. Figure 6.4 displays the results from such analyses. The first panel shows that support for overall government spending is positively related to engaged citizenship, even while controlling for the substantial impact of partisanship and the other predictors. Duty-based citizens have a slight, though statistically insignificant, tendency in the

FIGURE 6.4   Predictors of Spending Preferences

Overall Government Spending

▶ *Engaged citizens and Democratic partisanship strongly favor more spending overall.*

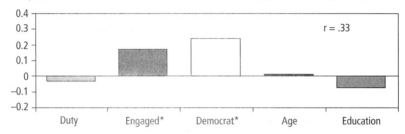

Spending on Social Programs

▶ *Engaged citizens and Democratic partisans strongly favor spending on social programs.*

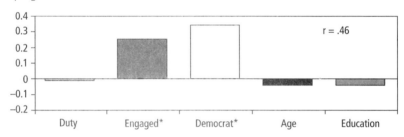

Spending on Infrastructure

▶ *People high in citizen duty, older, and better-educated Americans favor more spending on infrastructure policies.*

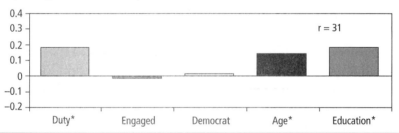

Note: Table entries are standardized coefficients from a multiple regression analysis; each bar represents whether the predictor has a positive or negative effect on citizenship norms. Statistically significant effects (more than .05) are noted by an asterisk.

Source: 2004 General Social Survey.

opposite direction. Thus, the identities of citizenship norms shape how Americans view the appropriate scope of government.

The second panel in the figure examines support for spending on social programs that are most likely to reflect the solidarity aspects of citizenship.[13] Here, the positive stimulus of engaged citizenship is even more apparent because these policies tap social issues such as welfare spending, support for minorities, health care, and social security. In contrast, the third panel analyzes support for infrastructure spending: highways, mass transit, scientific research, and the space program. Duty-based citizenship favors more spending for these policies, even despite the general negativity of duty-based citizens toward spending overall.

In summary, citizenship norms shape how Americans think about the scope of government in general, and how they define the specific policy priorities of their government. Feelings of citizen duty lead to a more restrictive view of government overall, and a more limited policy mandate reflecting more libertarian traditions. In contrast, engaged citizenship encourages an activist image of government, especially on the social programs that reflect the values embedded in these norms of citizenship.

PUBLIC POLICY PREFERENCES

Spending priorities provide one aspect of the public's policy priorities, but often the goals of policy are more important than their funding levels. As this chapter was being drafted in 2006, the U.S. Congress was engaged in a series of policy debates that touched on a range of non-spending issues: a constitutional amendment on flag-burning, proposals to ban gay marriage, immigration policy, the rules of citizenship, and various policies to address international terrorism. Often the choice is not how much to spend, but which policies to pursue.

The Georgetown CDACS survey included a battery of questions that tap contemporary policy choices. To highlight the differences between citizen duty and engaged citizenship, Figure 6.5 organizes these policy items into three categories. The first category at the top of the figure includes those items where citizen duty strongly promotes approval of the policy (a positive correlation), and engaged citizenship generally stimulates disapproval (a negative correlation). This category includes four different policies that reflect a strong national security orientation: the United

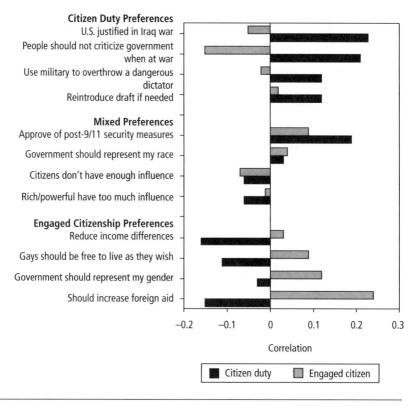

FIGURE 6.5 **Citizenship and Policy Preferences**

▶ *Citizen duty increases support for military action, while engaged citizenship increases support for social programs, multiculturalism, and foreign aid.*

Note: Figure entries are the correlations between each dimension of citizenship and favoring more spending in each policy area. A positive correlation means the norm is related to a preference for the policy; a negative correlation means the norm is related to opposition to the policy.

Source: Georgetown CDACS survey.

States was justified in the Iraq war, people should not criticize the government when at war, military force can be used to overthrow a dictator, and support for reintroduction of the military draft.

In contrast, the items at the bottom of the figure are policies favored by those high in engaged citizenship (a positive correlation), and generally opposed by those high in citizen duty (a negative correlation). This includes support for increased foreign aid, the representation of women in government, gay rights, and the reduction of income differences. (A third category in the middle of the figure includes issues where citizenship norms do not have strong effects).

The policy contrasts as a function of citizenship norms could not be starker. While citizen duty promotes support for national security and allegiance, engaged citizens are advocates for a liberal cultural agenda and economic liberalism. Perhaps the rhetoric and actions of the Bush administration have polarized citizenship norms around these contemporary issues and made images of citizenship more partisan in the current environment. One can imagine that many elements of public policy can appeal to both norms of citizenship or even be independent of such norms. The Bush administration developed its policies oriented by traditional norms of citizenship and government that encourage such images of national security, duty, and loyalty as their base. Its calls for a renewal of citizenship reflect a desire for Americans to develop values that will support such policies. Similarly, the Clinton administration pursued a different policy agenda because Bill Clinton and his top aides saw the role of government in terms of a different set of political norms. This shows how citizenship norms shape the policy preferences of Americans.

CITIZENSHIP AND PUBLIC POLICY

Norms of citizenship first shape individuals' political behavior and provide guidance on what they think a "good citizen" should do. So much of the discussion of citizenship focuses on its impact on political participation, civic engagement, and political tolerance—themes examined in previous chapters. This chapter illustrates how these citizenship norms also carry over to expectations of what a "good government" should do.

For example, norms of citizen duty encourage a more limited view of government, focusing on providing minimal policy outputs, such as national security, domestic order, and basic infrastructure needs. Engaged citizenship, meanwhile, stimulates a more expansive view of government and its role in society, including addressing the social concerns included in engaged citizenship. So this second group favors more government spending overall, especially on social programs, minority aid, foreign aid, education, and the environment. These preferences exist even independently of the partisan leanings of individuals.

Ronald Inglehart has extensively described how this pattern of changing styles of action and policy goals is a common feature in most advanced industrial democracies.[14] He similarly describes how new postmaterial values are increasing support for contentious and direct forms of political action, at the same time that they are generating support for new social and quality-of-life issues. As a result, individuals concerned about nuclear power or genetically modified foods often tend toward contentious forms of action as well. I am arguing that the American public is following a similar course as shaped by the norms of citizenship.

Americans' changing citizenship norms are increasing acceptance of government's overall policy activity and specifically new social policies. Despite the imagery that Americans expect less from government—fueled by the presidential victories of recent Republican candidates—the trends in public spending preferences actually move steadily and consistently in the other direction. Americans today favor more government spending than they did a quarter century ago. Engaged citizenship is inevitably intertwined with a belief that government exists to address a range of societal needs. As the balance of citizen norms shifts within the American public, this increases expectations for a more active government, especially on social programs. The time trends from 1973 until 2004 show that the greatest growth for more government spending occurs for improving the educational system, protecting the nation's health, foreign aid, and improving the condition of blacks. The public is changing its policy priorities in ways that are not as apparent in every day political discourse.

Perhaps policy conflicts have become so harsh in contemporary American politics because they reflect these different images of citizenship. In earlier periods, when most Americans shared norms of citizen duty, policy debates drew upon a common value set. But now, some policies tap different sets of norms and different identities about what a good citizen and government should do. In part, this may arise because citizenship norms are becoming more closely linked to partisan leanings. It also presumably reflects a tension between contrasting citizenship norms that now exist within the American public. For instance, one can imagine returning to the Leisure World retirement community and discussing the norms of engaged citizenship—being active in associations, understanding others, buying products for political reasons, and being concerned with those less well off—and these seniors would broadly accept these values as part of the American creed. If one argued that this should lead to policies supporting gay rights, foreign aid, and gender equality, it is just as easy to imagine that they would sharply disagree. These are the value differences embedded in shifting norms of citizenship, and this may be why certain policies deeply divide sectors of American society.

IMAGES OF LEVIATHAN

Try an experiment. Sit in a Starbucks and start a conversation with the people at the next table. Ask them what they think about how the government in Washington is doing its job. Usually, if they will talk to a stranger who asks them about politics, they eventually share a list of complaints. Taxes are too high, services are too low; government is doing too much in one area and not enough in another area. And typically they cite a favorite example of where the government has done something foolish or even corrupt. I have done this experiment when Bill Clinton and then George W. Bush occupied the White House, and only the examples differ, not the overall pattern of dissatisfaction.

Dissatisfaction is now commonplace in politics. The average American is unhappy with the performance of government—almost no matter whether he or she is a Democrat or a Republican. The contemporary political culture features "critical citizens" and "dissatisfied democrats" who expect more of their elected officials.[1] We are Monday morning quarterbacks, complaining about the miscues and the missed opportunities and thinking that a skilled government could (and should) do better.

This cynicism has become a normal part of politics, but during the 1950s and early 1960s, good citizenship meant support for the political system and a strong sense of national pride. In comparison to the other nations in *The Civic Culture* study, Americans had "a high degree of pride in the political system. Americans' attachment to the political system also includes both generalized system affect as well as satisfaction with specific governmental performance." [2] At about the same time, the American National Election Study (ANES) found that 73 percent of those surveyed felt the government could be trusted most of the time to do what is right, 71 percent believed politicians cared what people think, and 64 percent thought government was run for the benefit of all. Indeed, political scientists described such supportive and allegiant attitudes as fundamental elements of a democratic civic culture. [3]

During the last third of the twentieth century, however, these positive images of government gave way to doubts about politicians and skepticism of our democratic political institutions. [4] In 1979, President Jimmy Carter warned that declining public confidence "was a fundamental threat to American democracy." Political trust ebbed and flowed over the subsequent years but never returned to the allegiant and supportive orientations that *The Civic Culture* had described. The 2004 ANES found that only 47 percent of Americans trusted the government to do right, 34 percent felt that politicians cared what people think, and only 40 percent thought government was run for the benefit of all. This diminished support for government and political institutions has stimulated widespread debate about the vitality of democracy, since allegiance and trust were once considered essential to a democratic political culture. [5]

How have changing norms of citizenship affected these images of government? A strong link exists—but in more complex forms than previously recognized. Your discussion partner at Starbucks is not just reacting to the actions of government, but these impressions are also shaped by citizenship norms that define what is expected of a good government, as well as a good citizen.

CHANGING IMAGES OF GOVERNMENT

Public doubts about the government normally begin with questions about the incumbents of public office. Americans might initially criticize Richard Nixon's actions during Watergate, Bill Clinton's marital indiscretions, or George W. Bush's representations of the facts leading up to the Iraqi war. If dissatisfaction persists, then these feelings might generalize beyond the specific politicians of the day. Cynics may begin to distrust politicians as a group, thinking that those who attain public office are generally untrustworthy or are corrupted by the temptations of office. If these sentiments deepen, they may touch the institutions of government beyond the individual office holders.[6]

These examples illustrate the point that political support includes several different orientations. We distinguish between political support at three levels:

- **Political authorities** are the incumbents of political office, or in a broader sense, the current government and the pool of political elites from which government leaders are drawn.
- **Regime** refers to the institutions and offices of government rather than the present officeholders. This level of support also involves public attitudes toward the procedures of government and political institutions, such as the principles of pluralist democracy.
- **Political community** implies a basic attachment to the nation and political system beyond the present institutions of government.

Attitudes may differ across these three levels, and we explore each in this chapter.

Trusting Political Authorities

You might be cynical about politicians and the government, and today you have lots of company. But you have nothing on William Hungate. A Democrat from Missouri, Hungate served as a member of the U.S. Congress from 1964 to 1977. He sat on the powerful Judiciary Committee and was one of the primary authors of the articles of impeachment against President Richard M. Nixon. He voluntarily left Congress in 1977, tired of the politics, the logrolling, and the shortcomings of government. In one of his last addresses to Congress he said his farewells: "May the future bring all the best to you, your family and friends—and may your mothers never find out where you work."

Cynicism about government has a long tradition in America and is deeply ingrained in political lore and humor.[7] Yet, in the 1950s and early 1960s, most Americans were positive toward their government. There was an enthusiasm in the American political spirit, and political analysts viewed such positivism as critical to a successful democracy.

However, public images of politicians and government have followed a downward spiral over the past several decades. The most extensive evi-

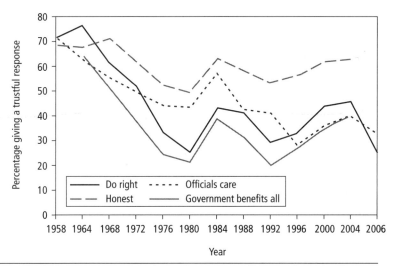

FIGURE 7.1   Trust in Government

▶ *Americans have become less trustful of politicians and government over time.*

Source: American National Election Studies.

dence comes from the American National Election Studies, which describes a deepening skepticism of politicians over time (Figure 7.1). Trust in political authorities started to decline in the late 1960s. Conflict over civil rights and Vietnam paralleled Americans' eroding public confidence in their leaders; in concert with Watergate and a seemingly endless stream of political scandals, support declined even further over the next decade.

Trust of government officials reached a low point in 1980, and then the trend temporarily reversed during the upbeat presidency of Ronald Reagan. The practiced symbolism of Reagan's administration, and the allegories that the "Great Communicator" himself used with the American public, stressed the positive aspects of American society and politics. Opinions rebounded in 1984, but the decline continued in later years. By the end of George Bush's presidency in 1992, the levels of trust hovered near their historic lows.

Trust levels improved somewhat by the end of the Clinton administration, following a decade of unprecedented economic growth and the end of the Cold War, but levels of support remained far below those of the late 1950s and early 1960s. Following the terrorist attacks on the World Trade Center and the Pentagon in September 2001, political support spiked upward. People were more trustful of politicians, more confident in political institutions, and felt greater national pride. As these events receded in time, however, opinions slipped back to their pre-9/11 levels. By the 2004 presidential election, trust in government was roughly the same as in 2000. As horrific as the terrorist attacks were, they did not reshape Americans' trust in government in an enduring way.

Nearly all other long-term public opinion series show the same downward trends in trust in government. For instance, the Pew Center for the People and the Press tracked evaluations of the ethical and moral practices of federal government officials; 34 percent of Americans were critical in 1964, and 60 percent in 2002.[8] The public has become increasingly skeptical and distrustful of the government and the individuals who hold political office.

The Sources of Change

These trends of decreasing trust in authorities are now well known, described by a host of academic and popular books. In most analyses, researchers point to unique and specific characteristics of American politics as the reasons for these trends. The presidency supposedly suffers from the accumulation of negative events that range from Watergate to Iran-Contra to Bill and Monica and now Iraq. Other explanations focus on the institutional structure of American government and the need for reform. The Congress suffers from its own set of scandals and various problems of the legislative process.[9] Reform Congress, the critics insist, and trust will improve. Politicians are now more concerned about pleasing special interests. Hence the calls to change the structure of campaigns and enact finance reform, so that political support can rebound. Other analysts suggest that the media are to blame, and the growth of investigative and attack journalism have demoralized the American public—thus the media should be reformed.[10] Perhaps the most perverse view is that the United States suffers from too much democracy and that limiting the democratic process will improve public images of government.[11]

While scandals, government performance, and institutional deficits may contribute to the decline in political support, broader forces of social change are also at work. Joseph Nye and his colleagues noted that these discrete explanations are not broadly consistent with the patterns of decreasing trust in government.[12] For instance, when scandals pass and the public votes a new government into office, the skepticism continues. In addition, cross-national studies document a similar trend of decreasing political trust in most advanced industrial democracies.[13] The breadth of this pattern, across a wide range of nations and different institutional structures, suggests that a common pattern of social change is affecting citizen images of government.

This book has argued that citizenship norms reflect broader changes in political values produced by the modernization of American society (and other Western advanced industrial democracies) over the past several decades. The decline of duty-based norms decreases respect for authority of all types, including respect for government officials and political institutions. So the erosion of duty-based citizenship may contribute to declining trust in government authorities. Such a relationship would be another reason why some politicians seek a revival of traditional, duty-based norms to create a more supportive and loyal public.

Engaged citizenship has a more uncertain impact on images of government. These citizens expect an activist government across a wide set of policies (see Chapter 6). So they may be more positive toward the politicians and government agencies that carry out these programs. However, engaged citizenship includes a desire for citizen autonomy and support for challenging political actions; this suggests that these individuals may be more critical of government. For instance, a growing emphasis on post-material and self-expressive values, which overlap with norms of engaged citizenship, stimulates criticism of the established leaders and institutions of government.[14]

To test these ideas, let's relate citizenship norms to several measures of authority support—images of politicians and the government—in the 2004 General Social Survey (Figure 7.2).[15] The first set of items in the figure tap images of government performance in the past, present, and future.[16] The contrast between duty-based and engaged citizenship is quite apparent. People who are high on citizenship duty are much more positive about the performance of the government—past, present, and future—with the weakest effect looking toward the future. In contrast, engaged citizenship is only weakly related to evaluations of the performance

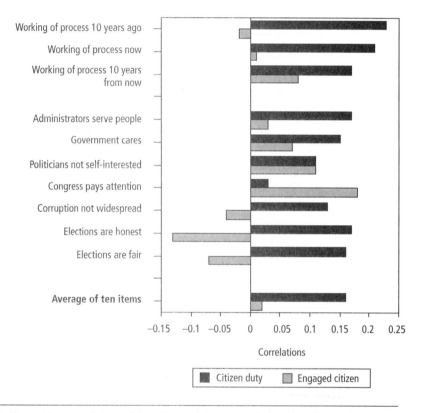

FIGURE 7.2 Citizenship and Evaluations of Government

▶ *Citizen duty promotes a more supportive image of government, while engaged citizens have mixed images of government.*

Note: Figure entries are correlation coefficients (Pearson *r*) that measure whether citizenship norms have a positive or negative effect on these evaluations of government.

Source: 2004 General Social Survey.

of government. Furthermore, these relationships flow in the opposite temporal direction; the evaluations of engaged citizens are most positive looking toward the future. In other words, duty-based citizenship leads to more positive images of government in the past, while engaged citizenship leads to more positive images of government in the future.

FIGURE 7.3   Citizenship and Satisfaction with the Process

▶ *Citizen duty increases satisfaction with the working of the political process, while engaged citizenship slightly decreases satisfaction.*

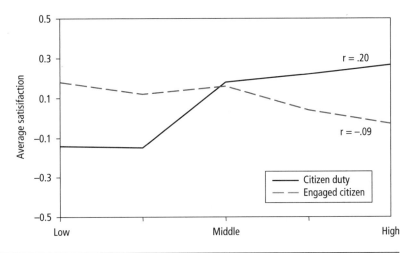

Note: See endnote 17 on the construction of the satisfaction index.

Source: 2004 General Social Survey.

Combining these three indicators of government performance makes the contrast between citizen duty and engaged citizenship even clearer.[17] Figure 7.3 shows that those high in citizen duty are more positive of government, while engaged citizens are more skeptical. These are not large differences, but when the contrasting effects of citizen duty and engaged citizenship are jointly considered, the cumulative effect is much larger. That is, each time an individual with a strong sense of citizen duty leaves the electorate and is replaced by one with a strong sense of engaged citizenship (such as through the generational changes discussed in Chapter 3), then positive images of government decrease.

A similar pattern appears across other political support questions (Figure 7.2). Norms of citizen duty increase beliefs that politicians are not self-interested, that Congress would pay attention if the respondent protested a law, that administrators serve the people, that government corruption is limited, and that elections are fair and honest. The Georgetown CDACS survey shows similar patterns.[18] In short, citizen duty taps the type of allegiant citizenship that earlier democratic theorists admired—citizens who have positive images of their government and the political authorities in office. Engaged citizens have mixed images of government and politicians. They are slightly more trustful of government and politicians, but their critical ethos appears in feelings that corruption is more common and in their doubts about the honesty and fairness of elections.

Americans are redefining what it means to be a good citizen, and this reshapes their images of government. If the person sitting next to you in Starbucks holds duty-based norms of citizenship, he or she will be more supportive of politicians and look back to an idyllic image of the past, when duty, social order, and allegiance were in greater supply. In contrast, if the next coffee drinker holds norms of engaged citizenship, he or she will be more skeptical of the current political authorities, but also be more optimistic about the political process working better in the future—better than it did in the past.

Democratic Values

On your next trip to Starbucks, if you began a new political conversation about the value of democracy, I suspect the conversation would be much different.[19] Despite their negative evaluations of government, Americans broadly endorse the democratic ideal. They readily agree with Churchill that democracy is better than other forms of government, even if it has its limitations. Americans believe that democracy ensures the pursuit of life, liberty, and happiness that is central to our political traditions. Indeed, public support for democratic values is essential in sustaining democracy.[20] Moreover, one would expect that social modernization, the expansion of education and other social trends have reinforced democratic values in the contemporary public, much as we saw in the spread of political tolerance in Chapter 5.

Public support for democracy is a complicated attitude to measure, however. Democracy contains several distinct political principles. Political tolerance, as examined in Chapter 5, is one central element of democratic values, but there are others. The 2004 General Social Survey tapped a set of democratic principles that were derived from previous research on democracy:[21]

- **Democratic inclusion and equality:** the importance of government treating everyone equally and protecting the rights of minorities.
- **Citizen participation:** the importance of giving people a chance to participate and citizens engaging in acts of civil disobedience.
- **Effective participation:** the importance of politicians considering the views of citizens.
- **Social democracy:** the importance of ensuring that people have an adequate standard of living.

One can think of other important democratic principles to measure, so this should not be treated as an exhaustive list. Still, this list includes many key themes discussed in the philosophical literature on democracy.

As you might expect, Americans broadly accept the importance of most of these democratic principles. On a seven-point importance scale, all but the item on civil disobedience have a mean score above six (the items are listed in Figure 7.4).[22] However, the main concern here is whether the norms of citizenship are related to support for democratic principles. Are there different relationships for duty-based and engaged citizenship? Duty-based citizenship promotes support for the politicians and the government as we have just seen, but do these norms also stimulate support for democratic values? Democratic norms possess an egalitarian and autonomous element that might conflict with the hierarchic and orderly norms of citizen duty. In contrast, norms of engaged citizenship should more openly embrace democratic values. The participatory norms, social concerns, and autonomy of engaged citizenship are broadly and directly compatible with democratic values as measured in this survey. Engaged citizenship may have an even stronger impact on democratic values.

Figure 7.4 presents the correlations between the two citizenship dimensions and the six democratic values items. The democratic values index combines all six items.[23] In every case but one, both sets of citizenship norms strengthen democratic values. However, citizen duty has a notably weaker relationship with most democratic values and a negative relationship with the civil disobedience item. Engaged citizenship, in

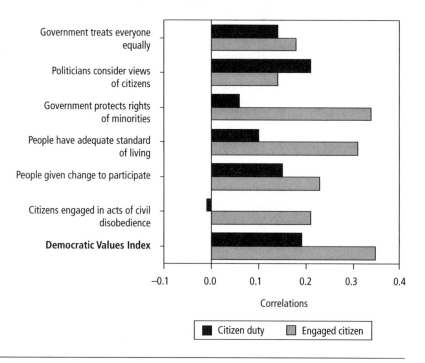

FIGURE 7.4   **Citizenship and Democratic Values**

▶ *Both sets of citizenship norms generally increase support for democratic values, and these effects are strongest for engaged citizenship.*

Note: Figure entries are correlation coefficients (Pearson *r*) that measure whether citizenship norms have a positive or negative effect on these democratic values.

Source: 2004 General Social Survey.

contrast, strongly correlates with all six items. Often this contrast is quite striking. For instance, engaged citizenship strongly encourages the protection of minority rights, but this is only slightly more common among those with duty-based citizenship. Similarly, engaged citizenship is clearly linked to defining democracy in terms of adequate living standards, but this is only weakly the case for duty-based citizenship.

Most Americans support democratic values when asked separately and in abstract terms. Who would disagree? Motherhood, apple pie, and democracy—this is the American way. A more robust way of measuring preferences is to ask people to choose between contrasting alternatives. The CDACS survey asked about the tradeoff between majority rights and social order on the one side and minority rights and preserving individual freedoms on the other. Both sets of options are reasonable and important goals of a democratic government, but they reflect values that can potentially come into conflict. Four items focused on these tradeoffs:[24]

> *For democracy to work best, the will of the majority must be followed,* **OR,**
>
> *For democracy to work best, the rights of minorities must be protected.*
>
> *In times of war, American should have a strong leader who unites the country,* **OR,**
>
> *In times of war, it is as important as ever to be able to disagree about our country's political direction.*
>
> *In order to curb terrorism in this country, it will be necessary to give up some civil liberties,* **OR,**
>
> *We should preserve our freedoms above all, because otherwise the terrorists will win.*
>
> *People should respect the rules/policies set by the government, even if they disagree with them,* **OR,**
>
> *When they disagree with the government, people should act according to their own sense of what is right/wrong.*

These are difficult questions to answer because both alternatives have a strong basis in democratic theory, and many people presumably agree with both of the choices given to them. The challenge for democracy is to find the appropriate balance between both. Indeed, in the post-9/11 world these items reflect the debates over issues such as the renewal of the Patriot Act, the domestic spying programs run by the National Security Agency, and the government's role in protecting the nation from further terrorist acts. Politics often means that we must choose between two desired goals, and citizenship norms shape the tradeoffs people are willing to make.

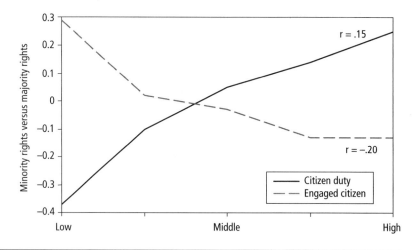

FIGURE 7.5   Citizenship and Majority/Minority Rights

▶ *Citizen duty increases support for majority rights over minority rights, and engaged citizenship increases support for minority rights over the majority.*

Note: Negative values indicate support for minority rights, and positive values indicate support for majority rights. See endnote 24 on the creation of this measure.

Source: 2005 CDACS Survey.

I've combined these four items into a single measure; at one end is greater support for minority rights and civil liberties, at the other end is support for majority rights and social order. As we might expect, those high on citizen duty support the majoritarian/order alternative on these four items (Figure 7.5). This is a very large difference as a function of duty-based norms. In contrast, engaged citizenship promotes support for minority rights and civil liberties when faced with these tradeoffs. The challenge of democracy is to balance both these sets of values, but when Americans are faced with these choices, citizenship norms shape the direction of their choices.

In summary, much as we saw for attitudes toward political tolerance and civil liberties in Chapter 5, duty-based citizenship produces a more restrictive image of democracy based on conformity and acceptance of authority. The good citizen is a loyal subject. In contrast, engaged citizenship reinforces Americans' commitment to norms of autonomous action and inclusion. Engaged citizens stress minority rights and the social dimensions of democratic politics in keeping with their self-definitions of good citizenship. Engaged citizens may be less trustful of contemporary politicians and political institutions because they have higher expectations for the democratic process.[25]

Feelings of National Pride

A European friend was visiting the University of California, Irvine, right after the terrorist attacks of September 11, 2001. He was amazed by the outpouring of generosity by Americans who lived three thousand miles away from New York. People contributed money to telethons, the businesses in Irvine had jars for contributions near their cash registers, and restaurants had a 9/11 night and donated the proceeds to New York. He was even more amazed by the patriotic outpouring of Americans. As has been often noted, the sales of American flags skyrocketed in the weeks after the terrorist attacks. Flags appeared on cars and homes. Even a few older 1960s generation secretaries in the university displayed the American flag on their office doors. The terrorist attacks brought Americans' deep feelings of patriotism to the surface.

Patriotism and strong feelings of national pride are a distinctive element of the American political culture—and were so even before September 11.[26] However, these sentiments may not be immune to the dissatisfactions that have affected other aspects of political support. Expressions of patriotism generally seem less common today than they did a generation ago—with the notable exception of the period immediately after September 11. Growing emphasis on multiculturalism and the spreading ethnic diversity of America raises questions about the breadth and depth of a common national identity. One of America's most vocal advocates of political tradition, Samuel Huntington, argues that there is a crisis of the American national identity and that the adherence to the founding creed of America is waning.[27]

To what extent are feelings of national identity linked to definitions of citizenship? Allegiance to the nation seems inimitably duty-based because it stresses loyalty, commitment, and support for the political order.

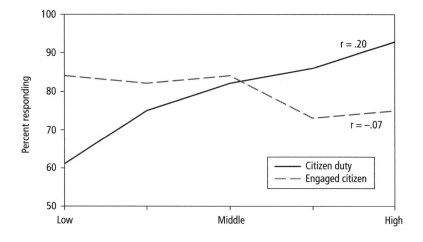

FIGURE 7.6   Citizenship and National Pride

▶ *Citizen duty spurs feelings of national pride, while engaged citizenship slightly decreases feelings of pride.*

Note: Figure entries are the percentage saying they are very proud to be American by citizenship norms.

Source: 2004 General Social Survey.

These orientations seem to form a single syndrome of political beliefs. In contrast, the link between engaged citizenship and national pride is more ambiguous. In abstract terms, a strong sense of citizenship should encourage attachment to the nation. However, engaged citizenship represents a questioning view of government, and these sentiments may be even clearer when measuring national attachments.

The General Social Survey asks a rich set of questions tapping different aspects of national attachments. The contrasting impact of citizenship norms is clearly seen in feelings of national pride (Figure 7.6). Barely 60 percent of people who are lowest in citizen duty say they are very proud to be American, and this increases to over 90 percent among those highest in citizen duty. In contrast, engaged citizenship decreases feelings of national pride. While duty-based citizenship may lead one to raise the flag on the Fourth of July and endorse national ambitions, the engaged citizen has a more reserved feeling toward the nation.

Certainly engaged citizens can be proud of their nation, but we expect that the nationalist and potentially ethno-centrist elements of national pride conflict with the inclusive solidarity aspects of engaged citizenship (being concerned with others in need in the nation and the world). For instance, another set of questions taps pride in various elements of the American experience (Figure 7.7). While citizen-duty positively stimulates pride in the U.S. armed forces and American history, engaged citizens see these same traits negatively. Conversely, engaged citizens are prouder of America's social programs, science, and the arts. As a result, these different groups of Americans think of the nation in terms of distinct parts of U.S. history and society. This is clearly illustrated in the last question in Figure 7.7: when asked if there are things in America today that make them ashamed, those high in citizen duty generally disagree, while engaged citizens tend to agree.

To one group of Americans, we are still the first new nation that reflects the positive potential of humankind; and they think of the nation's positive experiences. To another group of Americans, they see the nation's performance as falling short of its ideals; they look at America and see things that should be improved. Both are expressions of national pride, but one accepts the status quo and the other sees a need for change.

AMERICA, RIGHT OR WRONG

It is a slogan we have all seen many times. During the turbulent 1960s it was prominently used in the debates over the Vietnam War. It is still occasionally seen as a bumper sticker, or on a sign posted in a store (often in rural America), or in debates on the Iraq War. In its full form, it highlights the findings of this chapter.

> My country right or wrong.
> If right to defend it, if wrong to correct it.

This phrase, attributed to the late Senator Carl Schurz of Wisconsin, has unfortunately become politicized in the cultural divide about citizenship in America. Conservatives, who gloss over the second line, typically

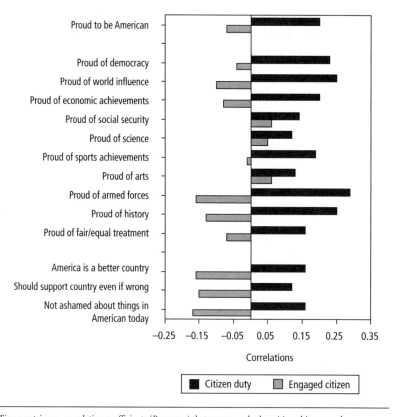

FIGURE 7.7   **Citizenship and Elements of National Pride**

▶ *Citizen duty strong encourages feelings of national pride, while engaged citizenship produces a mixed image of America's strengths and weaknesses.*

Note: Figure entries are correlation coefficients (Pearson *r*) that measure whether citizenship norms have a positive or negative effect on these quesions on national pride.

Source: 2004 General Social Survey.

embrace the first line. Liberals, who often skip over the first line, typically embrace the second. The strength of this credo is the combination of both elements, but politicians and political commentators often give them different emphasis.

This chapter shows that norms of citizenship lead to different images of government.[28] People holding duty-based norms of citizenship think of the United States as that shining city on the hill that Reagan and other conservative political figures describe. They are more trustful of government, more deferential to elites, and more enthusiastic in their national pride. They have a positive relationship to their government and nation—even while wanting a smaller government. Support and allegiance have first priority, much as in the first line of Schurz's phrase. So it is not surprising that expressions of trust and patriotism are stronger among those who accept duty-based norms of citizenship.

Engaged citizens, meanwhile, are less supportive of political elites and the government. They probably are also more skeptical of paying taxes, less willing to contribute to government, and less supportive of the institutions of representative democratic government. This creates the strains on democracy noted in recent scholarship.[29] The diminished political trust of engaged citizenship presents a challenge to government and the effective operation of the political system.

At the same time, engaged citizenship stimulates support for democratic values, especially an emphasis on equality and the protection of minority rights and expression. Consistent with their self-definition of citizenship, engaged citizens expect more of the government than social order and allegiance. In light of the evidence in previous chapters, these individuals have a more proactive and socially responsible view of citizenship. To a certain extent, these are the dissatisfied democrats or critical citizens who have higher expectations for their government.[30]

A democratic society needs both sets of norms to function effectively and function democratically. Ideally, these different orientations would be mixed within individual citizens who could see both the need to respect politicians and the need to question politicians and find the right balance between these two orientations: "My country right or wrong. If right to defend it, if wrong to correct it." In a democratic utopia, this might be the case. However, for contemporary American politics, these two beliefs are based in different groups of citizens. Some political analysts might lament the decline of duty-based citizenship; but if the consequence is a closer balance between these two elements of democracy, the process and the nation may benefit. Indeed, only through a desire that democracy better fulfills its ideals does the democratic experience progress, and the shift in citizenship norms contributes to this progress.

TABLE 7.1	Predicting Political Support

▶ Citizen duty, political satisfaction, democratic values, and national pride. Engaged citizenship decreases satisfaction, trust, and national pride—while even more strongly encouraging democratic values.

PREDICTOR	Satisfied with process	Trust in government	Democratic values	National pride
Citizen duty	.18*	.00	.16*	.18*
Engaged citizenship	−.16	−.18*	.34*	−.15*
Age	.01	.09	−.06	.11*
Education	.10*	−.18*	−.04	−.09*
Cognitive level	−.06	−.11*	.12*	−.04
Party identification (R)	.23*	.07*	−.16*	.22*
Multiple R	0.41	0.35	0.43	0.41

Note: Table entries are standardized regression coefficients.

*Coefficients significant at the more than .05 level.

Source: 2004 General Social Survey.

Appendix—Multivariate Analysis

To ensure that the impact of citizenship norms discussed in this chapter is independent of other influences on political support, I developed statistical analyses combining the citizenship variables with other potential predictors.

As a first step, the various survey questions were combined to create separate indices of political support. This factor analysis yielded four dimensions: satisfaction with working of the process (top three items in figure 7.2), trust in government (bottom items in figure 7.2), democratic values (figure 7.3), and national pride (figure 7.6). The factor analysis is available from the author.

Then, I conducted multiple regression analyses including the citizenship variables, age, education, cognitive level, and party identification. These multivariate analyses are similar to those presented and discussed more extensively in Chapters 4 and 5. Table 7.1 shows that the two dimensions have contrasting effects. Citizen duty is positively related to satisfaction with the political process, democratic values, and national pride—even while controlling for the other variables in the analysis. In contrast, engaged citizens are less satisfied or trustful of government, lower in national pride, and they are much more supportive of democratic values. In other words, the independent effects of these two citizenship dimensions are even more starkly contrasted while controlling for other characteristics.

Another significant feature of Table 7.1 is the impact of cognitive variables. Both education and cognitive level (a word skills test asked in the GSS) show a negative relationship with trust in government and lower levels of national pride, but cognitive level is positively related to democratic values. This is additional evidence that current skepticism of government comes from the sophisticated, educated citizen, rather than from those at the margins of politics.[31]

IN TOCQUEVILLE'S FOOTSTEPS

Imagine Alexis de Tocqueville's amazement as he traveled through the United States in 1830–32. He started in New York, then traveled on to Buffalo and Detroit, where he had his first contact with Native Americans, and then back to the East through Canada. The following year he headed west through Pennsylvania by horse, down the Ohio River on a steamboat (which nearly sank), eventually reaching the port of New Orleans after three months of travel.

In the midst of a rough and rugged new world, he saw a new democratic nation that differed dramatically from the autocratic political systems of Europe. *Democracy in America* was his tribute to the America public.[1] Tocqueville saw Americans' emphasis on participation, freedom, and equality as the foundation of this new democratic process. Americans were directly involved in governing and had created the modern world's first democracy. The special nature of the American polity is central to our ideas about nation and citizenship. From John Winthrop's description of colonial America as the City Upon a Hill to Ronald Reagan's reiteration of this imagery (as a "Shining City upon a Hill," no less), Americans view the United States as the first new nation.

Tocqueville's description of the American political culture was based on his knowledge of European politics. In other words, Tocqueville recognized what was distinct to Americans by comparing them to Europeans. There is a long history of such cross-national comparisons to gain insights into the American political culture (or the culture of any single nation).[2]

These past studies provide valuable evidence of the American political culture, but they often make conflicting claims. For instance, some observers stress the anti-statist and anti-government traditions, while others argue that Americans' sense of national pride and allegiance to government are exceptional.[3] Some repeat the Toquevillian observation about the participatory tendencies of Americans, but others lament the erosion of the very civil society that Tocqueville praised.[4] There are assertions about the tolerance and pluralism of the political culture, while others point to America's history of slavery and racial discrimination. We could easily expand this list.

Some of these contrasting images can coexist because the United States is a large and diverse nation, and different parts of the society can hold different political values. In addition, American society is changing. Some scholars discuss American traditions at the founding of the Republic, in the twentieth century, or in contemporary times. In addition, these descriptive studies often lack systematic evidence. Even an insightful observer such as Tocqueville was limited by the evidence he could collect and his inability to see beyond observable behavior of the Americans' he encountered to their individual inner values.

Many of these same debates about citizenship exist in Europe and other contemporary democracies.[5] Participation in election campaigns has decreased in most established democracies, and there are similar complaints about declining civic engagement. Analysts of European democracies cite the rise of individualism as a threat to the social compact of good citizenship. Indeed, if social modernization is altering citizenship in the United States, many of these patterns should be occurring in other established democracies.

We follow a Tocquevillian logic in this chapter—comparing American norms of citizenship to other democratic publics. Such comparisons should show what is distinctly American about the political values examined here. The great contemporary chronicler of American society and politics, Seymour Martin Lipset, repeated a common view among political analysts when he stated that "those who know only one country, know no country."[6] In addition, cross-national comparisons can identify common processes of social and political change that transcend any nation's unique historical experiences.

Our journey of comparison is much easier than Tocqueville's—no horses or steamboats—because the surveys of American public opinion are part of two larger cross-national studies of citizenship.[7] The 2004 General Social Survey is part of a larger International Social Survey Program (ISSP) studying these themes across dozens of nations. The 2005 CDACS survey replicates many questions included in the 2002 European Social Survey. So we can compare the meaning of citizenship between Americans and other publics and then examine how these norms shape other features of the political culture.

THE NORMS OF CITIZENSHIP

Do Americans think of citizenship differently than most Europeans? In recent years many observers have stressed the supposed differences across the Atlantic. Robert Kagan's popular book, *Of Paradise and Power*, summarizes these sentiments: "It is time to stop pretending that Europeans and Americans share a common view of the world. . . . Americans are from Mars and Europeans are from Venus."[8] Kagan was writing primarily about international orientations, but it reflects a broader comparison of the social elements of citizenship that supposedly vary between Americans and Europeans. This harks back to the tradition of treating the United States as exceptional in its social and political values.[9]

So let's focus on the norms of citizenship and how they compare across contemporary democracies. Before comparing American and European opinions, it's important to ask what differences might be expected in citizenship norms. Comparisons may vary between specific pairs of nations: Americans may be stronger adherents of one trait than the British, and less than the Japanese. But should we expect broad differences in citizenship norms between Americans and other democratic publics?

Citizen Duty. These norms are the foundation of citizenship in almost any nation (Chapter 2). Previous research yields an ambiguous image of Americans as distinctly high on norms of duty. On the one hand, analysts frequently cite the revolutionary origins of the United States as the basis of a populist and anti-statist tradition, in which people question the government and their duty to obey.[10] The framers structured government to limit its actions. We can see this anti-establishment tradition in current elections when even incumbents run as outsiders and rail against the government in Washington. On the other hand, it is unclear whether this anti-statist tradition affects feelings of citizen duty. For instance, the World Values Survey finds that Americans are less likely than the French, Germans, or British to say that cheating on one's taxes or falsely claiming government benefits can be justified.[11] Americans' strong religious traditions may also stimulate feelings of duty in the political realm. Allegiance and patriotism are also commonly cited elements of the American political culture. This is a paradox of the American political culture: the praise for autonomy and resistance to government appears as common as feelings of allegiance and duty. Perhaps the explanation, as presented in previous chapters, is that different individuals emphasize these two, differing sets of norms.

Citizen duty also embraces the responsibility to vote. Americans might score low on this norm because we know that turnout in U.S. elections is quite low. Yet, Chapter 3 found that Americans strongly endorse a norm that people should vote—even if they do not vote themselves. Low turnout partially reflects how elections are managed in America. Again, the evidence from previous research is ambiguous.

Engaged Citizenship. This combines several different elements: participation, autonomy, and solidarity (see Chapter 2). Election turnout aside, most analysts stress the participatory traditions in the United States. America is supposedly the nation of joiners and doers, spurred on the populist spirit of the American political culture. The political creed of activism is interlaced throughout U.S. history, as portrayed in Tocqueville's early description. In addition, populist traditions should stimulate norms of autonomy. Good citizens will believe that they should be informed and politically independent. Previous cross-national surveys generally find that Americans are more politically active than other democratic publics, and we similarly expect stronger participatory and autonomy norms.[12]

Engaged citizenship also includes solidarity norms promoting a concern for others. Such sentiments are widely identified with European democracies in sync with their large social welfare programs. Such values flow from the Social Democratic and Christian Democratic traditions in Europe.[13] Typically, analysts portray the United States as a contrasting case. America is the land of rugged individualism, and critics cite underdeveloped social policies and income inequality as consequences of these American values. We expect that Americans should give less importance to solidarity norms than European publics.

Taken together, we have unclear expectations about how Americans should compare to other democratic publics on both dimensions of citizenship. In terms of citizen duty, previous studies yield mixed advice on how Americans might position themselves. In terms of engaged citizenship, the expectations are clearer but move in opposite directions for different elements of these norms. Americans should stress the importance of participation and autonomy, while giving less importance to solidarity. Thus, the mix of these contrasting elements will determine the overall level of engaged citizenship.

These contrasting images of citizenship between Americans and Europeans would provide a rich basis for theoretical debate—which would never be resolved if it remained a debate between pundits and philosophers. In fact, Tocqueville himself saw these contradictions and said America was "a mixture of vices and virtues that is rather difficult to classify and that does not form a single picture." However, we can compare Americans' citizenship norms to other nations using a cross-national survey that includes the citizenship questions. The 2004 International Social Survey Program included the citizenship questions in coordinated surveys of 19 established democracies including the United States.[14]

Figure 8.1 presents the average importance Americans attach to each of the ten citizenship norms (see Chapter 2) and the average for the other eighteen established democracies. The duty-oriented items are to the left of the figure, and the engaged citizenship items to the right. Americans broadly place more importance on citizenship, ranking almost all the items as more important than other democratic publics. In a few instances the gap is substantial—serving in the military, keeping watch on government, social activism—and these items span both duty and engagement norms. There is one exception. Concern for the needy in the world is significantly lower among Americans when compared to other publics. This may reflect the stronger traditions of social citizenship in many European democracies, as well as their large welfare state programs.

The distinct national patterns of citizenship are seen in Figure 8.2. To create this figure, we first calculate the two dimensions of citizenship for

| FIGURE 8.1 | Comparing the United States to Other Democracies |

▶ *Americans attach more importance to most citizenship items than do people in other advanced industrial democracies.*

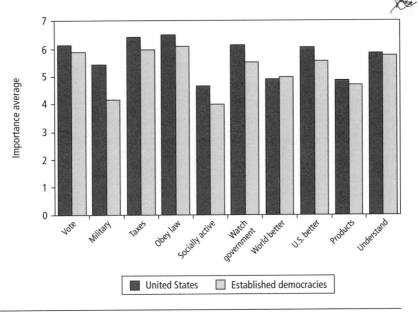

| United States   Established democracies |

Note: Eighteen nations are combined for the established democracies scores (N is approximately 24,000).

Source: 2004 International Social Survey Program.

all nineteen nations.[15] Then, we compute the average score for each nation on both indices. The horizontal dimension in the figure represents a nation's score on the citizen duty index; the vertical dimension is the nation's score on engaged citizenship.

American citizenship norms are not unique, but they are distinctive. Americans are second highest in citizen duty. More than most other publics, Americans believe a good citizen pays taxes, serves in the military, obeys the laws, and votes. Several other nations that are high in citizen duty also share a British heritage—Canada, Australia, and Ireland, plus Britain itself. This suggests that cultural elements of citizen duty derive from this legacy, perhaps from a tradition of popular sovereignty an' expectation of citizen allegiance in response. Most Scandir

FIGURE 8.2   Citizen Duty and Engaged Citizenship

▶ *Americans are very high in feelings of citizen duty and above average in feelings of engaged citizenship.*

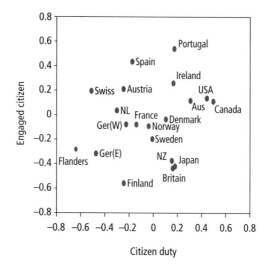

Note: Figure entries are national positions based on mean scores on the citizen duty and engaged citizenship factor scores.

Source: 2004 International Social Survey Program.

are located near the midpoint on citizen duty, and the lowest nations include several that have a German background: East and West Germany, Austria, and Switzerland.

Americans also score above most nations in engaged citizenship as shown on the vertical axis. Given the tradition of social citizenship in Europe, the relatively high placement of the United States is surprising, since the public in several welfare states (such as Britain, Germany, Sweden, and Norway) score at or below the overall average. As Figure 8.1 suggests, Americans' positive scores on engaged citizenship reflect participatory norms beyond voting and feelings of political autonomy. However, Americans are not dramatically different from Europeans on the two combined measures of social citizenship.

The high levels of citizenship among Americans—both citizen duty and engaged citizenship—are surprising. This book opened by citing the mounting claims that citizenship and democracy are at risk in the United States. Yet, Americans display a stronger sense of citizen duty than most other established Western democracies. And despite claims of the individualism of the American political culture, the norms of engaged citizenship are also relatively strong in the United States. In short, if democracy is supposedly at risk because of its citizens, there is little cross-national evidence that the American public holds citizenship norms that deviate from the range of other established democracies.

Because we have a cross-national public opinion survey from only a single time point, we cannot track how citizenship norms have changed over the years. However, as noted in Chapter 3, generational comparisons can suggest how these norms may be changing—and thus show the citizenship trajectories of nations over time. It is presumed that citizenship norms reflect core values that become fixed in political identities early in life, and then generally persist over time. Comparing the distribution of citizenship norms across generations suggests how norms have shifted across the decades.

Figure 8.3 displays the citizenship norms for five generations in the United States and for the other established democracies.[16] The dashed lines represent American generations. Two findings stand out. First, the norms of citizen duty decline among younger generations for both Americans and other nationalities. The oldest U.S. generation is significantly above the overall average in citizen duty, the youngest generation is below the average. This is a large change across generations that span several decades of U.S. history. In fact, the size of the decline in duty-based norms in the other democracies ($r=-.24$) is even greater than among Americans ($r=-.17$). This common trend reinforces this book's thesis that social modernization is producing a norm shift through changing generational experiences, increased affluence and education, changing economic and social structures, and the other forces of modernization.

Second, patterns of generational change differ for engaged citizenship. Support for engaged citizenship increases fairly steadily between older and younger Americans. In contrast, there is little generational change in these norms in other democracies. It's possible that this pattern reflects

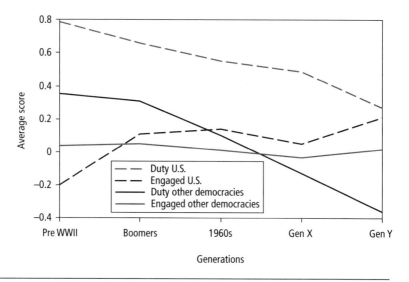

FIGURE 8.3 **Generations and Citizenship Norms**

▶ *Citizen duty decreases among the young in the United States and other democracies, while engaged citizenship increases among younger Americans.*

Source: 2004 International Social Survey Programs.

the stronger commitment to social citizenship that is ingrained in European political cultures. As some elements of engaged citizenship have decreased over time, others have grown—so little changes over time.[17]

If we combine both findings, this may explain why the process of generational change—and political change—is so apparent in the United States. The norms of the "greatest generation" of Americans heavily emphasize citizen duty and give much less importance to engaged citizenship. Younger Americans are sharply different; they give roughly equal weight to both sets of norms. Thus, generational change in the United States has markedly altered citizenship norms, and this is more easily noticed by political analysts and has more obvious effects on the style of politics. In Europe and most other established democracies, in contrast, the generation shift in citizenship norms is more modest. These publics have slowly shifted toward engaged citizenship, but at a slower rate. The pace of social and political change is slower than in the United States.

In summary, although generational change in citizenship norms is more modest outside the United States, the shift from citizen duty to engaged citizenship is broadly occurring across most advanced industrial democracies. Consequently, norm shift is not a unique American experience, but reflects the forces of social modernization touching all these nations. The following section compares whether citizenship norms have similar cross-national effects for participation, tolerance, and democratic values.

COMPARING THE CONSEQUENCES OF CITIZENSHIP

Political culture theory implies that citizenship norms should shape peoples' attitudes and behaviors, since these norms define what individuals feel is expected of them in political life. Having examined a host of effects for the American public, we can now extend these analyses to other established democracies. While Americans may be distinct in the levels of citizenship norms or the specific social conditions that shapes these norms, the effects of citizenship norms should be similar across nations. For instance, if engaged citizenship generally encourages contentious political action in America, then we should also see this in other nations. So let's examine three traits that are central to this study's descriptions of the impact of citizenship norms in the United States: political participation, political tolerance, and democratic values.

Participation since Tocqueville

On his travels through America, Tocqueville was struck by the participatory tendencies of Americans, especially compared to Europeans. This has remained a common description of the American political culture until recently (see Chapter 4). In the past decade, however, a growing number of politicians, pundits, and political scientists have asserted that the American political spirit has fundamentally changed. For instance, a 2006 report by the National Conference on Citizenship warns that "without strong habits of social and political participation, the world's longest and most successful experiment in democracy is at risk of losing the very norms, networks, and institutions of civic life that have made us the most emulated and respected nation in history."[18] The report then updates its 2000 findings to allow that "some aspects of civic health have modestly improved since 2000. Many more have worsened."[19] This notion that

| FIGURE 8.4 | **Political Participation in the United States and Other Democracies** |

▶ *Except for voting, Americans are as active or more active than other democratic publics.*

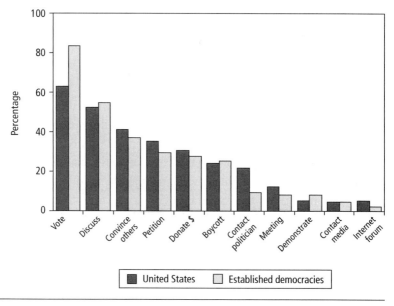

Note: Eighteen nations are combined for the established democracies scores.

Source: 2004 International Social Survey Program.

political participation is dropping to unprecedented levels has become the clarion call of those who see American democracy at risk.

Chapter 4 presented several trends suggesting that non-electoral forms of participation are actually increasing among Americans, while election turnout is decreasing. Indeed, similar patterns are occurring in many other advanced industrial democracies.[20] The 2004 International Social Survey Program (ISSP) compares Americans to other democratic citizens—much as Tocqueville did on the basis of his personal impressions.[21]

Figure 8.4 displays the percentage of Americans who have engaged in eleven different political activities in comparison to citizens in other established democracies. Clearly, Americans fall behind most other nations in voting; only 63 percent of Americans say they voted in the last national

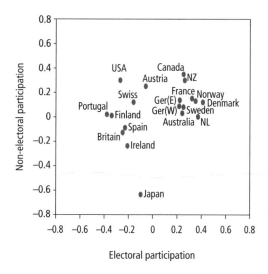

FIGURE 8.5   Political Participation

▶ *Americans score relatively low on electoral participation, but near the top on non-electoral participation.*

Note: Figure entries are national mean scores on electoral and non-electoral participation indices.

Source: 2004 International Social Survey Program.

elections, compared to 84 percent in the other democracies. Looking at participation beyond voting, however, Americans generally participate more than other democratic publics. For example, Americans are more active in signing petitions, donating funds to political groups, contacting politicians, attending meetings, and participating in Internet forums. This high level of American participation beyond elections is documented in other recent comparative studies.[22]

Another perspective on participation patterns compares the United States to each of the other established democracies in the ISSP. To simplify the presentation, I've constructed two participation indices (Figure 8.5).[23] Electoral participation is displayed on the horizontal axis. Americans score third from the bottom among these nineteen democracies (to the far left of the horizontal axis). This is a common pattern, reflecting the low turnout in U.S. elections. The second index combines all the forms of non-electoral participation, and this is the vertical dimension in the figure. In these terms, Americans score second highest in non-electoral action, higher than Swedes, Danes, the Dutch, and other publics that typically have high levels of voting. In other words, Americans are politically engaged, but not so much in electoral politics.

Chapter 3 suggested that participation patterns are changing because of changing citizenship norms. In the United States, duty-based citizenship encourages participation in elections and party politics, but discourages direct action and contentious action. Conversely, engaged citizenship stimulates participation in direct actions and protests, while only modestly encouraging electoral participation. So changing citizenship norms should also shift participation patterns.

This relationship between norms and participation should not be a distinctly American experience, however. If our general idea is correct, these norms should affect political action in other democracies. For instance, Swedes who define their citizen role in terms of engaged citizenship should be more likely to protest, pursue methods of direct action, and perhaps vote at a lower rate than duty-oriented citizens.

Figure 8.6 shows the cross-national link between citizenship norms and participation for all nineteen nations. The top panel of the figure presents the relationship between citizen duty and the two participation indices in Figure 8.5. As citizen duty increases, so also does participation in electoral politics, since one of the first duties of citizenship is to vote. Simultaneously, citizen duty diminishes non-electoral forms of action. These contrasting relationships are quite strong, and generally apply across the specific activities included in both indices.

Engaged citizenship has very different implications for political participation. As engaged citizenship increases, this modestly stimulates electoral participation. Elections are the foundation of democracy, and both norms of citizenship encourage voting. However, engaged citizenship even more strongly encourages non-electoral activities, such as boycotts, demonstrations, direct contact with politicians and the media, and internet activism.

The contrasts between the two panels of Figure 8.6 graphically illustrate the impact of citizenship norms on participation. As demographic change alters the balance of duty-based and engaged citizenship, a shift in partic-

FIGURE 8.6   **Citizenship and Electoral Participation**

▶ *Citizen duty increases electoral participation but decreases non-electoral
participation, while engaged citizenship increases both forms of participation.*

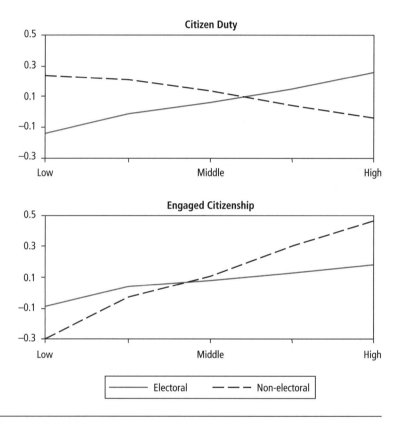

Note: All nineteen advanced democracies.

Source: 2004 International Social Survey Program.

ipation patterns should follow. If an individual high in citizen duty from
the "greatest generation" leaves the electorate, and is replaced by an individual high in engaged citizenship, the repertoire of political action will
also change. The likelihood of voting will decrease slightly between these
two individuals. But the use of direct and contentious forms of action will
markedly increase. This shift has been occurring in most established

democracies, even if at different rates and within different institutional settings. Changing citizenship norms are reshaping how democratic citizens relate to government and participate in the democratic process.

Tolerance

Tolerance lies at the very heart of a democratic political culture (see Chapter 5). However, analysts and philosophers debate the nature and measurement of political tolerance. Many people say they are committed to tolerance in the abstract but have difficulty applying this to groups that they dislike. Moreover, one might debate what tolerance really means. Is it tolerant to allow free expression to hatred and violence? The Germans outlaw Nazi propaganda and paraphernalia; it is illegal to deny the Holocaust, to sell a copy of Hitler's *Mein Kampf* or to even display a swastika. Would a good democrat prefer that Germany tolerate fascists goose-stepping down their streets wearing swastikas? Is America more democratic because we allow fascist parades, even when they run through Jewish communities? Or does this public action have different meaning for Germans and Americans? Does tolerance really mean we should ignore ideas of right or wrong because we are democrats or because we assume the political correctness logic that all viewpoints are equal?

I raise these difficult questions because the cross-national study of tolerance often evokes such issues. If there are problems in theorizing and measuring the tolerance of Americans, how do we compare American tolerance to that of Swedes or Germans? The best cross-nationally comparable method is probably the "content-controlled" measures of tolerance discussed in Chapter 5. This method asks individuals which groups they dislike the most and then asks about tolerance toward these groups.[24] Accordingly, it is tempting to compare Germans' tolerance toward their least-liked groups with Americans' tolerance toward the groups they dislike the most.

However, the 2004 ISSP used a simpler and more direct measure of asking whether the following three groups should be allowed to hold public meetings: religious extremists, people who want to overthrow the government by force, and people prejudiced against any racial or ethnic group. Without looking at the empirical findings, one might think that this list would severely test the tolerance of Americans. The ISSP survey

FIGURE 8.7   **Political Tolerance**

▶ *Americans score higher than other democratic publics on tolerance toward religious extremists and even those who want to overthrow the government.*

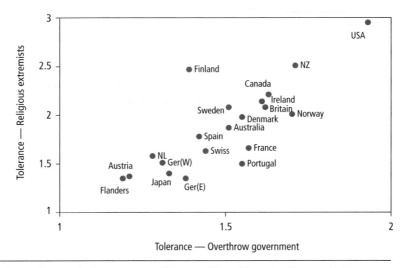

Note: Figure entries are national mean scores on willingness to allow public meetings by a) people who want to overthrow the government by force, or b) religious extremists. The scale was scored: 1) should definitely not be allowed, to 4) should definitely be allowed.

Source: 2004 International Social Survey Program.

was completed when memories of the September 11 terrorist attacks by Islamic extremists were still fresh in most people's minds. Racial tensions also have deep roots in the American historical experience.

Figure 8.7 displays the tolerance toward religious extremists and those who want to overthrow the government for the established democracies in the ISSP survey. Perhaps surprisingly, Americans are the most tolerant nation on both dimensions (and the same applies to the racial tolerance question). For instance, even in the wake of September 11, a full 73 percent of Americans say a public meeting by religious extremists should be allowed, compared to an average of only 29 percent across all nineteen nations. In addition, 30 percent of Americans would allow a p̶ ing by a group trying to overthrow the government, compar̶ cent among all these democracies. Moreover, this is not simp̶ of the groups included in the ISSP survey, since an earlier cross-national comparison of tolerance using a content-controlled method also ranked the American public quite high.[25]

One should interpret such percentages with a dose of skepticism because tolerance is such a complex attitude. Yet, these results may be surprising because there is so little systematic evidence of such attitudes, and many pundits stake their claims without systematic evidence. Or perhaps this is surprising because Americans so quickly accept the often-critical comments about this aspect of the American political culture, proffered routinely by pundits both at home and abroad. Certainly there are aspects of the American political culture that deserve criticism. But far from an example of the erosion of democratic values, Americans express more support for the political rights of negative social groups than do most other democratic publics.

Tolerance is best learned through the experience of living in a democratic society where tolerance is practiced. Tolerance is also linked to the processes of social modernization discussed throughout this book (see Chapter 5). Consequently, tolerance in the United States and other democracies should generally increase over time, and it should be linked to social characteristics and citizenship norms that reflect social modernization.[26] Figure 8.8 shows that across all these nations in the ISSP, strong feelings of citizen duty systematically decrease political tolerance. The relationship in the United States is almost identical to the average of the other 18 nations. Simultaneously, engaged citizenship increases political tolerance in general and for each of these three groups.

Citizenship norms do not have equal and strong effects across all democracies, but they function in the expected direction. The variability across nations may reflect the differential salience of these challenging groups or specific national conditions.[27] In addition, the levels of tolerance are much higher among the better educated, and distinctly higher among younger generations. Across all Western democracies, for instance, 41 percent of the World War II generation scores at the lowest tolerance level, compared to only 28 percent among Generation Y. This suggests that the same general forces of social modernization that are at play in the United States are also increasing tolerance in other democracies.

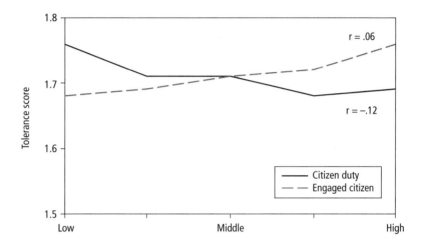

FIGURE 8.8   **Citizenship and Political Tolerance**

▶ *Citizen duty decreases political tolerance, and engaged citizenship increases tolerance.*

Note: The figure plots the mean score on the three-item tolerance scale.

Source: 2004 International Social Survey Program, all nineteen advanced democracies.

Democratic Norms

Perhaps the harshest claims of the crisis-of-American-democracy literature are those asserting that Americans are losing faith in their democratic system. The list of pessimists includes an impressive roster of American politics scholars.[28] If you want to lose faith in government, you need go no further than the conclusions of these researchers. The sentiments are shared by many political elites, and they have repeated this refrain over the past several decades. For instance, U.S. Supreme Court Justice Stephen G. Breyer recently said: "I worry about indifference and cynicism because indifference means nonparticipation and cynicism means a withdrawal of trust. . . . [W]ithout trust and participation, the Constitution cannot work."[29]

Can the state of democracy really be so fragile? Has so much changed since Tocqueville's description of the democratic spirit of America or the early studies extolling America's civic culture?[30] In a recent book, I tracked the decreases in political support in most established democracies.[31] Trust of political elites and key democratic institutions has clearly eroded over the past two generations. Where once most Americans trusted their government to do right, now a majority doubt its trustworthiness. Instead of the loyal and supportive citizen, the political skeptic is now more common.

Yet, we should not jump to simple conclusions. A thorough analysis of opinion data shows that people today are more skeptical about political elites, and even some political institutions—given the nefarious actions of some elected political officials, such skepticism might seem warranted. However, these publics are also committed to democratic ideals and core democratic principles. People have become "critical citizens" or "dissatisfied democrats" who expect more of their government, and they express their dissatisfaction when politics falls short of its democratic ideal. In many ways, commitment to democratic values is more important than trust in the politicians who currently hold office.

Therefore, we should compare support for democratic principles across the nations included in the International Social Survey Program using the same set of items that we examined for the American public in Figure 7.4. Several of the questions tap support for political rights identified with democracy: government authorities respect and protect the rights of minorities; government authorities treat everyone equally; politicians take into account the views of the citizens; and people should be given more opportunities to participate. In addition, another item taps a potential dimension of social rights that is often stressed in European conceptions of democracy: all citizens should have an adequate standard of living.

Even if contemporary publics have doubts about politicians and governments, people remain strongly supportive of democratic principles (Figure 8.9). On a 7-point scale of importance, most people rate both political rights and social rights as very important. The horizontal dimension shows that Americans rank fairly high in their support for political rights, which should be reassuring for those who wonder if current political tensions and the strains of battling international terrorism have eroded these democratic values. In fact, several of the nations that score

---

FIGURE 8.9   Democratic Values

▶ *Americans score above average in support for political rights and about average on support for social rights.*

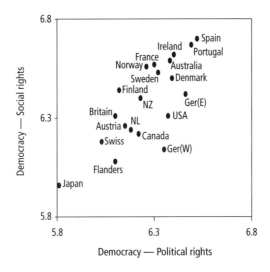

Democracy — Political rights

Note: Figure entries are national mean scores on four questions on the importance of political rights in a democracy and one question on the importance of an adequate standard of living. The scale was scored from 1=not at all important to 7=very important.

Source: 2004 International Social Survey Program.

---

above the United States—East Germany, Spain, and Portugal—might place such emphasis on political rights because they have experienced autocratic governments in their recent past. Americans' commitment to democratic principles is alive and well (although I recognize that further improvements should be encouraged).

The vertical dimension in the figure measures support for social rights as a democratic principle. One might expect that the individualist orientation of Americans will be most apparent here, which is linked to the limited welfare state policies of the United States. Many European political figures often criticize the United States for being an "elbow society" where people are pushing each other aside in their efforts to gain materialist success and where social protections are limited. Yet even on the

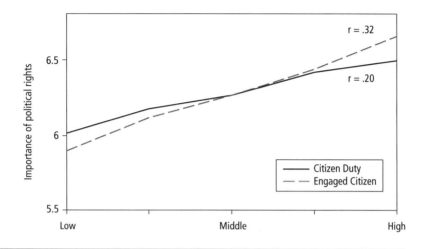

FIGURE 8.10 **Citizenship and Democratic Rights**

▶ *Both norms of citizenship increase support for political rights.*

Note: Figure entries are national mean scores on four questions of the importance of political rights in a democracy. The scale is scored from 1= not at all important to 7 = very important.

Source: 2004 International Social Survey Program, all nineteen advanced democracies.

social rights dimension, Americans rank near the middle of these other democracies.

I have focused on democratic values in part to emphasize the positive aspect of the political culture in most democracies—a theme that is often overlooked in the crisis-of-democracy literature. In addition, citizenship norms can reinforce these values. As argued in Chapter 7, good citizenship in a democracy should be positively related to support for democratic principles. However, engaged citizenship more strongly embraces the values of democracy because it emphasizes the participatory norms and autonomy underlying democratic values. Duty-based citizenship encourages support for democratic principles, but these partially conflict with the majoritarian and social order elements of these norms.

Figure 8.10 displays the relationship between citizenship norms and the index of democratic political rights for these democracies. Both citizenship norms strengthen democratic values. However, engaged citizenship has a notably stronger impact than citizen duty.[32] This means that either definition of good citizenship reinforces democratic political rights among the public. However, norms of engaged citizenship stimulate key democratic rights more strongly than citizen duty. Thus, norm shift reinforces the principles of democracy, a fact that hardly seems a source of political crisis.[33] A good democrat can criticize the government for its failings, while remaining committed to democratic principles. Indeed, democratic principles provide a valuable framework for judging the performance of governments. And in a world where some politicians seem preoccupied with security and order to the detriment of civil liberties, such a commitment to democratic values by the public should be applauded.

CITIZENSHIP IN COMPARATIVE PERSPECTIVE

This chapter represents what might be called a social science version of Einstein's relativity theory. In public opinion there are few absolutes, and we can best understand any single nation by comparing it to other reference points. So, determining the political health of the American polity requires either a comparison relative to other times (are we getting better or worse?) or a comparison to other nations (how are we doing relative to other democracies?).

While other chapters described the citizenship norms of Americans, this chapter compared American public opinion to other established democracies. The implicit logic is that if the opinions and political actions of Americans are placing democracy at risk, then this should be apparent in the United States ranking low in key elements of a democratic political culture. For instance, Americans would be less supportive of democratic values or distinctly less participatory than other established democracies. Such comparisons are often lacking from the American political science literature, but these comparisons are often made by European scholars who think more comparatively.[34]

Our cross-national comparisons provide little evidence of basic flaws in the American political culture—at least on the dimensions we compared. Americans are less active in elections, but they participate more frequently in a range of other political activities. American levels of tolerance and democratic values should be a source of reassurance about the vitality of American democracy, not a cause of concern.

This does not mean that the American political culture is a shining model that all should emulate; I never intended this chapter to be a "USA first!" presentation. There are problems and challenges that face the American public and polity, and this applies to any contemporary democracy. For instance, French bookstores are filled with titles such as *France in Freefall*, *Gallic Illusions* and *France's Misfortune*. "Declinism" has become a school of thought among French intellectuals. The British democracy audit is equally critical of the state of that nation.[35] Throughout the 1990s, the Japanese were offered a series of books that explained the decline of the nation. In most democracies, it seems, political analysts clamor to discuss what is wrong with politics in their nation. Such criticism is how governments and democracy improve, to be sure, but accurate criticism is the most valuable of all.

Cross-national comparisons can highlight the strengths and weaknesses of a polity—while domestic analysts often focus on only the negative side of the scorecard. If one compares the United States to Britain or Germany, for example, one typically sees positive and negative features of both democratic systems. Certainly there are features of the American political culture that represent potential problems for the nation, such as the low levels of voting. However, only by comparing Americans' opinions to other democracies can we develop a reference point for judging political realities. In comparison to other democracies, the American political culture still contains many of the values that make for vibrant democracy, and these may have even increased over the past several decades. Tocqueville would not recognize contemporary America, but he still might conclude that his observations about the democracy in America generally hold true today.

THE TWO FACES OF CITIZENSHIP

> There is no doubt that democracy has lost a clear
> conception of the type of citizen it wants to create.
>
> Karl Mannheim[1]

Have you seen reruns of those old movie serials (or Saturday morning cartoons) with the heroine tied to the train rails and the threat of death looming on the horizon? Several of America's leading political scientists similarly claim that the vitality of American democracy is at risk, and the risk arises from the public's decreasing civic engagement, declining political participation, and growing alienation from the democratic process.[2] Like the heroine on the train tracks, the vitality of democracy in America is on the line, and the train is rapidly approaching.

Indeed, one can see the speeding train. The American public and the American polity have changed in fundamental ways over the past fifty years. We recognize these changes, and a large portion of this book has described, examined, and dissected these trends. But to restate a phrase from the introduction: our basic argument is that "the good news is . . . the bad news is wrong." Based on the evidence presented in this book, America of today is very different from America of the 1950s. I do not believe that American democracy is about to expire. Different does not necessarily mean worse.[3]

The key to understanding the changes transforming the American public are the two faces of citizenship examined in this book. Citizenship in America, and most other Western democracies, has traditionally emphasized the duties and responsibilities of a good citizen. This meant respect for the law, paying taxes, and asking not what your country can do for you, but what you can do for your country. A "good citizen" felt a duty to vote and support the government. Many Americans, especially older Americans, embrace this definition of good citizenship. The philosophical literature on citizenship advocates such norms (see Chapter 2). Indeed, the norms of citizen duty reinforce the political bonds that are one of the strengths of American democracy; they stimulate many people to participate in the political process, and they encourage the social capital that benefits the nation.

Over the past several decades, however, norms of engaged citizenship have become more common. This other face of citizenship stresses participation, but in a more direct, action-oriented, and collective framework. The "good citizen" is engaged in a variety of social and political activities beyond elections (and often views elections and parties negatively for several reasons). Engaged citizens put less stress on maintaining the social order, and they emphasize the need for autonomy and skepticism of government. Engaged citizenship stimulates a concern with the condition of those who are less well off, both in America and globally.

Many readers will see elements of themselves in both descriptions. Tom Brokaw's poetic praise of the "greatest generation" and their values reflects many of the positive aspects of citizen duty and its beneficial contributions to the nation.[4] In contrast, engaged citizenship is more common among members of Generation X and the Millennial generation, which came of age beginning in the 1980s. In public presentations I have humorously suggested social markers for these two sets of citizenship norms.[5] If you prefer vinyl records, like Frank Sinatra, don't cross the street when the light is red, pay your taxes promptly and fully, and answer the letter to serve on a jury—these are the bellwethers of duty-based norms of citizenship. If you own an iPod, know who Bono is, cross streets on the red if there is no traffic, don't vote but are a civic volunteer, and worry as much about the fate of the world as the fate of your city, then you probably lean toward norms of engaged citizenship. Neither description is completely accurate nor exclusive, but they tap into the essence of these two different faces of citizenship.

The "crisis of democracy" literature misdiagnoses the current situation because it focuses on the negative consequences of the shifting balance of these two norms, without paying sufficient attention to the full process of change. The decline in citizen duty will strain certain aspects of our current democratic process, but there are also positive consequences of lower levels of citizen duty. In addition, American society and politics can benefit from a growth of engaged citizenship among the public, but there are also negative consequences of these norms. Perhaps the greatest risk to democracy is to miss the full nature of the changes that are transforming the American polity—both positive and negative—and thus advocate reforms to recreate the behaviors of a bygone age that was not as idyllic as some now imply.

REBALANCING THE AMERICAN POLITICAL CULTURE

Gabriel Almond described it as the Goldilocks theory of a democratic political culture.[6] A stable democratic society benefits from a civic culture that balances a mix of traits. For instance, good democratic citizenship needs allegiance to the state and obedience to the lawful decisions of government. Good democratic citizenship also requires that individuals participate in politics and challenge the government to represent their interests and fulfill their democratic responsibilities. Too much of the former pattern of citizenship leads to a deferential and potentially passive citizenry, where government may become unresponsive to its citizens, or worse. Too much of the latter may produce a system where division and political conflict could impede even a well-intentioned government from providing for the collective good. Democracy benefits from a Goldilocks political culture, which is neither too hot nor too cold, neither too hard nor too soft, neither too allegiant nor too challenging. Tocqueville said it more poetically: "To love democracy, it is necessary to love it moderately."

Democratic theory and studies of political culture recognize this need for balancing diverse elements of a democratic system.[7] In principle, individuals might accept both value sets and find their own balance—understanding how order has to be balanced against autonomy, and how minority and majority interests must be balanced. While individuals do hold a mix of both norms, they tend to emphasize one pattern or another. Almond and Verba, for instance, maintained that some individuals thought of themselves as fulfilling a subject role, and others functioned in terms of a more participatory role.[8] Some people think of themselves as centrists, but most people either have a liberal or conservative identity. In other words, the balance in a democratic political culture often results from different people following distinct sets of norms—and articulating the importance of their views of citizenship—and then society and the polity reflect the relative weight of these distinct groups.

If we look back to the electorate of the 1950s, the balance was heavily weighted toward the norms of citizen duty. There are certainly positive consequences of these norms. Citizen duty encourages individuals to vote and participate in the electoral process as an expression of citizenship, and not just an instrumental means to influence government policy. Duty-based citizenship reinforces allegiance to government and the state, with strong feelings of patriotism and national pride. Many of Robert Putnam's examples of the positive aspects of community in America— participating in elections, paying taxes, obeying the law, and supporting the government—reflect these norms of duty and community.[9] Indeed, when contemporary analysts decry the decline of citizenship in America, they are often saying that the erosion of duty-based norms is undermining these positive features.

However, these analysts sometimes overlook the potential negative consequences of duty-based citizenship, as described in this study. Citizen duty discourages autonomous political action, especially contentious activities such as protests or direct action. Certainly protests challenge the government and disrupt political tranquility. Yet, if one looks back on the past several decades of American politics (or further), it is easy to see where our nation has benefited because some citizens were willing to protest against government policy. Democracy requires a citizenry that can be assertive as well as supportive.

Similarly, citizen duty reinforces a majoritarian view of society that sometimes can be carried to excess: individuals should conform, social order is important, dissidence is undesirable, and unconventional groups should not be tolerated. The lower support for democratic values, civil liberties, and political tolerance among individuals high in citizen duty is not a positive feature of these norms. Majority rights are part of the democratic equation, but an unqualified stress on majority rule can weaken true democracy. In other words, citizen duty may sometimes give elites too much latitude in their actions when they should be challenged, and limit minority rights when they should be tolerated or embraced.

Engaged citizenship counterbalances some of the patterns of duty-based citizenship. Engaged citizens have a broader definition of political participation, and they are especially drawn to civic action and more direct forms of participation. Their mantra is that there is more to politics than elections—and the expansion of political action is one consequence of these new norms. So engaged citizens are less likely to vote in elections, but they protest more often, are more active political consumers, and are developing new patterns of political action.

Often the response to these new patterns of citizenship is to insist that they are examples of individualism and self-centered indulgence. Young, engaged citizens, goes this thinking, are too concerned about their rights and their own well-being. Thoughtful social scientists have warned about the decline of duty and the rise of individualism for these reasons. Francis Fukuyama, for instance, warned that a "society dedicated to the constant upending of norms and rules in the name of increasing individual freedom of choice will find itself increasingly disorganized, atomized, isolated, and incapable of carrying out common goals and tasks." [10]

However, this stereotype of the self-centered, even selfish new citizen does not jibe with the concern for others that is central to engaged citizenship (see Chapter 2). Engaged citizenship has a broader view of social responsibility than the old norms of citizen duty. This orientation shows in the policy concerns and the behavior of engaged citizens.

Let me offer one final illustration by stepping beyond the political realm to examine examples of civic volunteerism that are non-political in nature. The CDACS survey asked four questions about volunteerism to test the civic spirit of Americans:

- Are you registered as an organ donor
- Have you donated blood in the last five years
- Have you given to charity in the last year
- Have you picked up someone else's litter in the last year

These are examples of the positive, social "habits of the heart" that Tocqueville would admire, doing good works for the society at large. Figure 9.1 shows that both norms of citizenship encourage such civic virtue. However, duty-based citizenship has a weak impact on volunteerism.

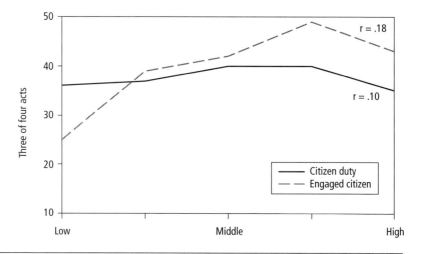

FIGURE 9.1   Doing "Good Works"

▶ *Citizen duty slightly increases the level of social good works, but engaged citizenship encourages these activities.*

Note: Figure presents the percentage who have done at least three of the following activities: registered as an organ donor, donated blood, gave to charity, or picked up litter in a public place.

Source: 2005 CDACS Survey.

One's duty to obey the law and vote in elections does not carry over into broader forms of social engagement. Ironically, then, the renewal of duty-based norms—which is often the message of contemporary pundits—may not produce the civic results they seek. In contrast, engaged citizenship encompasses norms of greater social concern and social engagement. Those who score high on engaged citizenship are about twice as likely as those at the low end of the scale to do at least three of these volunteer activities. This may explain why various studies point to an increase in volunteerism and civic action in America, even while conventional electoral participation is decreasing.[11]

Equally important, engaged citizenship encourages a deeper commitment to democratic values, tolerance toward political groups (of both the left and right), and civil liberties over social order. Engaged citizenship is also more inclusive in attitudes toward minorities and immigrants. These sentiments are joined by strong social concerns, expressed as policies to take care of those in need at home and abroad. Thus, engaged citizens want more government spending on a range of social programs. For them, government is a solution to society's problems.

At the same time, engaged citizenship also has potential negative effects. Disaffection for political parties and elections leads many otherwise engaged citizens to sit home on Election Day. Since elections determine the make-up governments and the broad parameters of public policy, absence from the voting booth actually limits their policy impact in ways that are inconsistent with the logic of political engagement. If young people and engaged citizens participated at equal rates as duty-based citizens, for example, the outcome of the last two U.S. presidential elections would have changed.[12] The government spends more on environmental protection, aid to Africa, or health care for the poor than any non-governmental organization. Participation in elections can shape public policy in these areas in important ways that youthful non-voters are missing. One might not have to protest so frequently if a more sympathetic government was elected in the first place.

Similarly, feelings of political distrust and alienation can limit the activities that are essential for democracy to function as a social contract between citizens and their government. For instance, we expect that engaged citizens will comply less often with the government when their own views differ from stated policies.[13] This might be as trivial as crossing a street on a red light, but it also includes paying taxes, filling out census forms, not exploiting government programs, or even a willingness to take a job in the public sector. At the same time, these individuals expect the government to pursue a more active policy agenda. Without more acceptance of government, and the compromises required by democratic politics, political dissatisfaction can erode the democratic social contract.

So, both aspects of citizenship have positive and negative features. We would not want a polity comprised solely of duty-based citizens any more than we would want only engaged citizens. Democracy functions best when there is a diversity of values within this general framework of democratic citizenship. Many previous writers have stressed this need for balance in various aspects of a democratic civic culture—my argument simply extends this logic to norms of good citizenship.

If we look back to the 1950s, with the hindsight of more than five decades of U.S. history, the balance of citizenship during that period was heavily weighted toward citizen duty. Americans may have been too allegiant, too deferential, too intolerant, and too majoritarian in their citizenship norms. This had some positive consequences for American politics, and political scientists saw these effects and focused on these beneficial consequences. And without a clear alternative, this was presented as how democratic politics ought to function. So when the balance of citizenship norms changed, political scientists and politicians became concerned that democracy was at risk—because the values identified with an earlier era of American politics were changing.

Despite what these critics say, the rebalancing of the American political culture has had positive consequences that should be recognized as closer to a Goldilocks balance. The contemporary American public is now more engaged, more tolerant, and more aware of minority rights, and this has strengthened democracy in America.

One might ask if the trend toward engaged citizenship has shifted the balance too much, encouraging Americans to be too critical, too skeptical, and too assertive. Indeed, in the Goldilocks analogy, she at first careened from one extreme to the other. This is a valid issue, but it is different from the one raised by critics who insist that we should return to a bygone era. The answer to this question partially depends on how governments and other political actors respond to these changes in citizenship norms. If we can first correctly understand how norms are changing, then the polity can adapt to accentuate the positive features of norm shift and lessen the negative features. More on this in the last section of this chapter.

UNDERSTANDING GENERATION X

One of the most surprising features of writing this book was to see the nearly universal pessimism of older political analysts toward today's youth. Even members of Generation X seem persuaded by the negative characterizations and join this critical bandwagon.[14] Similarly, psychologist Jean Twenge has recently written about the psychological tendencies of *Generation Me*.[15] She argues that young Americans are excessively self-indulgent to the point of narcissism, individualistic and oblivious to social rules, materialistic, and sad and depressed by their situation. Twenge sees Britney Spears, Kevin Federline, and self-obsessed contestants on *American Idol* as representative of today's youth. Twenge is obviously talking to different people than those interviewed in the surveys presented here.

Generations are a key element in the socio-historical trends that are transforming the American public. Those individuals who came of age during the Great Depression had their political values and behaviors shaped by these social forces. World War II was a similar formative event, leaving its legacy on all those who experienced and survived the war. The turbulent events in American politics in the 1960s and 1970s created a generation whose identity and values were shaped by the civil rights movement, the Vietnam War, Woodstock, and the other signature events of that decade.

Today, a new generation—Generation X (and soon the Millennials)—is reshaping the American public. Political analysts, especially those of older generations, often worry about the impact of Generation X on the democratic process. They argue that Generation X is less active in elections and that this is contributing to growing political disengagement. Generation X is less trustful of politicians, political parties, and the established institutions of representative democracy, and this is seen as a spreading political malaise. The young are supposedly self-centered, ill-informed, and lacking in social capital and collective values. If older Americans are heralded as the "greatest generation," the young are stigmatized as the "Doofus generation" or worse.[16]

Similarly, complaints about the work ethic of the young have come back in vogue. Sen. Hillary Rodham Clinton, D-N.Y., joined the assault on the young with the sound bite that "young people think 'work' is a four-letter word." She is like the old fogy who grumbles that when she was young, she did her chores before dawn and trudged ten miles to school (the law school at Yale?). Through the snow. Uphill. Both ways. Fortunately, Chelsea Clinton reminded her mother about the problems of such stereotypes and perhaps the empirical evidence that many young people are hard at work.[17]

Citizenship norms are changing, and generations are the vehicle for these changes. The young are different from their elders. But in these differences lay positive potential as well as negative challenges for the democratic process. It is too easy for older American citizens to complain that younger Americans are not like them, and therefore democracy will suffer. The evidence presented here hopefully offers a corrective to narrow claims that young Americans should be like their parents (or better yet, their grandparents) and that democracy will be strengthened in the process.

Generation X is the most educated generation in American history, educated by the best university system in the world, with access to an amazing array of information, a more cosmopolitan life experience, with a standard of living unimaginable by their grandparents at a similar stage in life. And they have benefited from the experiences of their elders (even if they are loathe to admit this). Looked at in these terms, we should hopefully await the entry of Generation X and the Millennials into the American electorate.

Similarly, young Americans subscribe to a range of values and behaviors that should benefit the democratic process. They are more supportive of autonomy and social solidarity as norms of citizenship, and more supportive of participation beyond elections. Younger generations are also more politically tolerant, and they more likely to favor the protection of civil liberties. They are also more likely to endorse strong democratic norms. These traits hardly sound like a threat to the democratic order.

Why, then, is there such widespread negativity toward young Americans? There are two possible reasons. First, this criticism is partially based on the erosion of duty-based citizenship among the young and the positive traits linked to these norms. Since we are familiar with the political behaviors linked to citizen duty, such as voting in elections and patriotic behavior, the decline of these behaviors is easily recognized and lamented. And when many young Americans act on their values—such as not voting, using the rhetoric of Jon Stewart's *Daily Show*, and trusting Bono more than the president of the United States—this challenges the duty-based sensibilities of their elders. In many ways, young people clearly do not act like their grandparents, and researchers focus on the negative examples that are readily apparent.

Second, the criticism of the young (and the praise of their elders) partially overlooks the positive consequences of engaged citizenship that we find among the young. Part of the corrective of this book has been to draw attention to both the positive and negative aspects of generational change. Even when these positive traits are realized, however, they are often discounted as expressions of self-interest or self-indulgence. Yet, the measures of volunteerism in Figure 9.1 decrease with age as do the social aspects of citizenship (see Chapter 2).

American youth thus have a different image of government and a different relationship to politics. It is not that they are apathetic and unconcerned about politics—they are often involved and they show their concern in different ways than their elders. It is not that they are disaffected and cynical about politics—they are cynical about politicians and how the political system currently functions, but supportive of the democratic ideal. So the current challenge for American democracy is not to convince young people to act like their grandparents, but for us to understand their changing values and norms and respond in ways that integrate them into the political process—and potentially change the process to better match this new electorate.

TOCQUEVILLE REVISITED

In addition to describing norm shift within America, we also followed in Tocqueville's example to compare American norms and behaviors to those of other democratic publics (see Chapter 8).

At one level, these cross-national comparisons show that norm shift is not unique to America, but is generally occurring in other advanced industrial democracies. Youth in Sweden, Germany, Japan, and other affluent democracies also differ from their elders. This implies that the unique features of American history are not the driving force in the process of norm shift, since generations are also changing in nations that did not experience the "greatest generation," the turbulence of American politics in the 1960s, or the various government administrations over these past fifty years. Instead, norm shift evolves from the general processes of social modernization that we summarized in Chapter 1. Generational change, educational effects, and the reshaping of life experiences are producing a similar norm shift across the affluent democracies. This is consistent with the large body of research on value change in advanced industrial societies, which argues that citizens are shifting to post-material and self-expressive values that are analogous to the norm shift described here.[18] In short, the United States is not alone in experiencing a shift from duty-based norms to engaged citizenship, and so the implications of many of the findings of this book broadly apply to these other democracies.

At another level, these cross-national comparisons allow us to judge the state of the American political culture relative to other democracies. If there is a political culture that indicates an underlying illness of democracy, it does not appear to be the United States. I found few signs that the American political culture was noticeably less democratic than other nations. With the exception of elections, Americans remain a highly participatory public, especially in the forms of collective action that Tocqueville most admired. The American public is strikingly positive in terms of political tolerance, and much like other nations, strongly supportive of democratic values. Even the social concerns of Americans are not as materialistic and individualistic as are often assumed.

Perhaps the cynics will next claim that all democracies are at risk, so comparisons to the other unhealthy cases is not relevant. I think a more reasonable conclusion is that the American political culture has retained—and even strengthened—many of the democratic elements that Tocqueville once admired. Moreover, most other advanced industrial democracies are also improving. A participatory public of critical citizens who display growing levels of political tolerance and social concern are positive signs, showing us the benefits of changing citizenship norms to the advancement of the democratic ideal.

NORM SHIFT AND AMERICAN DEMOCRACY

I wish I could conclude with a list of reforms to "fix" the American public and American democracy. But I can't. In part, it is not clear to me that the American public and/or democracy is broken and therefore needs fixing. I am not a Pollyanna when it comes to politics. Certainly we have problems, and there are major challenges to maintain a democratic order and to develop it further. In many ways, however, American democracy is stronger today than during the 1950s and 1960s. In addition, if we understand the processes of social change that have transformed citizenship norms, then this argues that we cannot recreate the norms and behavior of another age—nor should we want to recreate them. Thus, reforms to renew traditional norms of citizen duty seem near-sighted and doomed to failure because the changing balance of citizenship norms reflects the restructuring of American society and social relations on a broad scale.[19]

I do not have the answers. But the first step in getting the right answers is to ask the right questions. The current democratic challenge does not arise because Americans are now disinterested in politics or lacking in civic spirit. We should not be asking how we can turn back the clock, restore the norms of citizen duty, and change the underlying values of the American public—although this is the refrain from the Democracy-at-Risk chorus. Instead, we should be asking a different question: *how does the democratic process adjust to changing norms, mitigating the problems and maximizing the benefits?*

If you accept that norm shift is an enduring feature of American politics, then we can outline four examples of how the political process might adapt to the shifting balance of citizenship norms.

A first area of change involves parties and elections. In the United States and most other advanced industrial democracies, participation in electoral democracy is decreasing and public trust in parties and government officials is decreasing. This trend diminishes the democratic process and erodes the political influence of those who forsake electoral politics. However, these analyses are often based on the misdiagnosis that Americans, and especially the young, are politically disengaged and so require a restoration of that sense of civic duty. For instance, one commonly advocated reform is to make voting compulsory.[20] Is this really the Jeffersonian vision of the democratic process? Such a regressive enforcement of citizenship duty is unlikely to resonate with those who hold norms of engaged citizenship. The democratic challenge is to think in new ways to more successfully integrate these new norms into the electoral process.

If you want to increase electoral participation among the young, you should begin by recognizing their different citizenship norms. Reforms would be more effective if they are embedded in a framework of engaged citizenship, rather than appeals to citizenship as a duty. Just as parties adjust their turnout strategy for minority voters, the elderly, and union workers, they are more likely to involve young Americans through themes and approaches that appeal to youthful interests. For instance, parties could develop campaigns to show how elections can have an even greater impact on the issues for which youth now volunteer. Political parties have also tended to ignore the youth vote in their programs, campaigns, and even advertising, and these patterns could be reversed.[21] The New Voters Project argues that personal contacts through schools and the workplace can be effective in mobilizing young voters. A report by the American Political Science Association offered a long list of policy reforms to re-engage Americans in elections process—but it did not mention Internet voting, which might engage more young people.[22] Ironically, rapper P. Diddy's admonition to "Vote or Die" or MTV's "Choose or Lose" campaign might be more effective in mobilizing the young than the traditional duty-based approach that many analysts put forward.

Even more challenging is the need to integrate people with norms of engaged citizenship into partisan politics beyond casting a vote. Parties are essential institutions of democratic governance and it is difficult to imagine how democracy can function without them. However, those who have experienced norm shift often see political parties as dinosaurs from another political age. For instance, when our political science department set up a student internship program, students were eager to intern with a public interest group, but there was less interest in working for a political party—even if it was the party they supported. Political parties have to change if they want to be successful in the new political climate. Political parties have to show (or change their procedures so they can show) that they are as politically relevant and effective as working for a non-governmental organization, and as rewarding to their participants. Party leaders and elected officials need to think about how to demonstrate the continuing relevance of parties in new and creative ways. For instance, the retired prime ministers of Canada have hosted an annual reality TV show to select *The Next Prime Minister*, which is a way to demonstrate the relevance of government and public office to young TV viewers. The winner does not get to be prime minister, but the show does help launch careers in public service for many of the participants.

Second, norm shift implies that politics will be more contentious. The model of a loyal, passive, and deferential culture is decreasing. There are likely to be tensions between these different norms of citizenship and how they are translated into political action and public policy. For instance: is government the solution to policy problems or the source of the problem? This is a basic issue that divides duty-based and engaged citizens. In addition, engaged citizenship encourages a more challenging orientation toward government. These individuals are more likely to use contentious forms of direct action, be less deferential toward elites, and be more assertive in claiming their individual rights. Perhaps it is no wonder why politicians look back longingly to an earlier political era in American politics, but the current question is how to adapt to these new patterns. These shifts may have contributed to the erosion of political comity and impressions of increased polarization. So the second challenge is to define ways of moderating tensions and contentiousness so that it does not impede democratic decisionmaking.

Third, norm shift also implies that people will connect to their government in new ways, such as through direct action as well as public interest groups. We need to ask how this will happen and what are the consequences of new forms of democratic deliberation and decision-making? For instance, the increased demands for political access are already prompting governments to respond through institutional reforms to open new channels of expressing public interests ("interest articulation").[23] Recent reforms to facilitate these new participation channels—such as the expansion of referendums and initiatives, public-access administrative hearings, direct contact with policy makers, and new access through the courts—are perhaps as extensive as the populist reforms that transformed American democracy in the early 1900s. This is a beneficial development because voice and access are important elements of a strong democratic process.

But institutional reforms often have unintended consequences. As we experience these ongoing institutional reforms, it requires thoughtful attention to how these new forms of access alter the democratic process. For example, as interests proliferate and gain greater political voice through new forms of access, it becomes more challenging to reach a collective solution to political questions. We are developing a system of complex governance with multiple access points and decision-making nodes. The result is increased articulation of interests (more voice), but less aggregation and comparison of interests (the balancing of contending voices). Political parties were initially created to provide such interest aggregation as mass democracy first developed, and groups within the party coalition negotiated on a common governing program. This worked well when electoral democracy was the dominant channel of both voice and interest aggregation. But as the role of parties has declined within the contemporary political process, and voice and the venues for political articulation have increased, the aggregation process has weakened. Good democratic politics is based on a reasonable judgment among contending voices, not just on who can clamor the loudest for their interests. Today, we need new institutional structures to find ways to aggregate interests into coherent public policy.

Finally, changes in the mix of political activity raise new questions about the equality of citizen influence. Many of these new political channels place higher demands on the skills and resources of activists. The "one person, one vote" rule also does not apply to these new forms of non-electoral participation, where individuals can write as many letters as they want, be active in multiple community groups, and attend more than one protest. While the opportunities for participation are equal, these activities are disproportionately used by the politically sophisticated who possess political skills and resources. Educational differences in participation are much greater for protest or community activity as compared to voting turnout.[24] This has real implications for the voices expressed within the political process. For example, when people organize to prevent polluting industries or to gain government benefits, those with higher education and political skills are likely to have greater voice; the "politically rich" may become even richer using these new forms of action. Simultaneously, those without these same resources may lose influence, and democracy will suffer as a result. Consequently, a change in the mix of political participation can increase the inequality of different sectors of the public.[25] Yet in other areas—such as political tolerance—norm shift may decrease social-status differences. So the question is not how to deal with a disinterested and apathetic public, but how to allow for expanding citizen voice while monitoring how this affects inequality in participation, political values, and other political behaviors.

In summary, I do not believe that democracy is at risk in America, unless we reject our own traditions and the positive values represented in the norms of engaged citizenship. This is not a time for retrenchment. It should be a time of democratic reform and expansion. There is a renewed spirit of our age, and it is reflected not in the rhetoric of Washington politicians or political scientists, but in those outside Washington who are more sensitive to the changing norms of citizenship. Citing a rock star is unusual for an academic book, but Bono's graduation address at the University of Pennsylvania in May 2004 reflects a more positive view of our age than the rhetoric from most political experts:

> There's a truly great Irish poet, his name is Brendan Kennelly, and he has this epic poem called "The Book of Judas," and there's a line in that poem that never leaves my mind, it says: "If you want to serve the age, betray it." What does that mean to betray the age?
>
> Well to me betraying the age means exposing its conceits, its foibles; its phony moral certitudes. It means telling the secrets of the age and facing harsher truths.
>
> Every age has its massive moral blind spots. We might not see them, but our children will. Slavery was one of them and the people who best served that age were the ones who called it as it was—which was ungodly and inhuman. Ben Franklin called it what it was when he became president of the Pennsylvania Abolition Society. . . .
>
> I'm in love with this country called America. I'm a huge fan of America, I'm one of those annoying fans, you know the ones that read the CD notes and follow you into bathrooms and ask you all kinds of annoying questions about why you didn't live up to that.
>
> I'm that kind of fan. I read the Declaration of Independence and I've read the Constitution of the United States, and they are some liner notes, dude. As I said, yesterday I made my pilgrimage to Independence Hall, and I love America because America is not just a country, it's an idea. You see my country, Ireland, is a great country, but it's not an idea. America is an idea, but it's an idea that brings with it some baggage, like power brings responsibility. It's an idea that brings with it equality, but equality even though it's the highest calling, is the hardest to reach. The idea that anything is possible, that's one of the reasons why I'm a fan of America. . . .

Adams said about Ben Franklin, "He does not hesitate at our boldest measures, but rather seems to think us too irresolute."

Well this is the time for bold measures. This is the country, and you are the generation.

If the American polity responds to this seismic shift in its political norms, the democratic ideal can be even stronger.

EPILOGUE: ENGAGED CITIZENS AND THE 2008 PRESIDENTIAL ELECTION

Lyse P. was attending her first major political event. Sen. Tom Harkin annually hosts a fundraising event, the Harkin Steak Fry, in an open field outside of Indianola, Iowa. At this 2007 event six hopefuls in the 2008 Democratic presidential primary would address the crowd. Two weeks earlier Lyse had been at a rock concert in the same field listening to the music of Papa Roach and Saliva, two of her favorite bands. Today, she was looking forward to hearing from a star of a different sort—Barack Obama.[1]

Lyse's attendance illustrates how young engaged citizens influenced the course of American politics in the 2008 election. She was only 17, not yet old enough to vote, but here she was at an election event wearing an Obama T-shirt adorned with Obama stickers and buttons. She was an example of the BarackStars, a network of high school students the campaign was recruiting in Iowa. By the time of the Iowa caucuses in January, most high schools in Iowa had a branch of the BarackStars. The University of Iowa, Iowa State University, Grinnell, and other college campuses had well-organized Obama groups. Through the Myspace, Facebook, and My.BarackObama.com Web sites, young people shared information about their candidate and connected to other Obama supporters, and the campaign connected to them.

Recruiting Lyse and other young people to the Iowa caucuses was a core strategy of the Obama campaign. The campaign strategists planned to bring new participants into the political process to increase Obama's support in the caucuses, and they were recruiting these new supporters from the ranks of young Iowans. Just a few days after the Harkin Steak Fry, Obama's campaign manager circulated a memo describing this youth-oriented strategy.[2] The campaign was following the same plan in the early primaries in New Hampshire, Nevada, and South Carolina. Even in Indiana, a late primary state, supporters were already staffing an information booth at Bloomington's Community Farmers' Market to attract students at Indiana University. This pattern was repeated in college towns across the nation. Young America, especially the student population, was to be a central part of the Obama electorate.

Most political scientists believed this strategy was unlikely to generate success. They saw it almost as a sign of desperation in the face of the Hillary Clinton juggernaut. These analysts knew about all the negative reports regarding young Americans (see Chapter 4). The young supposedly are disinterested in politics, concerned only with voting for the next *American Idol* winner and unlikely to show up on election day. Indeed, a week before the Iowa caucuses in January 2008, *Time* magazine quoted a political science expert on voter turnout: "Conventional wisdom has a name for candidates who rely on the youth vote: loser."[3] Clinton's chief strategist was also reassured by the young faces at Obama events in Iowa. He, too, expected these young people to stay home on caucus night and predicted the median age of caucus goers would approach 60.

But Obama won the Iowa caucuses, besting a field of other distinguished Democrats, each of whom had more experience in national politics. Obama's victory in Iowa launched a stream of commentaries about young people's surprising support for him and their surprising participation in the campaign. Some of these analysts suggested that the Iowa results were an anomaly, expecting that young people would stay home in the subsequent primaries. Some of these experts were still surprised when Obama won the Democratic Party's presidential nomination at the end of the primary season.

This epilogue asks whether we should have been so surprised by Obama's successful appeal to young Americans—especially given the description of engaged citizens throughout the book. This is not a discussion of the 2008 campaign overall. Hillary Clinton's campaign for the Democratic Party nomination and John McCain's journey to the presidential election are also important stories that others will tell, but those accounts are not the story of youth and politics in 2008. Our focus is on young people in the elections and their attraction to the Obama candidacy.[4] We want to assess what the election says about the changing nature of American politics.

THE PRIMARY CAMPAIGN

As described in Chapter 4, voting turnout by the young had decreased in the United States and most other established democracies over the past several decades. Political scientists debated what could be done to reverse this trend, offering solutions such as changing registration laws, changing the day for elections, or even requiring all eligible citizens to vote. This book suggested that a more likely solution was to understand how young engaged citizens think about politics and change politics to address these new orientations. Is that what happened in 2008?

Iowa was the first sign that young Americans could be more engaged in the electoral process. Young people turned out at events like the Harkin Steak Fry and rallies at university campuses. Still, many pundits claimed that the students who flocked to Obama rallies (and to a lesser extent the rallies of the other candidates) would stay home on caucus night. For instance, experts criticized the Obama campaign when the candidate skipped an AARP meeting of senior citizens to attend an Usher concert and speak to young voters; the experts scoffed that the seniors would attend the caucuses and the young would not. One of the most cynical reporters opined that young people would miss the caucuses to attend football-watching parties for the Orange Bowl that was being played on the same night.

Approximately 124,000 Democrats had participated in the 2004 Iowa caucuses, and the party predicted 150,000 caucus-goers for 2008. Party officials were overwhelmed when almost 240,000 showed up on caucus night. A total of 87,000 Republicans had participated in the last contested primary in 2000, and 120,000 came in 2008. Turnout rates in the caucuses had doubled since 2004.

Turnout increased among all age groups, but especially among the young. CIRCLE (Center for Information and Research on Civic Learning and Engagement) estimates that the combined youth turnout in both party caucuses increased from 4 percent in the 2004 caucuses to 13 percent in 2008.[5] On the Democratic side, 17- to 29-year-olds represented 22 percent of all participants, up from 17 percent in 2004. Clinton's historic race for the presidency motivated many Iowans to participate, and John Edwards's campaign brought others to the caucuses. But the greatest surge came from young Obama supporters. In a crowded field of candidates, 57 percent of caucus-goers under age 30 favored Obama, compared to only 18 percent among those age 65 or older. Obama had built a significant part of his campaign around young people, and they showed up. On the Republican side, young Iowans tended toward Mike Huckabee.

Lyse P. was a good example of the enthusiasm for Obama in action. She pretty much spent the fall of her senior year in high school working for her candidate, making phone calls, canvassing, making walk packets, and generally volunteering for the campaign. She organized a chapter of BarackStars at her high school and linked these students through a group on Facebook. And she was not the only one. Every Thursday at the local Obama headquarters was high school night, where young people came to connect to the campaign. On the night of the caucuses, she was a precinct captain for Obama in her home precinct—at age 17. Lyse's story retold across Iowa changed the face of the caucuses.

Still, the analysts' cynicism persisted, and some cautioned that the Iowa results were a fluke, even though young people continued to participate in subsequent Democratic primaries. In the first two dozen Democratic contests, youth turnout was nearly 50 percent higher than in 2004, and it grew even as a share of the total turnout.[6] For instance, exit polls reported that young people were 14 percent of the Democratic primary electorate in South Carolina, up from 9 percent in the 2004 exit polls. Even in Ohio, a primary Obama lost to Clinton by 10 points, exit polls indicated that youth participation increased from 9 percent of the electorate in 2004 to 16 percent in 2008. These percentages are astonishing, given that overall turnout in the primaries rose dramatically. Moreover, young voters continued to break heavily for Obama.

The profile of Obama supporters mirrored the patterns of engaged citizenship described in this book. Figure E.1 displays the average support for Obama by age from exit/entrance polls conducted for the first nineteen primaries and caucuses up to the March 5 Super Tuesday primaries

FIGURE E.1	Age and Support for Obama

▶ *Support for Obama is highest among younger voters in the Democratic primaries.*

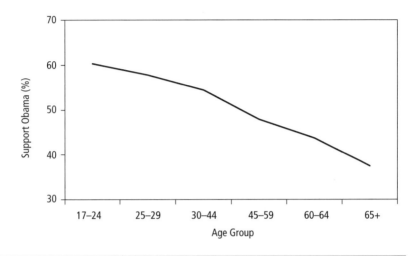

Note: Figure averages percent voting for Obama in 19 states up to March 5, 2008 primaries.

Source: National Election Pool of exit/entrance group surveys accessed from MSNBC.COM.

(Edwards dropped out of the campaign on January 30 after the first four primaries).[7] In these contests, Obama garnered more than 60 percent of the vote among those under age 25 compared to only 38 percent among seniors over age 65. One would have to look back to Gary Hart's generational appeal in 1988 or Robert Kennedy's 1968 campaign to find such a large generation gap within the Democratic primaries. As a female running for president, Clinton also was making history, but generational change seemed to trump gender; younger women leaned toward Obama, and older women endorsed Clinton. In Iowa, for instance, Obama received twice as much support among women under 45 as those older than 45 (50 percent versus 24 percent), and Clinton's appeal was smaller among the young than among women over age 45 (21 percent versus 36 percent).

Obama's support was not limited to the young, however. He also drew disproportionately from the better-educated, independents, and other groups linked to the norms of engaged citizenship. In nine northern

Super Tuesday states, for instance, Obama gained nearly 20 percent more votes among those with postgraduate degrees compared to Democratic voters with a high school education or less. If one combined age and education, Obama's special appeal to young better-educated Democrats is even more striking. These are the groups most closely identified with the new style of engaged citizenship discussed in this book, and they were strong Obama supporters in the primaries.

Obama's success in recruiting youthful supporters in the caucuses and primaries helped him win the Democratic Party presidential nomination. Something obviously had changed among young Americans who were supposedly apathetic, ill-informed, and unwilling to vote. What? Some analysts suggest that the "Millennials" who first voted in 2008 are substantially different from youth in earlier elections.[8] I disagree. As Figure 1 shows, the support for Obama is not an abrupt shift from one age group to another; rather, it is a fairly steady generational progression—consistent with the value shift argument of this book. Similarly, as shown in Figure 3.1, the generational patterns in rising turnout do not show an abrupt shift among Millennials, but a steady generational progression from old to young. The forces that came into play in the 2008 campaign are not unique to this election, but the Obama campaign uniquely tapped into the changes in American society that we describe in this book.

I think four major factors contributed to Obama's success in mobilizing young Americans in the primaries in 2008. First, one of the realities of campaigns is that many people vote because someone asks them to, and the Obama campaign asked the young to participate. The Obama team hired the former director of the "Rock the Vote" campaign from MTV and had one of the founders of Facebook as an adviser. This campaign was the first that fully embraced the Internet age to reach young citizens. Seven months before Obama declared his candidacy, supporters had established an "Obama for President" page on Facebook. The campaign used the technology of the new millennium to attract the Millennial generation. Facebook, Myspace, YouTube, and My.BarackObama.com were communication channels to the young. More than one million people viewed Obama's Iowa victory speech on YouTube, and millions more watched on BarackObama.com. A range of YouTube videos—from Obama girl to will.i.am—were part of his appeal to the young.[9] As noted above, the campaign consciously organized college and high school students who personally contacted other young people.[10] Attendees at early Obama rallies were asked to add their names, e-mail addresses, and cell phone numbers to the list at the door. These lists provided a database of potential supporters who received information via e-mails from the campaign and requests to participate and donate, and who could be mobilized as the election approached. Political networks exist to mobilize union members, church members, and other voter blocs; the Obama campaign created a network for its young supporters.

The new technology was not enough, however. In 2004 Howard Dean had demonstrated that creating an Internet network did not ensure that people would show up to vote. The Obama campaign's organizational strategy was to combine the new technology of the Internet with old-style grassroots politics.[11] The campaign's unprecedented success in on-line fund-raising provided the resources to build a participatory campaign.[12] As organizers began working in a state, they could turn to e-mail lists and online networks to recruit local supporters as precinct captains and then provide these organizers with contact information for Obama supporters in the precinct. Even more important, people began talking to each other directly through the Obama Web site ("MyBO"), social networking sites, and blogs. The Obama campaign used the enthusiasm of these young (and older) volunteers to out-organize the competition. One Democratic strategist observed, "They've married the incredibly powerful online community they built with real on-the-ground field operations. We've never seen anything like this before in American political history."[13]

But more than organization is needed. Past electoral reforms that tried to increase turnout, such as registering to vote while renewing a driver's license, had less impact than intended. Institutional fixes alone will not work, even though they are on the usual menu of advice from political experts. If Clinton or McCain had used the identical organization structure, they would have been less successful in mobilizing young voters. One has to understand what motivates people to vote.

A second rule of campaigns holds that people participate because they want to. Previous studies of youth turnout (see Chapter 4) noted that young people are less interested in electoral politics. This behavior is considered normal because political interest and involvement generally increase as people establish careers and families. In addition, most campaigns focus on older Americans and their priorities and often overlook the issue interests of the young.[14] By leaving young people out of the process, the campaigns tended to create a reinforcing spiral of decreasing electoral interest and involvement by younger voters. Public interest groups, MTV, and other groups had tried to engage the young in previous elections, but the parties and candidates themselves seemed to repeat the politics of catering to the AARP generation while overlooking the MTV generation.

This book argues that engaged citizens are not disinterested in politics, but they are less interested in electoral politics and instead participate in other ways (Chapter 4). The Obama campaign recognized this broader political engagement and convinced the young who volunteered in their local community center, senior center, or local public interest group to volunteer for the campaign phone banks, to walk the precincts, and to persuade their friends to participate.

The campaign did this by discussing the political issues motivating the young. It described climate change as "one of the great moral challenges of our generation," voiced consistent opposition to the Iraq war, recognized the distinct health care needs of young people, and discussed other youth-related issues such as the costs of college or the uncertainty of the job market. The campaign held town hall meetings in the schools to hear the concerns of young voters and then discuss the campaign's position on these matters. The Obama campaign told young Americans that voting was a way to address their interests through a government responsive to their concerns.

Third, American youth have been raised in a society where tolerance and diversity are applauded. Compared to their elders, the young are much more likely to accept racial and ethnic diversity and the rights of minorities (see Chapter 5). For young people who grew up with President David Palmer on the TV program *24* and Tiger Woods as a role model for golf, an African American presidential candidate is not extraordinary.[15] (The same holds for their images of a woman as president.) Engaged citizens do not merely accept diversity; they view Obama's biracial heritage as a positive trait—different from the views of many older Americans.[16] The Obama message and his personal story were a strong attraction to young engaged citizens in the Democratic primaries. Older voters grew up when racial prejudice was openly displayed and segregation was still legally sanctioned in the United States. For many older citizens, voting for an African American must have created some cognitive dissonance.

Fourth, Obama is a candidate of a different sort. He is very young for a presidential candidate, handsome, and charismatic. His oratorical skills turned a campaign stump speech into a "happening." Although his critics claimed Obama was substituting style for substance, it was clear that young people (and many older voters) were responding to these stylistic differences. Obama also adopted a different style of campaigning. He eschewed the politics of division, negativity, and the permanent campaign that had become the standards of American electoral politics and that may still appeal to old-style partisans and duty-oriented citizens. Obama's approach was especially appealing to many voters after the experiences of the Bush presidency and the rise of the permanent campaign that extended back to earlier administrations. The Obama campaign's emphasis on unity, cooperation, and hope tapped into the political norms of engaged citizens. When members of the Kennedy family endorsed Obama in January 2008, they created a link to the mystique of John F. Kennedy's legacy. Here was a candidate who said he would change America, and many young people voting in the Democratic primaries responded to that promise.

In short, the Obama organization ran a different type of campaign in the Democratic primaries in relation to the young. The campaign consciously mobilized young people as no other had previously done. It expressed the issues and political style that appealed to youthful engaged citizens. By including the issues of interest to young people and connecting to them on their own terms, the Obama campaign also showed that past electoral disinterest among the young at least partially reflected the nature of past campaigns rather than an intrinsic feature of a generation raised on television and a pop culture mass media.[17] Perhaps most important, the Obama campaign recognized that young Americans are interested in their nation and would participate if politics changed to reflect their views.

THE GENERAL ELECTION CAMPAIGN

On August 28 Barack Obama accepted the Democratic nomination for president. Instead of speaking only to the Denver convention-goers, Obama gave his acceptance speech to more than 80,000 supporters in a football stadium. It was exactly forty-five years to the day since Martin Luther King Jr. delivered his famous "I have a dream" speech to civil rights demonstrators on the Washington Mall. Obama's nomination as the Democratic Party's presidential candidate is perhaps this book's clearest example of how much American politics has changed over the previous half-century.

Sen. Joseph Biden was chosen as Obama's running mate. A week later, Sen. John McCain and Gov. Sarah Palin accepted the Republican nominations for president and vice president, respectively, at their convention in Minneapolis. The general election campaigns had begun.

General elections are much different from primaries. The electorate is different. Candidates no longer face only citizens from their own party (and crossovers in some primary states); the successful candidate has to attract support from independents and even from members of the opposing party. The electorate in the general election is also much larger and more diverse than in the primaries. The voting coalitions that were successful within a particular party often change in the general election. For instance, Obama's win in the Utah primary was unlikely to translate into statewide victory in November, and although Obama lost the California primary to Clinton, it was unlikely that McCain would win California's electoral votes. These contrasts apply as well to the McCain campaign. In short, the election cycle is like winning a game of checkers (the primaries) and then having to play a new game of chess (the general election) with a different player and different rules. There are broad similarities between both games, but also important differences. It is inherently difficult to predict election outcomes from primary election results: both major party candidates have won in their party's primaries, but half of these candidates eventually lose general elections.

The presidential election offered a clear ideological choice between the two candidates, especially on the issues that most concern young engaged citizens. The Obama-Biden campaign discussed environmental quality, education, the Iraq war, and genocide in Darfur. The campaign's themes also broadened to attract the 18 million people who had voted for Clinton and the independents who would be needed for victory; but the appeal to youth continued as well. The McCain-Palin ticket stressed a different agenda of cutting taxes, military victory in Iraq, and drilling for oil. McCain's political style seemed oriented toward adherents of duty-based citizenship, with the claims of placing country first, the emphasis on patriotism, and his distinguished military record. The candidates themselves epitomized the generational contrast: an energetic 47-year-old Democratic candidate who was the advocate for progressive change versus the 71-year-old Republican candidate who seemed to long for the good old days. McCain's selection of Palin as a running mate did little to change the image of the Republican ticket; despite her youth and gender she advocated the same ideological positions as McCain—with even greater intensity.

A thought experiment might make this contrast clearer. Turn to the list of citizenship norms on page 26. From the GSS column in Table 2.1, select five norms that you think McCain might pick and then select five norms for Obama. Comparing these two lists, I suspect that McCain would closely fit the norms of duty-based citizenship, while Obama would be closer to engaged citizenship. In other words, the contrasts in 2008 reflected the differences in citizenship norms we have discussed in this volume.

The Obama campaign also continued its strategy of youth engagement from the primary season. It announced a summer fellowship program to train young people in campaign organizing; more than 10,000 applied for the 3,600 slots. The fellows participated in a six-week training session that prepared them for the fall campaign. The Internet and text messaging were important communication tools. Supporters signed up to receive the text message announcing Obama's vice-presidential nomination—and therefore had their cell numbers entered into the campaign's database. Viral messaging encouraged people to download information on how to register to vote, and then forward it to friends. With Obama leading 2 to 1 among citizens under age 30, registering young people and getting them out to vote was a major campaign goal. Rock the Vote claimed to have registered more than 2.5 million voters by election day. The Obama campaign continued to use the Internet as an unprecedented fund-raising tool, eventually collecting roughly $650 million in donations from more than 2.5 million donors. Enthusiasm, organizing, and funding created a powerful campaign for Obama that had a special appeal to young engaged citizens.

Party strategies changed during the general election campaign, partly in response to the actions of the opposition and partly in response to unfolding political and economic events. The meltdown of the financial sector and the dramatic downturn of the stock market in October focused attention on economic issues and clearly benefited Obama and most Democratic candidates because voters saw the Democrats as more likely to address the challenges. These economic issues cemented Obama's rapidly growing lead in the polls in the month before the election. At the same time, as the focus shifted to the economy, the campaign devoted less attention to the youth-oriented issues that had been prominent in the primaries. With a rapidly worsening economy, an unpopular president, and the continuing war in Iraq, any Republican candidate would have had difficulty attracting voter support. Except for a week immediately after the Republican National Convention in early September, Obama had led McCain since May in the average of national public opinion polls (see www.pollster.com).

Election Day

Approximately 130 million Americans cast votes for president and a host of other political offices on November 4. Turnout in the election was the highest in forty years, and some votes are still being tallied as this epilogue is written. Lyse P. was there as well. She volunteered during the election and especially during the final weeks of the campaign, even skipping classes the last two weeks to work full-time for Obama.

The experts had made their predictions, and the vote results started to roll in as the polls closed in the East and Midwest. The first indication of the outcome was the closeness of the contest in the battleground states of Indiana, North Carolina, Ohio, and Virginia. All four states had voted for George W. Bush in 2000 and 2004. When the networks called Pennsylvania for Obama, it signaled the outcome of the night. At 8 p.m. Pacific Standard time, the polls closed in California, Hawaii, Oregon, and Washington, and all the networks announced that Obama had surpassed the

270 electoral votes needed for election and would become the forty-fourth president of the United States.

Obama delivered his victory speech to more than 200,000 supporters in Chicago as most of the nation watched in admiration. Equally impressive was McCain's concession speech, in which he outlined the historic nature of the outcome and the fundamental changes in America's political history it represented. He also encouraged his supporters to find ways to come together with the new administration to address the country's common needs. It was a powerful statement of democracy at its best; it ended a hard-fought campaign with a recognition and acceptance of the public's decision. The election results prompted unprecedented spontaneous public celebrations outside the White House in Washington, D.C., in Times Square in New York City, at a block party on First Street in Seattle, and in millions of family living rooms. Americans had exercised their right to vote, and a feeling of change was in the air.

Turnout

One of the central questions of the 2008 general election was whether young people would turn out in greater numbers than in the past. The heightened campaign interest and activity on college campuses and other youth forums was obvious. In addition, the Obama campaign continued to reach out to the young to encourage them to vote.[18] A network of foundations and public interest groups—Rock the Vote, First Time Voters Project, BotherVoting.org, and others—worked to increase youth turnout. The outcome was uncertain, however, and naysayers claimed that most young people would once again stay home on election day. A week before the election NBC journalist Campbell Brown told her CNN viewers that early voting evidence from Florida "suggests that young voters just might do what they always do: blow it off, stay home, space out, get a better offer."

Figure E.2 displays the changes in turnout between presidential elections starting with 1996. The first bar represents the change in turnout for the entire electorate, and the second bar is the change in turnout for citizens under age 30. Turnout for the whole public has been generally increasing—in part because of the efforts of political parties and other groups. Turnout was up 2.5 percent in 2000 and almost 6 percent in 2004.

FIGURE E.2   **Increasing Election Turnout**

▶ *Youth turnout has been growing more than the overall public since 1996.*

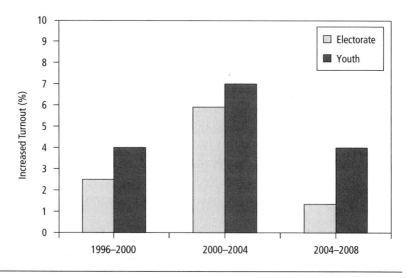

Source: Electorate data from the United States Election Project (*elections.gmu.edu/voter_turnout.htm*); youth turnout data from CIRCLE, "Youth Turnout Rate Rises to at Least 52%" (*www.civicyouth.org*).

Final statistics for 2008 are not yet available as this epilogue is being written, but the best estimates are that turnout grew by another 1.3 percent. It was surprising that overall turnout did not increase more given the historic nature of the 2008 election, but apparently the greater Democratic turnout was partially counterbalanced by a decrease in the number of Republicans who voted.

And what about youth? Youth turnout has grown more than the overall electorate for each of these comparisons. In 1996 only 37 percent of citizens under age 30 voted, a situation that stimulated the calls and programs to reengage younger voters in electoral politics. Youth turnout increased 4 percent by 2000, and an additional 7 percent in 2004.

Estimates for youth turnout in the 2008 election are still tentative, but the best available statistics indicate a 4 to 6 percent increase.[19] The growth in turnout among the young is several times that of the overall public. Indeed, CIRCLE claims that almost two-thirds of the overall increase in turnout in 2008 was due to the surge among the young.

These gains in youth turnout considerably narrow the difference between young and middle-aged voters. Even in 2008, however, there was probably a 10 percent gap between the turnout rates of those under age 30 and those over age 30. We expect that the gap between the youngest age groups and older voters will persist, as it is an enduring pattern in most democratic electorates. Turnout rises with increasing family responsibility, careers, geographic and social stability, and other life cycle effects. It cannot be reversed, only moderated. But the efforts to mobilize young people in 2008, especially by the Obama campaign, have shown that most members of Gen X and the Millennials can become participants in the electoral process.

Vote Choice

Our other major question is who these young voters supported in 2008, and what the entire electoral base for Obama and McCain tells us about the politics of America. A preliminary analysis of the exit poll findings gives us insights into voting patterns; more precise information will become available in the months ahead.[20]

Table E.1 compares the 2008 voting results for various demographic groups to the results from 2000, the last time a Democrat won the popular vote. Obama received roughly 52 percent of the national popular vote, compared to 49 percent for Al Gore. Obama's share of the vote is the largest a Democrat has received since the 1964 election of Lyndon Johnson. In broad terms, many of the traditional patterns of party support were repeated in the 2008 election. For instance, the vast majority of Democratic Party identifiers (89 percent) voted for the Obama-Biden ticket, and the vast majority of Republicans voted for McCain-Palin (91 percent). Electoral change occurred at the margins—yielding enough votes to produce a 3 percent increase for Obama compared to Gore.

The shift in voting patterns across age groups is the largest contrast in Table E.1. Voters under age 30 gave two-thirds of their vote to Obama and Biden. The Obama surge was apparent on election night as the Democrats' vote share jumped in many counties with a large university, especially in

TABLE E.1	**Comparing Social Group Voting for Gore and Obama**

▶ *Obama gains more support than Gore from youth, the better educated, and minorities*

Group	Percent of 2008 Electorate	Gore 2000 (Percent)	Obama 2008 (Percent)	Percent Difference
Total	100%	49	52	+3
Age				
18–24	10	55	66	+11
25–29	8	54	66	+12
30–44	29	46	54	+8
45–64	37	51	50	−1
65 and over	16	46	45	−1
Men	47	43	49	+6
Women	53	55	56	+1
White	74	43	43	0
Black	13	90	95	+5
Hispanic	8	61	66	+5
Asian	2	62	62	0
HS or less	25	54	55	+1
Some college	31	46	51	+5
College degree	27	45	50	+5
Graduate school	17	52	58	+6
Protestant	54	38	45	+8
Catholic	27	52	53	+1
Jewish	2	77	77	0
No religion	12	66	75	+9
Union member in Household	21	61	58	−3
No member	79	45	51	+6
Northeast	22	56	58	+2
Midwest	24	48	53	+5
South	32	43	47	+4
West	22	49	55	+6
Liberal	22	79	88	+8
Middle-of-road	44	54	60	+6
Conservative	34	20	20	0
Democrat	40	88	89	+1
Independent	28	43	51	+8
Republican	32	7	9	+2

Sources: 2000 *Los Angeles Times* Exit Poll; 2008 Edison Media Research Exit Poll.

battleground states: Durham County, North Carolina (Duke University and North Carolina Central University), was up 13 percent for the Democrats compared to 2000; Albemarle County, Virginia (University of Virginia), up 15 percent; Monroe County, Indiana (Indiana University), up 19 percent; Johnson County, Iowa (University of Iowa), up 11 percent; and Boulder County, Colorado (University of Colorado), up 24 percent. Nationwide, voters under age 30 shifted toward the Democrats by 12 percent compared to 2000, and this number is essentially the same if we compare 2008 to John Kerry's vote share in 2004. With a 12 percent rise in youth turnout since 2000, the shift toward the Democrats had an even larger impact on the electoral result. We see, however, that this shift decreases somewhat across age groups: 30–44 years old (+8 percent for Obama), 45–64 (–1 percent), 65 and over (–1 percent).

The swing to Obama is also proportionally larger among people with social characteristics we have linked to engaged citizenship. Obama gained among voters with university or graduate degrees, while receiving virtually the same vote share as Gore among voters with a high school diploma or less. Those who identify with either of the two parties displayed about the same loyalty rates in 2000 and 2008, but independents had an 8 percent swing toward Obama. Not all young Americans adhere to the norms of engaged citizenship, and not all engaged citizens are young. Still, engaged citizens seem to be one of the important swing groups behind the Obama victory.

The other obvious keys to Obama's victory are race and ethnicity. Black Americans are among the most loyal supporters of the Democratic Party; Gore garnered 90 percent of their votes, and John Kerry received 88 percent. Although there is not much room for growth, the black vote for Obama rose to 95 percent. The major change in 2008 was the increase in black turnout because of the Obama candidacy. Early postelection estimates suggest that black turnout increased significantly since 2004, which contributed to Obama's victory in Michigan, North Carolina, and Virginia. Obama also did better than either Gore (up 5 percent) or Kerry (up 13 percent) among Hispanic voters. The ethnic diversity of the American electorate—white voters decreased from 81 percent of the 2000 electorate to 74 percent in 2008—is a long-term demographic shift that will continue. Obama drew together a multiethnic coalition with implications for the future of the Democratic Party.[21]

THE LEGACY OF 2008

The 2008 presidential election was exceptional in many ways. Obama's charisma and the historic nature of his candidacy generated unusual interest in the election, especially among engaged citizens. Hillary Clinton's run for the nomination was a major political step forward for women. The nomination of Sarah Palin as the Republican candidate for vice president mobilized conservative voters. The ongoing conflicts in Iraq and Afghanistan further stimulated political interest. And then the meltdown of the credit market and the losses on Wall Street increased economic concerns and interest in politics. It is unlikely that the next presidential election will reflect such a convergence of factors—at least we hope the nation will be in better shape.

What are the likely enduring consequences of the 2008 contest in terms of American public opinion, the norms of citizenship, and the workings of the American political process? Political scientists are not very good at forecasting the future, but let me suggest a few points to consider.

Participation is one important change. Because of the historic nature of the 2008 election, I suspect that overall participation levels may dip in future elections. At the same time, previous research maintains that lifelong voting patterns tend to build upon early life experiences.[22] When Gen X was participating less, researchers predicted that this generation would continue to lag behind earlier generations even as they aged. By the same token, the increased turnout among Millennials in 2008 should foretell their higher involvement in the future, all else being equal. Many young people are now registered to vote, which is an important first hurdle. They participated in 2008 and therefore have a stake in supporting their preferred candidate or party. Many of them participated beyond voting by donating money, working for a campaign, or contacting friends to support a candidate. Furthermore, the 2008 election demonstrated that young people will participate if the candidate's message addresses their concerns and the campaigns use appropriate techniques to communicate with them. In other words, 2008 provides a baseline from which participation may expand as members of the millennial generation finish their studies, begin a career, purchase a home, and share the other life experiences that foster attention to government and politics.

The Obama campaign also introduced new techniques to reach young (and other) voters. Blending the Internet with traditional in-person contacting was successful in spreading the campaign's message and in getting people to the polls on election day. Proposed reforms to simplify registration for first-time voters and remove institutional barriers to youth voting can also increase youth turnout in the future.[23] And voters should not have to wait hours in line to cast their ballot, as many did in 2004 and 2008. Electoral reforms can benefit turnout in the long term, and future elections should build on the positive lessons of the 2008 experience.

There are limits to institutional reforms, however. Spending more money, using the Internet creatively, and developing a new style of campaign organization are not enough. An important change in 2008 was a conscious effort by the Obama campaign to motivate young voters by discussing the issues that concern them and crafting a campaign to engage them. If a candidate adopted the institutional structure of the Obama campaign without the content, she or he would be less successful in mobilizing youth. The importance of motivation is often missed in calls to "fix" turnout primarily through institutional reforms. The motivational factor is especially important for young engaged citizens who are unlikely to vote simply out of sense of citizen duty. As I discussed in Chapter 9, campaigns need to show engaged citizens how elections can affect the issues of concern to them—and then follow through on these policy promises. People need a reason to vote, and simply reforming the institutions is not enough.

Another question is whether the 2008 election will shift the overall political balance in American politics. Repeatedly, it seems, political scientists and pundits predict a fundamental realignment in American politics. By the next election, however, the issues will be different. By the next election, the candidates will be different. This should lead us to be cautious about projecting from one election into the future. The outcome of future elections largely depends on what the government, the Democratic Party, and the Republican Party do in the interim. The good thing about democratic elections is that they give the electorate the opportunity to take stock of the past and to change their votes.

One bit of evidence on future party alignments, however, is the party identities of voters in the latest election. Party identification is a long-term

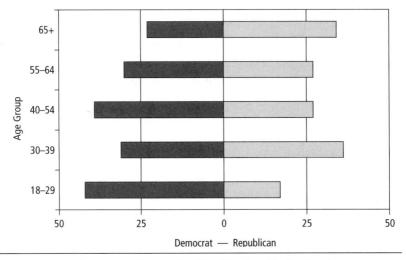

FIGURE E.3   Party Identification

▶ *Youth were the most Democratic of all age groups in 2008.*

Note: Figure entries are the percentage of Democratic and Republican Party identifiers in each age group.

Source: Time magazine Abt SRBI Poll, *America by the Numbers* (October 3–8, 2008), N = 1053.

affective identification with a preferred party, even if some voters occasionally switch sides. It is a main variable in predicting turnout, vote outcomes, and opinions toward the issues and candidates of the day.[24] As such, a shift in party identification could indicate a shift in the baseline of party politics in the future.

Figure E.3 presents the distribution of Democratic and Republican Party identifiers based on a *Time* magazine survey conducted in October 2008. This survey includes only self-identified registered voters and therefore misses people who are not registered. The patterns highlight the impact of the 2008 campaign on the party identities of the young.[25] The highest percentage of Democratic partisans (42 percent) is among registered voters under age 30. The proportion of engaged citizens is higher among young, better-educated individuals; this group is even more heavily Democratic (47 percent). Moreover, voters under 30 report the smallest number of Republican partisans (17 percent), which yields a large 25 percent gap in the Democratic-Republican balance. Voters over age 55, in contrast, are disproportionately Republican.

Social science research suggests that some young citizens will change their partisan loyalties over time; these identities are not immutable. But as the Millennial generation becomes a larger share of the electorate (see Figure 1.2), and older voters depart, the partisan balance should shift toward the Democratic Party. The same applies to the patterns among engaged citizens for policy orientations (Chapter 6) and other political values discussed in this book (Chapters 5 and 7). Young engaged citizens favor a more activist government, a more socially liberal government, and an environmentally conscious government. Generational demography can shape the nation's political destiny unless new forces change this balance.

The day after the election, people and pundits were discussing its larger implications for the racial divisions in America. Before the vote, older Americans, both white and black, often said that previously they could not have imagined a black person being elected president of the United States during their lifetime. For all ethnic groups, Obama's victory is a sign of how much America has changed over the past half-century and how some of the negative stereotypes about race (on all sides) were proven wrong.

The nation took a dramatic step forward on its long journey, and many Americans now hope that the 2008 election will transform the country's race relations and politics. This election should affect U.S. society and politics because a barrier has been breeched. Change comes slowly, however, and real change requires a deeper shift in how we think of ourselves and how we live our lives. As Obama himself stated in his *A More Perfect Union* speech: "I have never been so naïve as to believe that we can get beyond our racial divisions in a single election cycle, or with a single candidacy—particularly a candidacy as imperfect as my own." This is a journey that engaged citizens are willing and able to take. A post-racial society is unlikely, but a more harmonious and improving society is clearly possible.

Finally, the experiences of the 2008 election have the potential to reshape how we think of our fellow citizens and our government. Since the

1970s, Americans' trust of their fellow citizens and their trust in their government has diminished. This trend was exacerbated at the elite level in heightened partisan polarization, partisan hostility, and open displays of political intolerance.

The 2008 election was a sign that many Americans want a new style of politics. People can disagree, but they can do so respectfully. To be a member of a different party or social group should not mean an end to civility. The 2008 election was an example of a politics of inclusion triumphing over a politics of playing to the base. And it selected a president who says he will follow a different course. He will have the difficult task of restoring social and political trust in America, which many politicians have tried unsuccessfully to do. The Obama administration may not be able to restore trust, especially in an enduring way, because the causes of distrust are broad and complex. Engaged citizens also might be quick to criticize Obama's pragmatic choices that fall short of a theoretical ideal. But a new style in Washington may lessen the sharpness of political division and perhaps build new bridges. Engaged citizens favor a more-inclusive and less-combative political style, and they will press for these changes in Washington and their local communities.* They want to change the political culture in the ways we have described in this book. They believe in the closing words of Obama's acceptance speech on November 4 in Chicago:

> *This is our time, to put our people back to work and open doors of opportunity for our kids; to restore prosperity and promote the cause of peace; to reclaim the American dream and reaffirm that fundamental truth, that, out of many, we are one; that while we breathe, we hope. And where we are met with cynicism and doubts and those who tell us that we can't, we will respond with that timeless creed that sums up the spirit of a people: Yes, we can.*

---

*We have linked engaged citizenship to support for Obama in 2008, and most young engaged citizens probably did vote for Obama. At the same time, there are also young conservatives who are engaged citizens, who work with their church or conservative groups on issues of global poverty, climate change, and family issues. Engaged citizenship can exist separate from party orientation.

APPENDIX A: STATISTICAL PRIMER

Anyone who reads newspapers knows that their reporting regularly features public opinion polls. Because such information is often presented in tables and graphs, the informed citizen needs to understand how to read and interpret them.

This book offers similar analyses of public opinion. I often present the relationship between two or more public opinion questions to determine the sources of citizen norms and their impact on political behavior. For instance, what factors are related to levels of citizen duty or engaged citizenship, or how do these two types of citizenship norms affect political participation or images of government? These relationships may be shown in graphic terms. Figure 3.1, for instance, indicates that citizen duty is higher among older Americans, but engaged citizenship is lower. Figure 7.3 shows that higher levels of citizen duty increase satisfaction with the political process, but higher levels of engaged citizenship decrease satisfaction.

Implicitly, at least, there is a presumption of causality. For instance, when citizen duty is related to higher turnout, we presume that the reason is that these norms encourage people to vote as part of their civic duty.

Often tables and figures include lots of comparisons, such as many levels of education or many levels of church attendance—and it can become difficult to see the overall pattern amid a blur of numbers. In such cases I use correlation statistics to summarize relationships (they are often included in the figures). Even if you are not numerically inclined, statistics are tools to help you understand relationships. These correlations summarize the extent to which responses on one survey question (such as levels of education) are related to responses on another question (such as turnout).

Statisticians might feel faint after reading the quick summaries that follow and from the limited attention devoted to the assumptions underlying the use of these statistics. Statistics is a complex field, and data analysis is a complicated research methodology. Nevertheless, this primer provides a quick reference guide on how to use the statistics presented in the book, with the hope that it helps you understand the presentation of findings.

CORRELATION STATISTICS

I most commonly use three correlation statistics:

- **Cramer's V correlation.** This correlation measures the relationship between two variables when at least one of them is a "categoric" variable, that is, just a set of categories with no distinct order. An example of a categoric variable would be region, race, religious denomination, or any measure that does not follow a natural order from low to high, agree to disagree, or some other underlying order. Racial differences in citizenship norms in Figure 3.3 is a categoric example.
- **Pearson's _r_ correlation.** This correlation measures the relationship between two variables when both have an ordered pattern of categories, such as from low to high or from agree to disagree. This correlation statistic is more powerful and demanding than Cramer's V because it does not just see if categories differ on the predicted variable, but presumes an ordered pattern to these differences. For instance, as educational levels increase, so too does adherence to the norms of citizen duty and engaged citizenship (Figure 3.2).

  The Pearson's _r_ also measures the _direction_ of a relationship because there is a distinction between higher and lower values. For instance, citizen duty increases voting turnout, but the same norms decrease participation in demonstrations. The first example would produce a positive correlation, and the second a negative correlation.

- **Regression coefficient** (β). This statistic is the most complex. Often we want to examine the relationship between two variables, but we think this relationship might partially depend on another variable(s). Multiple regression is a statistical method to simultaneously examine the relationships of several variables with a dependent variable, so that we can assess the separate effects of each. The regression coefficient describes the relationship between two variables, while "statistically controlling for" the other variables in the model. For instance, what is the separate effect of engaged citizenship on protesting while simultaneously controlling for (or statistically removing) the fact that engaged citizens are younger and better educated, which can have separate effects of participation patterns.

This book presents standardized regression coefficients from several such regression analyses (see Figure 3.7 and Table 4.4). These statistics are comparable to the Pearson r and are calculated in a similar way. They signify the direction and strength of a relationship. The differences between a Pearson r and a regression coefficient indicate how much a relationship changes by controlling for the other variables in the model.

A simple example illustrates the logic of regression analysis. We begin with the question of whether engaged citizenship is related to higher participation in protest activity. Figure A.1 shows there is a strong relationship between these two traits.

If we stopped here, we would conclude that engaged citizenship stimulates people to participate in challenging political activities, such as demonstrations. The correlation between these two variables is a substantial .23. But a skeptic might ask if this result is because of the norms of engaged citizenship or because these individuals also possess other traits—younger age, higher education, and higher cognitive skills—that might be the real source of this relationship.

You already know the answer to this question if you have correctly interpreted Table 4.4. This table presents a regression analysis in which engaged citizenship is used to predict participation in demonstrations, while statistically controlling for differences attributable to age, education, cognitive skills, and the other predictors in the analyses. The regression coefficient of .21 indicates that the effect of engaged citizenship is

FIGURE A.1   **Engaged Citizenship and Participation in Demonstrations**

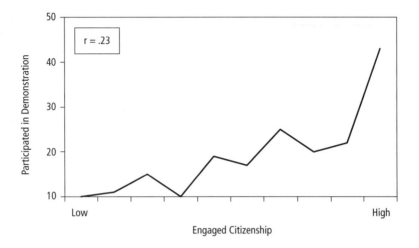

essentially unchanged even when these other factors are taken into account. In other words, it is citizenship norms, rather than these other predictors, that produced the relationship in Figure A.1.

WHAT IS BIG?

Correlations are designed to summarize the strength of the relationship between two variables, which raises the question of what is a strong relationship versus a weak relationship. I chose the three correlation statistics in this text because they give comparable values for similar relationships, even if they are calculated differently:

- **Cramer's V correlation.** This statistic ranges from a value of 0.0 when there are no differences across categories (that is, each comparison in a table has the same percentage distribution) to a value of 1.00 when categories in a table differ by a maximum possible 100 percent. Typically, we interpret coefficients of .10 or less as a weak relationship, .10–.20 as a modest relationship, and .20 or larger as a strong relationship.
- **Pearson's r correlation.** This statistic measures three properties that are apparent in Figure A.1. First, how strongly does one variable pre-

dict differences in the dependent variable; in Figure A.1 this means how steep is the angle of the line describing this relationship. Second, how are individuals within each category clustered around the mean score plotted in the figure, or how well does the line represent the overall pattern. Third, relationships can be positive or negative. For instance, demonstrations increase with higher levels of engaged citizenship (a positive relationship), but voting turnout decreases (a negative relationship) (see Table 4.4).

Thus, the Pearson r ranges from a value of -1.0 when there is a perfect negative relationship (a sharp negatively sloped line with all the points clustered on the line), to 0.0 when there are no differences across categories (that is, scores of the predictor variable are unrelated to the dependent variable) to a value of 1.00 when there is a perfect positive correlation. As with Cramer's V, we interpret coefficients of .10 or less as a weak relationship, .10–.20 as a modest relationship, and .20 or larger as a strong relationship.

- **Regression coefficient** (β). This statistic is comparable to the Pearson r, except that it measures the relationship between two variables while controlling for the relationships shared by other variables in the model. Like the Pearson r, it ranges from -1.0 for a perfect negative relationship to 1.0 for a perfect positive relationship. As with the other two statistics, we interpret coefficients of .10 or less as a weak relationship, .10–.20 as a modest relationship, and .20 or larger as a strong relationship.

Statistics presented in graphs and tables can sometimes seem complex, but statistics are simply a shortcut for summarizing a picture like Figure A.1 that describes how much one variable is related to another—and with this guide these relationships should be easier to interpret than trying to understand all the percentages in a statistical table or points in a graph.

ENDNOTES

CHAPTER 1

1. Stuart Silverstein, "More freshmen help others, survey finds." *Los Angeles Times*, January 26, 2006.
2. Ronald Inglehart and Christian Welzel. *Modernization, Cultural Change and Democracy*. New York: Cambridge University Press, 2005; Wayne Baker, *America's Crisis of Values Reality and Perception*. Princeton: Princeton University Press, 2004; Russell Dalton, *Citizen Politics*, 4th ed. Washington, DC: CQ Press, 2006.
3. Stephen Macedo et al., *Democracy at Risk: How Political Choices Undermine Citizen Participation, and What We Can Do about It*. Washington, DC: Brookings Institution Press, 2005: 1.
4. Some of the most prominent examples of this genre are Alan Wolfe, *Does American Democracy Still Work?* New Haven: Yale University Press, 2006; Fareed Zakaria, *The Future of Freedom: Illiberal Democracy at Home and Abroad*. New York: Norton, 2003; Samuel Huntington, *Who Are We? The Challenges to America's Identity*. New York: Simon & Schuster, 2004; Stephen Craig, *The Malevolent Leaders: Popular Discontent in America*. Boulder, CO: Westview Press, 1993; E. J. Dionne, *Why Americans Hate Politics*. New York: Simon & Schuster, 1991; John Hibbing and Elizabeth Theiss-Morse, *Congress as Public Enemy: Public Attitudes toward American Political Institutions*. New York: Cambridge University Press, 1995; Joseph Nye, Philip Zelikow, and David King, eds., *Why Americans Mistrust Government*. Cambridge, MA: Harvard University Press, 1997; and perhaps the best-researched and most well-reasoned project, Robert Putnam, *Bowling Alone: The Collapse and Renewal of American Community*. New York: Simon and Schuster, 2000. Some might add to this list Russell Dalton, *Democratic Challenges, Democratic Choices*. Oxford: Oxford University Press, 2004; but I disagree.
5. Putnam, *Bowling Alone*; Tom Brokaw, *The Greatest Generation*. New York: Random House, 1998.
6. Putnam, *Bowling Alone*, 283.
7. William Damon, "To not fade away: Restoring civil identity among the young." In Diane Ravitch and Joseph Viteritti, eds., *Making Good Citizens: Education and Civil Society*. New Haven: Yale University Press, 2001. Also see Wattenberg, *Is Voting for the Young?* New York: Longman, 2006; Jean Twenge, *Generation Me: Why Today's Young Americans Are More Confident, Assertive, Entitled—and More Miserable Than Ever Before*. New York: Free Press, 2006.
8. Ronald Inglehart, *Culture Shift in Advanced Industrial Society*; Baker, *America's Crisis of Values*; Inglehart and Welzel. *Modernization, Cultural Change and Democracy*; Terry Clark and Michael Rempel, eds., *Citizen Politics in Post-Industrial Societies*. Boulder, CO: Westview Press, 1998.
9. Clark and Rempel, *Citizen Politics in Post-Industrial Societies*; Inglehart, *Culture Shift in Advanced Industrial Society*.
10. Richard Florida, *The Rise of the Creative Class: And How It's Transforming Work, Leisure, Community and Everyday Life*. New York: Perseus Books, 2002: 1–3.
11. Angus Campbell et al., *The American Voter*. New York: Wiley, 1960; Angus Campbell et al., *Elections and the Political Order*. New York: Wiley, 1966.
12. Neil Nevitte, *The Decline of Deference*. Petersborough, Canada: Broadview Press, 1996.
13. Norman Nie, Jane Junn, and Kenneth Stehlik-Barry, *Education and Democratic Citizenship in America*. Chicago: Chicago University Press, 1996.
14. Samuel Popkin, *The Reasoning Voter*. Chicago: University of Chicago Press, 1991.
15. Peter Drucker, *Post-Capitalist Society*. New York: Harper Business, 1993; also see Erik Wright, *Class Counts: Comparative Studies in Class Analysis*. Cambridge: Cambridge University Press, 1996. The comparative politics literature notes a similar development in most other Western democracies,

labeling this group as the "new middle class," or the "salatariat." Oddbjørn Knutsen, *Class Voting in Western Europe.* Lanham, MD: Lexington Books, 2006.

16. Florida, *The Rise of the Creative Class*, 77–80; also see Morley Winograd and Dudley Buffa, *Taking Control: Politics in the Information Age.* New York Henry Holt, 1996.

17. Florida, *The Rise of the Creative Class*, ch. 3.

18. I used the ANES data to describe the public; this is a major survey project that I use in subsequent chapters. I did not include retirees in this figure because their prior employment status was often ambiguous, and the number choosing this retirement category rises significantly over this five-decade span. If retirement is meant to imply previous employment, then the trends in Figure 1.4 are even sharper.

19. The Center for American Women and Politics (www.cawp.rutgers.edu) reports that only twenty-six women were members of the 83rd U.S. Congress in 1953, and by the 108th Congress (elected in 2004) this had increased to 172 women—a six-fold increase. Twenty-three women held statewide elective offices in 1969; this increased to eighty-one in 2004. In 1971, there were 244 women in all the state legislatures combined, and by 2003 this increased to 1,654—also a six-fold increase.

20. Katherine Tate, *From Protest to Politics: The New Black Voters in American Elections.* Cambridge: Harvard University Press, 1993.

21. Daniel Bell, *Postindustrial Society.* New York: Free Press, 1973; Ronald Inglehart, *The Silent Revolution.* Princeton: Princeton University Press, 1977; Inglehart, *Culture Shift in Advanced Industrial Society.*

22. There is a tendency, however, to idealize the past, implying that Americans had access to more and better information in the past, when newspaper readership was higher and television was still uncommon; Putnam, *Bowling Alone*; Wattenberg, *Is Voting for Young People?* Certainly access to information is much greater today than in the 1950s: this seems indisputable.

23. The citizenship battery was included in the 2004 General Social Survey (GSS), and the American analyses in this volume are based on the 1972–2004 cumulative GSS file provided by the Roper Center archive. The 2004 International Social Survey also includes a module on citizenship, and the cross-national analyses are based on the 2004 ISSP file provided by the Zentralarchiv für empirische Sozialforschung. I thank the principal investigators and the archives for providing these data: all the interpretations and analyses are my responsibility.

24. I greatly appreciate the willingness of the Center for Democracy and Civil Society and Marc Howard, director of the project, to share these data. The CDACS/CID replicated a battery of citizenship questions also asked in the 2002 European Social Survey. In-person interviews were conducted with 1,001 American respondents between May 16 and July 19, 2005. The International Communications Research (ICR) conducted the interviews using a clustered, area-probability sample of households and random selection of respondents. For additional information see: http://www.georgetown.edu/centers/CDACS/cid.htm.

CHAPTER 2

1. See, for example, Derek Heater, *What Is Citizenship?* Cambridge, UK: Polity Press, 1999; Derek Heater, *Citizenship: The Civic Ideal in World History, Politics and Education,* 32. ed. Manchester: Manchester University Press, 2004.

2. I try to link my research to the rich philosophical literature on citizenship. Unfortunately, much of the recent literature is of uncertain value. The communitarian and critical theory literature in particular seems intent on creating an alternative reality and espousing ideologically based critiques of the current political situation. Moreover, few of these authors look for systematic evidence to support their statements.

3. Gabriel Almond and Sidney Verba, *The Civic Culture: Political Attitudes and Democracy in Five Nations.* Princeton: Princeton University Press, 1963.

4. Aristotle, *Politics,* translated by E. Barker. Oxford: Clarendon Press, 1946: 1283b, italics added.

5. Robert Dahl, *On Democracy.* New Haven: Yale University Press, 1998; Sidney Verba, Kay Schlozman, and Henry Brady, *Voice and Equality: Civic Voluntarism in American Politics.* Cambridge: Harvard University Press, 1995; Carole Pateman, *Participation and Democratic Theory.* Cambridge: Cambridge University Press, 1970; Dennis Thompson, *The Democratic Citizen: Social Science and Democratic Theory in the Twentieth Century.* Cambridge: Cambridge University Press, 1970.

Even with the near universal acceptance of the mass franchise, many analysts still prescribe a narrow role for the citizen. The elitist critique of democracy typically argues that too many citizens lack the knowledge or interests to make informed decisions, and thus limited participation is desirable; Almond and Verba, *The Civic Culture;* Samuel Huntington, *American Politics: The Promise of Disharmony.* Cambridge: Harvard University Press, 1981; Michael Delli Carpini and Scott Keeter, *What Americans Know about Politics and Why It Matters.* New Haven: Yale University Press, 1996; Henry Milner, *Civic Literacy: How Informed Citizens Make Democracy Work.* Hanover, NH: Tufts University Press, 2002.

6. Robert Putnam, *Bowling Alone: The Collapse and Renewal of American Community.* New York: Simon and Schuster, 2000; Stephen Macedo et al., *Democracy at Risk: How Political Choices Undermine Citizen Participation, and What We Can Do about It.* Washington, DC: Brookings Institution Press, 2005; National Conference on Citizenship, *America's Civic Health Index: Broken Engagement.* Washington: National Conference on Citizenship, 2006 (www.ncoc.net).

7. Ronald Inglehart, *Culture Shift in Advanced Industrial Society.* Princeton: Princeton University, 1990; Wayne Baker, *America's Crisis of Values: Reality and Perception.* Princeton: Princeton University Press, 2004; Terry Clark and Vincent Hoffmann-Martinot eds., *The New Political Culture.* Boulder, CO: Westview Press, 1998.

8. Cliff Zukin, Scott Keeter, Moly Andolina, Krista Jenkins, and Michael X. Delli Carpini, *A New Engagement? Political Participation, Civic Life, and the Changing American Citizen.* New York: Oxford University Press, 2006; Bruce Cain, Russell Dalton, and Susan Scarrow eds., *Democracy Transformed? Expanding Political Access in Advanced Industrial Democracies.* Oxford: Oxford University Press, 2003.

9. Immigration and Naturalization Service, *Citizenship Education and Naturalization Information.* Washington DC: U.S. Government Printing Office, 1987: 3.

10. Ibid., 12–13. To point out a small irony, the Prussian government of the nineteenth century also stressed three norms for a "good citizen": pay your taxes, serve in the army, and keep your mouth shut. This example suggests that citizenship norms in authoritarian and democratic governments share state sovereignty as a core principle.

11. T.H. Marshall, *Citizenship and Social Class,* ed. T. Bottomore. London: Pluto Press, 1992; originally published 1950.

12. Although this book emphasizes the modern roots of social citizenship, these concepts were part of the discussion of citizenship beginning with Aristotle. See Heater, *Citizenship,* 270–284.

13. Judith Shklar, *American Citizenship.* Cambridge: Harvard University Press, 1991; D. Harris, *Justifying State Welfare.* Oxford: Blackwell, 1987; Michael Walzer, *Spheres of Justice: A Defense of Pluralism and Equality.* Oxford: Blackwell, 1983.

14. David Held, *Democracy and the Global Order: From the Modern State to Cosmopolitan Governance.* Cambridge, UK: Polity Press, 1995; Michael Walzer ed., *Toward a Global Civil Society.* Providence: Berghahn Books, 1995.

15. For example, see Putnam, *Bowling Alone;* Macedo et al., *Democracy at Risk;* Martin Wattenberg, *Where Have All the Voters Gone?* Cambridge: Harvard University Press, 2002; Tom Tyler, *Why People Obey the Law.* New Haven: Yale University Press, 1990; Amitai Etzioni. *The Spirit of Community: Rights, Responsibilities and the Communitarian Agenda.* London: Fontana Press, 1995.

16. The 1984 General Social Survey and the 1987 Swedish Citizenship Survey included some questions on citizenship norms. The 1998 Swedish Democracy Audit was the first systematic assessment of these norms. For additional information see Linda Bennett and Stephen Bennett, *Living with Leviathan: Americans Coming to Terms with Big Government.* Lawrence, KS: University Press of Kansas, 1990; Olof Petersson, Anders Westholm, and Göran Blomberg, *Medborgarnas makt* (Citizen Power). Stockholm: Carlssons, 1989: ch. 8; Olof Petersson, J. Hermansson, Michelle Micheletti, J. Teorell, and Anders Westholm, *Demokrati och Medborgarskap. Demokratiradets Rapport 1998.* Stockholm: SNS Förlag, 1998.

The "Citizens, Involvement and Democracy" (CID) project replicated several of these items in a set of European nations in the late 1990s; and the European Social Survey (ESS) asked a subset of these items for twenty-two European nations in 2002. See Sigrid Rossteutscher, "Die Rückkehr der Tugend?" In Jan van Deth, ed., *Deutschland in Europa.* Wiesbaden: VS-Verlag, 2005; B. Denters, Oscar Gabriel, and Mariano Torcal, "Norms of good citizenship." In Jan van Deth, J. Ramón Montero, and Anders Westholm, eds., *Citizenship and Involvement in Europe.* London: Routledge, 2006.

17. The GSS asked this citizenship battery in the United States, and the same items were asked in the International Social Survey Program survey (see Chapter 8). The U.S. survey has a sample size of 1,472 who were interviewed as part of the ISSP module. This limits the number of cases available for analysis. In addition, the GSS also used split samples for other questions, and thus some of the items from the 2004 GSS were not asked of the sub sample that also included the citizenship battery.

18. Almond and Verba, *The Civic Culture*, 13.

19. The CDACS asks a similar question to define the norms of good citizenship, and respondents reply on an 11 point importance scale. For additional information on the survey see: www.georgetown.edu/centers/CDACS/cid.htm.

20. Petersson, et al., *Demokrati och Medborgarskap.*

21. Denters, Gabriel, and Torcal, "Norms of good citizenship."

22. Marshall, *Citizenship and Social Class.*

23. These dimensions were empirically determined using factor analysis. Factor analysis is an iterative statistical method, balancing theory and empirical patterns. I explored several options before deciding on the results in Table 2.2. An unrotated analysis has all items loading positively on the first dimension, which normally occurs when a battery of items are rated on a single scale such as importance; the second dimension separates the duty versus social activism items. I use a varimax rotated factor analysis to distinguished between different aspects of citizenship. I first explored four dimensions to match the categories in Table 2.1, but this did not recover the four clusters and instead produced a fourth dimension with a single variable (military service). An arbitrary cutting point based on eigenvalues would yield three dimensions, and the third dimension barely passed the normal threshhold of 1.0 (3.01, 1.32, 1.16). The second and third dimensions also had several overlapping variables. Therefore, I decided on a two dimensional solution of the GSS items. The CDACS has one fewer items and only two dimensions have eigenvalues greater than 1.0.

    I also conducted an oblique rotation. This produced the same basic clustering of variables. However, the pattern was a bit more distinct. The two dimensions in an oblique rotation are correlated at .30.

24. In overall terms, the analyses suggest that the GSS battery produces a more "balanced" measure of both dimensions because it has a more even set of items across the four categories. The CDACS, for instance, had only one autonomy and one solidarity question, but four social order questions. But both surveys yield high comparable dimensions and empirical results, as I will demonstrate in the analyses.

25. See Chapter 4.

26. Immigration and Naturalization Service, *Citizenship Education and Naturalization Information*, 11.

27. Bennett and Stephen Bennett, *Living with Leviathan*, ch. 5; Neil Nevitte, *The Decline of Deference.* Petersborough, Canada: Broadview Press; Ronald Inglehart, "Postmodernization, authority and democracy," in Pippa Norris, ed., *Critical Citizens.* Oxford: Oxford University Press, 1999.

28. Wattenberg, *Where Have All the Voters Gone?*; Martin Wattenberg, *Is Voting for the Young?* New York: Longman, 2006.

29. Benjamin Barber, *Strong Democracy. Participatory Politics for a New Age.* Berkeley: University of California Press, 1984.

30. Inglehart, *Culture Shift in Advanced Industrial Society*; Inglehart and Welzel. *Modernization, Cultural Change and Democracy.*

31. Nevitte, *The Decline of Deference.*

32. Almond and Verba, *The Civic Culture*, 24–26.

33. Charles Merriam and Robert Merriam, *American Government.* Boston: Ginn, 1954, 805.

CHAPTER 3

1. A photo from this meeting is included in Sen. Lugar's December 2005 newsletter to constituents posted at http://lugar.senate.gov/newsletter/2005/december.html.

2. Tom Brokaw, *The Greatest Generation.* New York: Random House, 1998; Robert Putnam, *Bowling Alone: The Collapse and Renewal of American Community.* New York: Simon and Schuster, 2000.

3. Brokaw, *The Greatest Generation*, xix–xx.

4. Linda Bennett and Stephen Bennett, *Living with Leviathan: Americans Coming to Terms with Big Government.* Lawrence, KS: University Press of Kansas, 1990, 126–130; Sigrid Rossteutscher, "Die Rückkehr der Tugend?" In Jan van Deth, ed., *Deutschland in Europa.* Wiesbaden: VS—Verlag, 2005.

5. Jonathan Cohn, "A lost political generation?" *New Prospect* (1992) 9:
6. For instance, the director of the Center on Adolescence at Stanford University writes about the moral decline of the young: "In the aggregate, young people's behavior has grown increasingly uncivil year by year according to practically every indicator that we can muster: physical assault, verbal aggression, cheating, lying, stealing, sexual harassment, vandalism, drunkenness, discourtesy, and so on, down to a panoply of major and minor assaults on the social fabric"; William Damon, "To not fade away: Restoring civil identity among the young." In Diane Ravitch and Joseph Viteritti, eds. *Making Good Citizens: Education and Civil Society.* New Haven: Yale University Press, 2001, 140. Damon is equally critical about the political engagement of the young: William Damon, *The Moral Child.* New York: Free Press, 1990.
7. National Conference on Citizenship, *America's Civic Health Index: Broken Engagement.* Washington, DC, 2006: 8.
8. See Ronald Inglehart, *Culture Shift in Advanced Industrial Society.* Princeton: Princeton University Press, 1990; Ronald Inglehart and Christian Welzel, *Modernization, Cultural Change and Democracy: The Human Development Sequence.* New York: Cambridge University Press, 2005.
9. Wayne Baker, *America's Crisis of Values: Reality and Perception.* Princeton: Princeton University Press, 2004.
10. Citizenship norms are measured by factor scores computed from the analyses in Table 2.2. Because of the construction method, a value of zero equals the position of the average American. The construction method also produces two dimensions that are statistically unrelated to each other.

    Generation was coded in two steps. I first defined five historical periods: until 1945, 1946–1960, 1961–1975, 1976–1990, and 1991 and later. Then I assigned respondents to a generation based on the period in which they turned 18 years of age and thus became more attuned to the norms of citizenship.

    It is also possible that the relationships in Figure 3.1 may reflect differences in the life-cycle position of individuals, with attention to duty increasing as people age and assume more family and career responsibilities. With a single time point we cannot disentangle generational and life cycle effects, but other evidence points to a strong generational component (Inglehart, *Culture Shift*).
11. If one separates the elements of duty-based citizenship, the strongest age differences appear for two items: importance of serving in the military (r=.24) and importance to always vote in elections (r=.15). The age correlations with other duty items are below .10. The CDACS survey yields similar findings. The correlation of age with citizen duty is .20, and with engaged citizenship it is –.05.
12. Gabriel Almond and Sidney Verba, *The Civic Culture.* Princeton: Princeton University Press, 1963, 163.
13. Philip Converse, "Change in the American electorate." In Angus Campbell and Philip Converse, eds. *The Human Meaning of Social Change.* New York: Russell Sage Foundation, 1972; Henry Milner, *Civic Literacy: How Informed Citizens Make Democracy Work.* Hanover, NH: Tufts University Press, 2002; Almond and Verba, *The Civic Culture,* ch. 6.
14. Norman Nie, Jane Junn, and Kenneth Stehlik-Barry. *Education and Democratic Citizenship in America.* Chicago: University of Chicago Press, 1996, ch. 2.
15. Almond and Verba, *The Civic Culture,* chs. 6 and 9.
16. Nie, Junn, and Stehlik-Barry, *Education and Democratic Citizenship in America,* ch. 4.
17. Bennett and Bennett, *Living with Leviathan,* 119.
18. The CDACS survey finds a weak negative correlation between education and citizen duty (–.05), and a positive correlation with engaged citizenship (+.13).
19. The respondent's income is negatively related to concern for those worse off in America (–.07) and those worse off in the world (–.14).
20. Putnam, *Bowling Alone.*
21. Pippa Norris and Ronald Inglehart, *A Rising Tide.* New York: Cambridge University Press, 2004. However, Almond and Verba found that men and women in 1959 were relatively similar in the norms of political activism (*Civic Culture,* 177).
22. For instance, other research shows that in the 1950s and early 1960s, women gave more support to the Republican Party, but by the 1900s women disproportionately support the Democratic Party: D. Studlar, Ian McAllister, and B. Hayes, "Explaining the gender gap in voting: A cross-national analysis." *Social Science Quarterly* (1998) 79:779–798.
23. Norris and Inglehart, *A Rising Tide.*

24. The correlation with citizen duty is r=−.01, and the correlation with citizen engagement is +.11. In comparison, homemakers score slightly above average on the duty-based dimension (+.05), while working women score below the average. This implies that shifts in the employment status of women (Figure 1.4) may have also changed citizenship norms. Another indication of changing gender patterns comes from generational comparisons. Women score significantly higher than men in citizen duty among older cohorts, but this relationship moderates and reverses in younger generations.

25. B. Denters, Oscar Gabriel, and Mariano Torcal, "Norms of good citizenship." In Jan van Deth, J. Ramón Montero, and Anders Westholm, eds., *Citizenship and Involvement in Europe*. London: Routledge, 2006.

26. For these three religious denominations, the eta correlation is statistically insignificant for citizen duty (.02) and engaged citizenship (.04).

27. The question asked: "Would you consider yourself a very strong (denomination) or a not very strong (denomination)?" The responses were 1) very strong, 2) not very strong, 3) somewhat strong, and 4) no religion. Broadly comparable results to Figure 3.4 occur if one uses frequency of church attendance to measure religiosity (correlation with citizen duty is .14).

28. This is broadly similar to the patterns that Denters, Gabriel, and Torcal identified among European publics: Denters, Gabriel, and Torcal, "Norms of good citizenship."

29. For instance, Laver and Budge included measures of social order, morality, and social welfare in defining the Left/Right orientation of political parties in Western democracies. Michael Laver and Ian Budge, *Party Policy and Government Coalitions*. New York: St. Martin's Press, 1992.

30. Charles Merriam, *American Political Ideas, 1865–1917*. New York: MacMillan, 1923: 28.

31. For example, see Stephen Macedo et al., *Democracy at Risk: How Political Choices Undermine Citizen Participation, and What We Can Do about It*. Washington, DC: Brookings Institution Press, 2005; William Bennett and Samuel Nunn, *A Nation of Spectators*. Washington, D.C.: National Commission on Civic Renewal, 1998.

32. These analyses are based on a multivariate regression analyses (OLS). All the predictors are included in a statistical model that estimates the indedependent influence of each predictor as a beta coefficient (ß). A positive ß indicates the predictor increases the citizenship norm, and a negative ß indicates a decrease in the norm. Coefficients significant at the .05 level are noted by an asterisk in Figure 3.7

33. Inglehart, *Culture Shift in Advanced Industrial Society; Inglehart and Welzel. Modernization, Cultural Change and Democracy; Baker, America's Crisis of Values.*

CHAPTER 4

1. Alexis de Tocqueville, *Democracy in America*. New York: Knopf, 1966: 249.

2. Sidney Verba and Norman Nie, *Participation in America*. New York: Harper and Row, 1972: 3.

3. Gabriel Almond and Sidney Verba, *The Civic Culture*. Princeton: Princeton University Press, 1963. Also see Samuel Barnes, Max Kaase et al., *Political Action*. Beverly Hills, CA: Sage, 1979; M. Kent Jennings and Jan van Deth, eds., *Continuities in Political Action*. Berlin: deGruyter, 1989.

4. Robert Putnam, *Bowling Alone: The Collapse and Renewal of American Community*. New York: Simon and Schuster, 2000: ch. 2; Martin Wattenberg, *Where Have All the Voters Gone?* Cambridge: Harvard University Press, 2002; Martin Wattenberg, *Is Voting for the Young?* New York: Longman, 2006; Andre Blais, *To Vote or Not to Vote? The Merits and Limits of Rational Choice Theory*. Pittsburgh: University of Pittsburgh Press, 2000; Thomas Patterson, *The Vanishing Voter: Public Involvement in an Age of Uncertainty*. New York: Vintage, 2003; National Conference on Citizenship, *America's Civic Health Index: Broken Engagement*. Washington: National Conference on Citizenship, 2006 (www.ncoc.net).

5. William J. Bennett and Samuel Nunn, *A Nation of Spectators*. Washington, DC: National Commission on Civic Renewal, 1998.

6. Robert Putnam, *Bowling Alone*, 35.

7. William Damon, "To not fade away: Restoring civil identity among the young." In Diane Ravitch and Joseph Viteritti eds., *Making Good Citizens: Education and Civil Society*. New Haven: Yale University Press, 2001. Also see Wattenberg, *Is Voting for the Young?*

8. Russell Dalton, *Citizen Politics: Public Opinion and Political Parties in Advanced Industrial Democracies*, 41. ed. Washington: CQ Press, 2006: ch. 2–4; Cliff Zukin, Scott Keeter, Moly Andolina, Krista Jenkins, and Michael X. Delli Carpini, *A New Engagement? Political Participation, Civic Life, and the Changing American Citizen*. New York: Oxford University Press, 2006; Pippa Norris, *Democratic Phoenix: Rein-*

venting Political Activism. Cambridge: Cambridge University Press, 2002, ch. 10; Robert Wuthnow, "United States: Bridging the privileged and marginalized?" In Robert Putnam, ed., *Democracies in Flux: The Evolution of Social Capital in Contemporary America.* Oxford: Oxford University Press, 2002.

9. Ronald Inglehart, *Modernization and Post-Modernization.* Princeton: Princeton University Press, 1997: 307.

10. There is a slight decrease in informal activity over time, although this might be due to the ambiguity of coding responses to such an open-ended question. Some of the examples of individual contacting in 1981 may also fit as examples of collective action involving an informal group.

11. Jeffrey Birnbaum, "On Capitol Hill, the inboxes are overflowing." *Washington Post* (July 11, 2005), D1.

12. Putnam, *Bowling Alone,* and Macedo et al., *Democracy at Risk,* present trends in participation in a wide variety of activities, but many of these trends are from commercial marketing polls of uncertain quality (see endnote 24).

13. For example, surveys often change the time reference of the question; asking whether individuals have done an activity over the past year, two years, or longer. The 1967 Verba-Nie survey, for example, did not have a clear time reference; their 1989 survey asked about activity over the previous twelve months. Other questionnaires vary the focus of activity or combine different activities in a single question. Neither the 1987 or 1989 surveys have been systematically replicated; the 2004 CSES is the closest approximation to the wording and time frame.

14. Verba, Schlozman and Brady, *Voice and Equality,* 72.

15. The Social Capital Benchmark Survey 2000 was conducted by the Saguaro Seminar at John F. Kennedy School of Government, Harvard University. These data were acquired from the Roper Center at the University of Connecticut. The Comparative Study of Electoral Systems is a consortium of election study surveys that include a common questionnaire in their post-election surveys. These data were downloaded from the CSES Web site (www.cses.org).

16. There is an anomaly with the 1967 data. The data distribution (which has only three categories) does not match the codebook (which has four response categories). In addition, it appears that some 200+ cases that are very low in political interest were mistakenly coded as missing data. After discussion with the principal investigator and analyst of these data, I recoded these missing data cases to the "no interest" category and recoded the other categories to regain the distribution of four categories. This is my best assumption on the actual distribution of responses in the 1967 survey. This reconstructed distribution is used in the table, although the results cannot be verified against the original survey findings.

17. Similarly, the American National Election Study finds a slight increase in general political interest since the early 1960s. See Dalton, *Citizen Politics,* 25. The percentage that follows "what's going on in government and public affairs" trends slightly upward over time. In contrast, a different question about interest in the specific election campaign trends downward since 1952. This reinforces my assertion that fewer Americans are engaged in elections, but general interest is increasing.

18. Gallup asked the question between 1952 and 1984; the Pew Center repeated the question in Sept./ October 1996 and October 2000. The question asks about general political interest, not tied to the campaign: "Generally speaking, how much interest would you say you have about politics—a great deal, a fair amount, only a little, or no interest at all?" There are eleven monthly time points between 1952 and 2000. Interest fluctuates within a fairly narrow band, and it tends to increase around elections. Political interest generally increases over time (r=.26). The source of these data is the IPOLL database at the Roper Center.

19. Wattenberg, *Where Have All the Voters Gone?;* Blais, *To Vote or Not to Vote?*

20. Michael McDonald and Samuel Popkin, "The myth of the vanishing voter." *American Political Science Review* (2001) 95(4): 963–974. Turnout increased by 6 percent in the 2004 nations elections (VAP; 4 percent for VEP), but the overall downward trend since the 1960s is still apparent.

21. Rosenstone and Hansen, *Mobilization, Participation and Democracy in America;* Putnam, *Bowling Alone,* ch. 2.

22. Evidence from a larger set of nations suggests that campaign activity is decreasing in most advanced industrial democracies; Russell Dalton and Martin Wattenberg, eds., Parties without Partisans. Oxford: Oxford University Press, 2000: ch. 3.

23. Changes in campaign finance laws have altered the way that people give money to campaigns. Table 4.3 presents only those who have given money to a party in the campaign. However, other funds go

directly to candidates or to political action groups. In 2004, for instance, 15 percent of the public gave to at least one of these sources, so the percentage in the table is a conservative estimate.

24. There are major methodological differences between these survey series. The Verba et al. surveys were conducted by the National Opinion Research Center at the University of Chicago, and the American National Election Study was conducted by the Institute for Social Research at the University of Michigan. Both of these academic surveys utilize random area-probability sampling selection, in-person interviews, and make extensive efforts to generate high response rates and representative samples.

    The Roper surveys used a mix of area probability sampling and quota or random-walk selection of respondents at the last stage; so these are not fully random samples; the sampling methods also changed during the time series collection. In addition, the short fieldwork time span and commercial orientation of the Roper Poll would imply less accuracy of these data. The DDB surveys used by Putnam and the National Conference on Citizenship are mail surveys. The initial lists of names are not generated on a systematic random sampling basis, interviews are sent and returned by mail, and the response rates are substantially below the GSS and ANES.

25. Verba and Nie, *Participation in America*, ch. 3.

26. In addition, the 2000–04 American National Election Studies asked whether the respondent had contacted a public official in the past year; approximately a quarter of the public responded positively.

27. Similarly, the World Values Survey finds that the number of Americans who belong to civic associations, environmental groups, women's groups, or peace groups increased from 6 percent in 1980, to 18 percent in 1990, to 33 percent in 1999; Dalton, Citizen Politics, ch. 3.

28. Stolle, Hooghe, and Micheletti. "Politics in the supermarket." *International Political Science Review* 26: 245–70; Russell Dalton, "Citizenship Norms and Political Participation in America," occasional research paper of the Center for Democracy and Civil Society, Georgetown University. (http://www8. georgetown.edu/centers/cdacs/cid/DaltonOccasionalPaper.pdf).

29. Barnes, Kaase et al., *Political Action;* Inglehart, *Culture Shift in Advanced Industrial Society.*

30. Bruce Bimber and Richard Davis, *The Internet and US Elections.* New York: Oxford University Press, 2003; Bruce Bimber, *Information and American Democracy: Technology in the Evolution of Political Power.* New York: Cambridge University Press, 2003;

31. Birnbaum, "On Capitol Hill."

32. The top ten groups reflect a mix of youthful ambitions and aspirations: 1) Reduce the drinking age to 18, 2) legalize same-sex marriages, 3) Americans for alternative energy, 4) support a woman's right to choose, 5) support stem cell research, 6) abolish abstinence-only sex education, 7) government + religion = disaster, 8) AIDS/HIV research, 9) pro-life, and 10) equal rights for gays (downloaded November 1, 2006).

33. Norman Nie, Jane Junn, and Kenneth Stehlik-Barry, *Education and Democratic Citizenship in America.* Chicago: Chicago University Press, 1996. They argue that education primarily marks the political stratification of the public, and thus the rise in education does not translate directly into an increase in participation. However, their analyses also show that education is related to democratic norms—much as we find in Chapter 2. This combination of education's resources component and norm component are what shifts the patterns of action.

34. Wattenberg, *Where Have All the Voters Gone?;* Wattenberg, *Is Voting for the Young?;* Mark Franklin, *Voter Turnout and the Dynamics of Electoral Competition in Established Democracies Since 1945.* New York: Cambridge University Press, 2004.

35. Verba and Nie, *Participation in America.*

36. William Damon, "To not fade away: Restoring civil identity among the young." In Diane Ravitch and Joseph Viteritti, eds., *Making Good Citizens: Education and Civil Society.* New Haven: Yale University Press, 2001: 123. In less polemic terms, the same sentiments have been expressed by Putnam in *Bowling Alone* and Macedo and his colleagues in *Democracy at Risk.*

37. Dalton, *Citizen Politics,* ch. 2–4; Robert Wuthnow, "United States: Bridging the privileged and marginalized?" In Robert Putnam, ed., *Democracies in Flux: The Evolution of Social Capital in Contemporary America.* Oxford: Oxford University Press, 2002; Zukin et al., *A New Engagement?*

38. Data from the GSS show that age is positively related to voting (r=.29) and belonging to a political party (r=.16), but the young are more active in boycotting products (r=–.09), attending demonstrations (–.12), and participating in Internet forums (r=–.11).

39. Zukin et al., *A New Engagement?,* 189.

40. The GSS participation items span a wide range of participation options, including new forms of action, and all the questions were asked in a common format of activity in the previous twelve months.

The survey found: 35 percent had signed a petition, 32 percent had donated money to a social or political cause, 25 percent had boycotted some product, 22 percent had contacted a government official, 13 percent had attended a rally or political meeting, and 6 percent had participated in a march or demonstration.

41. For the youngest age cohort, many are still in school or will complete additional years of schooling. Therefore, I estimated the eventual size of better/lesser educated within this cohort, rather than their present size in the survey.

42. Even the castigation of youth for their declining turnout is overstated. The turnout trend among the voting eligible electorate under age 30 has varied within a narrow band since 1976 (discounting the first youth enfranchisement election of 1972). Thomas Patterson, "Young voters and the 2004 election," 6. (www.ksg.harvard.edu/presspol/vanishvoter/).

43. In contrast, Putnam argues that protestors are an aging subset of the population and protest is becoming less common among the young; *Bowling Alone,* 165. This may be an artifact of the question he analyzes, which asks whether the respondent has *ever* protested. Someone who is under 30 has had fewer opportunities than those in their 40s and 50s. The GSS question is more direct and comparable, asking about protest over the previous twelve months.

44. See Elizabeth Theiss-Morse, "Conceptualizations of good citizenship and political participation." *Political Behavior* (1993) 15: 355–380; B. Denters, Oscar Gabriel, Mariano Torcal, "Norms of good citizenship." In Jan van Deth, Jose Ramón Montero, and Anders Westholm, eds., *Citizenship and Involvement in Europe.* London: Routledge, 2006.

45. Raymond Wolfinger and Stephen Rosenstone, *Who Votes?* New Haven: Yale University Press, 7–8.

46. Blaise, *To Vote or Not to Vote,* 92.

47. The GSS included a battery of ten words and asked respondents to identify the meaning of each. The cognitive skills measure in Table 4.4 is a count of the number of words that were correctly identified; also see Nie, Junn and Stehlik-Barry, *Education and Democratic Citizenship in America.*

48. Table 4.5 presents the correlation between citizen norms and participation for all the items in both the GSS and CDACS survey.

49. John Hibbing and Elizabeth Theiss-Morse, *Stealth Democracy: Americans' Beliefs about How Government Should Work.* New York: Cambridge University Press, 1.

50. Putnam, *Bowling Alone;* Macedo et al. *Democracy at Risk.*

51. Sharon Jayson, "Gen-next." *USA Today* (October 24, 2006); Janet Kornblum, "Ideas incubate on the Internet." *USA Today* (October 24, 2006).

52. A variety of groups worked explicitly to increase youth turnout in 2004. The New Voters Project (www.newvotersproject.org) is an alliance of state Public Interest Research Groups (PIRGs) that focused on increasing youth turnout; the Youth Vote Coalition was a coalition of more than 100 national organizations that encouraged youth voting; the Center for Information and Research on Civic Learning and Engagement (CIRCLE) at the University of Maryland has pursued a research program focusing on youth voting; MTV ran its "Choose or Lose" campaign on the air; and P. Diddy's "Vote or Die" rhetoric attempted to raise political awareness and add to electoral mobilization in 2004.

53. The 2004 GSS included questions on beliefs that parties encourage activism and support for referendums. Engaged citizens are slightly disapproving of the former and approving of the latter. However, I suspect that a forced choice between these two alternatives would produce an even clearer illustration of preferences, since people could not simply favor both, as do two-thirds of the respondents. Also see Chapter 7 below.

54. Verba and Nie, *Participation in America,* 52.

55. Bruce Cain, Russell Dalton, and Susan Scarrow, eds., *Democracy Transformed? Expanding Political Access in Advanced Industrial Democracies.* Oxford: Oxford University Press, 2003.

CHAPTER 5

1. Richard M. Fried, *Nightmare in Red: The McCarthy Era in Perspective.* New York: Oxford University Press, 1991.

2. David K. Johnson, *The Lavender Scare: The Coldwar Persecution of Gays and Lesbians in the Federal Government.* Chicago: University of Illinois Press, 2004.

3. James Gibson, "Political intolerance and political repression during the McCarthy Red Scare." *American Political Science Review* (June 1988) 82: 511–529.

4. The Motion Picture Producers and Distributors of America (MPPDA) required that all films pro-
    duced and distributed by its members have the seal of approval of its Production Code Admini-
    stration (PCA). The PCA had detailed guidelines to protect moral standards and reinforce "correct"
    standards of life. If you look at old movies from the era, many still display their PCA number.
5. Jerome Karabel, *The Chosen: The Hidden History of Admission and Exclusion at Harvard, Yale, and
    Princeton.* New York: Houghton Mifflin, 2005.
6. Jim Gibson, Enigmas of intolerance: Fifty years after Stouffer's *Communism, Conformity, and Civil
    Liberties, Perspectives on Politics,* (2005) 4: 21–34; Samuel Stouffer, *Communism, Conformity and Civil
    Liberties.* New York: Doubleday, 1955.
7. Clyde Nunn, Harry Crockett, and J. Williams, *Tolerance for Non-Conformity.* San Francisco: Jossey-
    Bass, 1978: 7.
8. Norman Nie, Jane Junn, and Kenneth Stehlik-Barry, *Education and Democratic Citizenship in Amer-
    ica.* Chicago: University of Chicago Press, 1996: 64.
9. Herbert McClosky and Alida Brill, *Dimensions of Tolerance: What Americans Believe about Civil Liber-
    ties.* New York: Russell Sage Foundation, 1983; and Nie, Junn, and Stehlik-Barry, *Education and Demo-
    cratic Citizenship in America.* Others have questioned the evidence of increasing tolerance, and I dis-
    cuss this critique below. See John Sullivan, James Piereson, and George Marcus, *Political Tolerance and
    American Democracy.* Chicago: University of Chicago Press, 1982; Jeffrey Mondak and Mitchell
    Sanders, Tolerance and intolerance, 1976–98. *American Journal of Political Science* (2003) 47: 492–502;
    James Gibson, Political tolerance. In Russell Dalton and Hans-Dieter Klingemann, eds., *Handbook of
    Political Behavior.* Oxford: Oxford University Press, 2007.
10. Stouffer, *Communism, Conformity and Civil Liberties.*
11. James Davis, "Communism, conformity, cohorts and categories: American tolerance in 1954 and
    1972–73." *American Journal of Sociology* (1975) 81: 491–513.
12. Nunn, Crockett, and Williams, *Tolerance for Non-Conformity.*
13. Nunn, Crockett, and Williams, *Tolerance for Non-Conformity,* 51.
14. Sullivan, Piereson, and Marcus, *Political Tolerance and American Democracy.*
15. Paul Sniderman et al., "Principled tolerance and the American mass public." *British Journal of Politi-
    cal Science* (1989) 19: 25–45.
16. James Gibson, "Alternative measures of political tolerance. Must tolerance be 'least-liked'?" *American
    Journal of Political Science* (1992) 36: 560–577.
17. To underscore this chapter's theme the rising political tolerance of Americans, the 2004 General
    Social Survey asked whether religious extremists should be allowed to hold a public meeting: 74 per-
    cent said they should be allowed. Even though the specific reference of this question is not clear, this
    extent of tolerance in the wake of September 11 is noteworthy.
18. I separated the samples into self-identified liberals, centrists, and conservatives. Using tolerance of
    speech as an example, there are comparable negative trends over time among all three ideological
    groups (pearson *r* correlation of tolerance of speech and year of study):

	Communist	Atheist	Homosexual	Militarist	Racist
Liberal	−.08	−.08	−.16	−.09	−.01
Center	−.09	−.11	−.17	−.10	−.01
Conservative	−.11	−.11	−.16	−.10	−.02

19. Russell Dalton, *Citizen Politics: Public Opinion and Political Parties in Advanced Industrial Democ-
    racies,* 4th ed. Washington: CQ Press, 2006, ch. 6.
20. Robert Putnam, *Bowling Alone: The Collapse and Renewal of American Community.* New York: Simon
    and Schuster, 2000, 352.
21. Another example of moderation in public opinion is Fiorina's analyses of ideological polarization in
    America: Morris Fiorina, *Culture Wars.* New York: Longman, 2004. Despite widespread media rhet-
    oric about the deep divisions within the American public, Fiorina describes a generally moderate
    and centrist public opinion even on issues that appear most divisive.
22. Lawrence Bobo and Frederick Licari, "Education and political tolerance: Testing the effects of cog-
    nitive sophistication and target group affect." *Public Opinion Quarterly* (1989) 53: 285–308.

23. Nie, Junn, and Stehlik-Barry, *Education and Democratic Citizenship in America,* ch. 7; also Paul Sniderman, Richard Brody, and Philip Tetlock, *Reasoning and Choice.* New York: Cambridge University Press, 1991; Nunn, Crockett, and Williams, *Tolerance for Non-Conformity,* ch. 4.
24. Nunn, Crockett, and Williams, *Tolerance for Non-Conformity,* ch. 5; McClosky and Brill, *Dimensions of Tolerance,* 387–403; Bobo and Licari, "Education and political tolerance."
25. Nunn, Crockett, and Williams, *Tolerance for Non-Conformity,* ch. 5.
26. Putnam, *Bowling Alone,* 357; also James Davis, "Changeable weather in a cooling climate atop the liberal plateau." *Public Opinion Quarterly* (1992) 56: 261–306.
27. Because education is increasing at a slower rate among recent cohorts, this may moderate age group differences in tolerance. However, the cumulative 1976–2004 GSS data do not show a statistically significant decline in tolerance among younger cohorts. Indeed, the cohort born 1940–45 has an average tolerance score about a full point lower than the cohort born in 1980–85. In contrast, those who think of citizenship primarily in terms of citizen duty are less likely to be political tolerant. Regardless of the values of a challenging group, citizenship duty displays a negative effect (even though two coefficients are not statistically significant).
28. Tocqueville discusses the potential tyranny of an omnipotent majority that leaves little space for dissident views. He cites examples of political opposition to the war of 1812 or racial prejudice in America as examples, and concludes: "what I find most repulsive in America is not the extreme freedom reigning there, but the shortage of guarantees against tyranny [of the majority] (*Democracy in America,* vol. I, ch. 7). Similarly, McClosky and Brill are equally critical of the historical absence of tolerance in American political practices, quoting Levy: "The persistent image of colonial America as a society that cherished freedom of expression is a sentimental hallucination that ignores history. . . . The American people and their representatives simply did not understand that freedom of thought and expression for the other fellows, particularly the fellow with the hated ideas." Leonard Levy, ed., *Legacy of Suppression: Freedom of Speech and Press in Early American History.* Cambridge: Harvard University Press, 1960: 9.
29. Herbert McClosky and John Schaar, "Psychological dimensions of anomie." *American Sociological Review* (1965) 30: 14–40.
30. McClosky and Brill, *Dimensions of Tolerance,* ch. 8.
31. Ewa Golebiowska, "Individual value priorities, education, and political tolerance." *Political Behavior* (1995) 17: 23–48; also see Mark Peffley and Robert Rohrschneider, "Democratization and political tolerance in seventeen countries: A multi-level model of democratic learning." *Political Research Quarterly* (2003) 56: 243–257.
32. The previous analyses were based on the 15-item tolerance battery in the General Social Surveys, but the citizenship module only included three questions on tolerance toward religious extremists, those who wish to overthrow the government, and racists. These three items attempt to balance the political orientations of groups so that tolerance is not an artifact of ideological position.
33. The survey included five items; the pearson r correlations between citizen-activism and citizen-duty follow:

	Engaged Citizenship	Citizen Duty
Immigrants improve society	.21	−.04
Government does not spend too much on immigrants	.26	−.09
Parents of children born in the U.S. should receive citizenship	.20	−.07
Children of U.S. parents born outside country should be citizens	.12	−.03
Legal immigrants should have same rights as native born	.14	−.08

34. The list included thirteen groups and an option to mention another disliked group that did not appear on the list. For this list see the CDACS Web site: www.georgetown.edu/centers/CDACS/cid. htm.

35. Richard C. Leone and Greg Anrig, eds., *The War on Our Freedoms: Civil Liberties in an Age of Terror.* New York: Twentieth Century Fund, 2003; Philip B. Heymann, *Terrorism, Freedom, and Security: Winning without War.* Cambridge: MIT Press, 2004; Darren W. Davis and Brian D. Silver, "Civil liberties vs. security: Public opinion in the context of the terrorist attacks on America." *American Journal of Political Science* 48 (2004): 28–46.

36. The items were developed by Jim Gibson, and I appreciate his willingness to share these data. This classification of items is based on a factor analysis that identified two dimensions in the responses to the civil liberties battery. The items are listed in Table 5.3 according to their loadings on the two respective factors.

37. Examples of this crisis of American politics literature include Samuel Huntington, *Who Are We? The Challenges to America's National Identity.* New York: Simon & Schuster, 2004; Stephen Macedo et al., *Democracy at Risk.* Washington, DC: Brookings Institution Press, 2005; John Hibbing and Elizabeth Theiss-Morse, *Stealth Democracy: Americans' Beliefs about How Government Should Work.* New York: Cambridge University Press, 2002. Also see discussion in Chapter 1.

38. Putnam, *Bowling Alone,* ch. 22.

CHAPTER 6

1. Derek Heater, *Citizenship: The Civic Ideal in World History, Politics and Education,* 3rd ed. Manchester: Manchester University Press, 2004: 274.

2. F. A. Hayak, *The Road to Serfdom.* Chicago: University of Chicago Press, 1944; F. A. Hayak, *The Constitution of Liberty.* Chicago: University of Chicago Press, 1960; Robert Nozick, *Anarchy, State and Utopia.* New York: Basic Books, 1977; Lawrence Mead, *Beyond Entitlement: Obligations of Citizenship.* New York: Free Press, 1986.

3. Ronald Reagan, Inaugural Address, 1981: 191.

4. T. H. Marshall, *Citizenship and Social Class,* ed. T. Bottomore. London: Pluto Press; 1992 originally published 1950.

5. Ole Borre and Elinor Scarbrough, eds., *The Scope of Government.* New York: Oxford University Press, 1995; Linda Bennett and Stephen Bennett, *Living with Leviathan: Americans Coming to Terms with Big Government.* Lawrence, KS: University Press of Kansas, 1990; Russell Dalton, *Citizen Politics: Public Opinion and Political Parties in Advanced Industrial Democracies,* 4th ed. Washington: CQ Press, 2006, ch. 6.

6. This would be a complex phenomenon to study. Duty-based citizenship includes the responsibility to pay taxes, but I suspect these same individuals would express great negativity about the high levels of taxation and how government spends their money. In contrast, engaged citizens may not feel such a duty to pay taxes, but then be more positive toward government programs that spend these taxes. How these two factors balance out is an ideal topic for further study when empirical evidence becomes available.

7. The question wording reads: "We are faced with many problems in this country, none of which can be solved easily or inexpensively. I'm going to name some of these problems, and for each one I'd like you to tell me whether you *think* we're spending too much money on it, too little money, or about the right amount. First (READ ITEM A) . . . are we spending too much, too little, or about the right amount on (ITEM)?"

8. Bennett and Bennett, *Living with Leviathan.*

9. Ibid., 137.

10. The wording of the spending choices can strongly impact the responses. The term "welfare," for instance, produces less support for social spending than a question about "helping the poor." Therefore, I focus on the broad trends in Table 6.1 rather than specific support for any single policy option.

11. Benjamin Page and Robert Shapiro, *The Rational Public: Fifty Years of Trends in Americans' Policy Preferences.* Chicago: University of Chicago Press, 1992.

12. Page and Shapiro, *The Rational Public;* also see Beate Huseby, "Attitudes toward the size of government." In Borre and Elinor Scarbrough, eds., *The Scope of Government.*

13. This classification of items is based on factor analyses that produced these two clusters of items. The social dimension has the highest loadings for dealing with drug addiction, education, programs to help blacks, health care, social security, and childcare. I constructed factor scores for both dimensions, and these are used in the regression analyses in Figure 6.4.

14. Ronald Inglehart, *Culture Shift in Advanced Industrial Societies.* Princeton: Princeton University Press, 1990; Ronald Inglehart, *Modernization and Postmodernization.* Princeton: Princeton University Press, 1997.

CHAPTER 7

1. Hans-Dieter Klingemann, "Mapping political support in the 1990s." In Pippa Norris, ed. *Critical Citizens.* Oxford: Oxford University Press, 1999; Pippa Norris, "Introduction." In Norris, ed., *Critical Citizens.*
2. Gabriel Almond and Sidney Verba. *The Civic Culture.* Boston: Little Brown, 1965, 313.
3. At the same time, American political thought and history often highlight the anti-government traditions in the United States. The nation was founded by those who opposed British government, and these sentiments are supposedly enshrined in the political culture. One approach stresses this anti-government element of American culture; Seymour Martin Lipset, *Continental Divide: The Values and Institutions of the United States and Canada.* New York: Routledge, 1990; Samuel Huntington, *American Politics: The Promise of Disharmony.* Cambridge: Harvard University Press, 1981; Anthony King, "Distrust of government: Explaining American exceptionalism." In Susan Pharr and Robert Putnam, eds., *Disaffected Democracies: What's Troubling the Trilateral Countries?* Princeton: Princeton University Press, 2000. King's essay, however, illustrates the contradictions of this claim by also citing Americans' patriotism and their admiration of government. When early empirical studies found high levels of political support in the United States, most political scientists argued that these patterns were an essential part of a democratic civic culture.
4. Seymour Martin Lipset and William Schneider, *The Confidence Gap.* New York: Free Press, 1983; E. J. Dionne, *Why Americans Hate Politics.* New York: Simon & Schuster, 1991; Stephen Craig, *The Malevolent Leaders: Popular Discontent in America.* Boulder, CO: Westview Press, 1993; John Hibbing and Elizabeth Theiss-Morse, *Congress as Public Enemy: Public Attitudes toward American Political Institutions.* New York: Cambridge University Press, 1995; Joseph Nye, Philip Zelikow, and David King, eds., *Why Americans Mistrust Government.* Cambridge: Harvard University Press, 1997.
5. For example, see the discussions in Russell Dalton, *Democratic Challenges, Democratic Choices.* Oxford: Oxford University Press, 2004, ch. 1; Stephen Macedo et al., *Democracy at Risk.* Washington, DC: Brookings Institution, 2005, ch. 1.
6. David Easton, *A Systems Analysis of Political Life.* New York: Wiley, 1965; David Easton, "A reassessment of the concept of political support." *British Journal of Political Science* (1975) 5:435–457.
7. Ridicule of government began even before the formation of the Republic. Mark Twain, for example, asked "Suppose you were an idiot. And suppose you were a member of Congress," and then he added, "But I repeat myself." Similarly, Will Rogers wrote that Americans feel the same way when Congress is in session as when the baby gets hold of a hammer: "It's just a question of how much damage he can do before we take it away from him." For a contemporary study of political humor see David Niven, S. Robert Lichter, and Daniel Amundson, "The political content of late night comedy," *The Harvard International Journal of Press/Politics,* (2003) 8: 118–133.
8. Pew Center for People and the Press. "Deconstructing distrust: How Americans view government (1998)"; Pew Center for People and the Press, "Americans Struggle with religion's role at home and abroad (2002)." (www.people-press.org).
9. Hibbing and Theiss-Morse, *Congress as Public Enemy;* Joseph Cooper, ed., *Congress and the Decline of Public Trust.* Boulder, CO: Westview, 1999; Jonathan Rauch, *Government's End: Why Washington Stopped Working.* New York: Public Affairs, 1999.
10. Thomas Patterson, *Out of Order.* New York: Knopf, 1993; Thomas Patterson, "Doing well and doing good: How soft news and critical journalism are shrinking the news audience and weakening democracy and what news outlets can do about it." Cambridge: Shorenstein Center, Harvard University, 2001.
11. John Hibbing and Elizabeth Theiss-Morse. *Stealth Democracy: Americans' Beliefs about How Government Should Work.* New York: Cambridge University Press, 2002.
12. Nye, *Why Americans Distrust Government,* ch. 12.
13. Dalton, *Democratic Challenges, Democratic Choices.*
14. Dalton, *Democratic Challenges, Democratic Choices:* ch. 5; Ronald Inglehart, "Postmodernization, authority and democracy." In Pippa Norris, ed., *Critical Citizens.*

15. I used factor analyses to determine the items that tap each dimension of political support. I relied on these analyses to group and interpret items in this chapter, as well as providing the basis for the multivariate analyses in the chapter appendix.

16. The question asks: "On the whole, on a scale of 0 to 10 where 0 is very poorly and 10 is very well, how well does democracy work in America today? And how about ten years ago? How well did democracy work in America then? And how about ten years from now? How well do you think democracy will work in America then?"

17. I added the three items together and divided by three. Thus, the resulting index runs from 0 to 10 (see the question in note 16).

18. Both duty-based and engaged citizenship is positively related to trust in politicians, political parties, and Congress. However, these relationships are generally stronger for duty-based citizenship than for engaged citizenship. The following table presents these correlations:

	Duty-based	Engaged
Trust politicians	.20	.18
Trust parties	.19	.16
Trust Congress	.23	.10
Trust Supreme Court	.16	.05
Trust legal system	.21	.07
Trust police	.34	.02

19. I should note that this chapter is not a paid advertisement for Starbucks. In fact, I routinely hold office hours at the Panera Bread near the UC Irvine campus and not the Starbucks.

20. Robert Dahl, *Polyarchy*. New Haven: Yale University Press, 1971; Robert Dahl, *On Democracy*. New Haven: Yale University Press, 1998; Almond and Verba, *The Civic Culture*.

21. Dahl, *On Democracy*, 37. In addition, these four categories clearly overlap with the ideas of citizenship discussed in Chapter 2. The degree of overlap is the point of the analyses here.

22. The question reads: "There are different opinions about people's rights in a democracy. On a scale of 1 to 7, where 1 is not at all important and 7 is very important, how important is it to. . . ."

23. The index is a factor score from factor analyses. The factor analysis finds that all six items are positively loaded on a first dimension: treat everyone equally (.75), politicians consider citizens (.73), protect minority rights (.70), adequate standard of living (.65), participate in decisions (.62), and civil disobedience (.18).

24. This clustering is based on a factor analysis of Q85 that yields two dimensions. The listing of items in the text reflects the size of their factor loadings. The second dimension deals with equality and participation, and this is not significantly related to either citizen duty (–.03) or engaged citizenship (–.04).

25. Such patterns also appear in analyses that compare democratic values and trust in government as a function of post-material values. Dalton, *Democratic Challenges, Democratic Choices*, ch. 5.

26. Dalton, *Citizen Politics*, ch. 12. Despite concerns about the erosion of patriotism, feelings of national pride have actually increased even prior to 9/11.

27. Samuel Huntington, *Who Are We? The Challenges to America's Identity*. New York: Simon & Schuster, 2004.

28. The chapter appendix shows that the impact of the two citizenship dimensions on images of government and other values is consistent even when controlling for other factors.

29. Marc Hetherington, *Why Trust Matters: Declining Political Trust and the Demise of American Liberalism*. Princeton: Princeton University Press, 2005.

30. See Klingemann, Mapping political support in the 1990s; Norris, "Introduction"; also Huntington, *American Politics*. Huntington viewed creedal passion as a negative feature of American political history, but in the conclusion I will argue that this is one of the positive driving forces of democratic growth.

31. Dalton, *Democratic Challenges, Democratic Choices*, ch. 3; Russell Dalton, "The social transformation of trust in government," *International Journal of Sociology* (March 2005) 15: 129–45.

CHAPTER 8

1. Alexis de Tocqueville, *Democracy in America*. New York: Knopf, 1960.
2. See the examples cited in Seymour Martin Lipset, *The First New Nation: The United States in Historical and Comparative Perspective*. New York: Basic Books, 1963; Seymour Martin Lipset, *American Exceptionalism: A Double-Edged Sword*. New York: W. Norton, 1997. Lipset includes Max Weber, Friedrich Engels, James Bryce, Gunnar Martial, Louis Hart, and other great social commentators in this list.
3. Seymour Martin Lipset, *Continental Divide*. New York: Routledge, 1990; Anthony King, "Distrust of government: Explaining American exceptionalism." In Susan Pharr and Robert Putnam, eds., *Disaffected Democracies*. Princeton: Princeton University Press, 2000.
4. These points are discussed extensively in Chapter 4 in this book.
5. Bas Denters, Oscar Gabriel, Mariano Torcal. "Norms of good citizenship." In Jan van Deth, J. Ramón Montero, and Anders Westholm, eds., *Citizenship and Involvement in Europe*. London: Routledge, 2006; Robert Putnam, *Democracies in Flux*. Oxford: Oxford University Press, 2002; Dietlind Stolle, "The sources of social capital." In Marc Hooghe and Dietlind Stolle, eds., *Generating Social Capital. Civil Society and Institutions in Comparative Perspective*. New York: Palgrave, 2003; Helmut Klages, "Engagementpotenzial in Deutschland." In Bundesministerium für Familie, Senioren, Frauen und Jugend, eds., *Freiwilliges Engagement in Deutschland*. Stuttgart: Kohlhammer.
6. Lipset, *American Exceptionalism*, 17; Rudyard Kipling perhaps stated it more eloquently when he said, "And what should they know of England, who only England know?" from "The English Flag," in *Barrack-Room Ballads and Other Verses* (London: Methuen, 1892), stanza 1.
7. The other chapters of this volume were written and reviewed by CQ Press while I waited for the release of the 2004 ISSP. So this chapter is really a test/comparison of cross-national patterns after the U.S. survey had been analyzed and described.
8. Robert Kagan, *Of Paradise and Power: America and Europe in the New World Order*. New York: Knopf, 2003.
9. Lipset, *American Exceptionalism;* Deborah Madsen, *American Exceptionalism*. Edinburgh: Edinburgh University Press, 1998; Charles Lockhart, *The Roots of American Exceptionalism: History, Institutions and Culture*. New York: Palgrave Macmillan.
10. Lipset, *American Exceptionalism*, ch. 1; Lipset, *Continental Divide*, ch. 2.
11. Ronald Inglehart et al. *Human Beliefs and Values*. Madrid: Siglo XXI Editores, 2004.
12. Gabriel Almond and Sidney Verba, *The Civic Culture*. Princeton: Princeton University Press, 1963; Sidney Verba, Norman Nie, and Jae-on Kim, *Participation and Political Equality*. New York: Cambridge University Press, 1978; Samuel Barnes, Max Kaase et al., *Political Action*. Beverly Hills: Sage Publications, 1979; Pippa Norris, *The Democratic Phoenix*. New York: Cambridge University Press, 1999; Russell Dalton, *Citizen Politics*, 4th ed. Washington, DC: CQ Press, 2006.
13. T. H. Marshall, *Citizenship and Social Class*, ed. T. Bottomore. London: Pluto Press; 1992 originally published 1950; Ole Borre and Elinor Scarbrough, eds., *The Scope of Government*. Oxford: Oxford University Press, 1995.
14. The ISSP data were provided by the Zentralarchiv für empirische Sozialforschung at the University of Cologne (ZA 3950). The 2004 ISSP includes: the United States, Australia, Austria, Britain, Canada, Denmark, Finland, Flanders, France, Germany, Ireland, Japan, New Zealand, Netherlands, Norway, Portugal, Spain, Sweden, and Switzerland. I do not include the new democracies in this survey because we are focusing on how citizenship has evolved in affluent, established democracies. Different causal processes are likely at work in new democracies as people first learn democratic citizenship.
15. I replicated the two-dimensional factor structure described in Chapter 2. Engaged citizenship was the first dimension, explaining 25.9 percent of the variance in these ten items; and citizen duty was the second dimension (21.7 percent variance). In general terms, the factor analysis for these nineteen nations produced the same general structure as for the U.S. analyses. I then computed factor scores for the two dimensions, and the average scores for each nation locate nations in Figure 8.2.
16. The U.S. patterns in Figure 8.1 are slightly different in absolute values from the generational comparisons of Figure 3.1 because the citizenship scores were recalculated based on the pooled factor analysis of all nineteen nations. Generation groups are defined in the same way as in Figure 3.1: Pre-WWII are those who came of age before 1946; boomers came of age between 1946 and 1960; the

Sixties generation was between 1961 and 1975; Generation X was between 1976 and 1990; Generation Y was after 1990.

17. For instance, there are small age differences in the importance attached to understanding the opinions of others or helping those in need throughout the world, but the young are distinctly more likely to say it is important to keep watch on government and be active in associations.

18. National Conference on Citizenship, *America's Civic Health Index: Broken Engagement*. Washington: National Conference on Citizenship, 2006 (www.ncoc.org): 4. The report also presents a measure of America's civic health, which shows an improvement since 2000; but then the report drops "three controversial measures" to produce a continuing decline since 2000: 8.

19. Ibid., 4.

20. Martin Wattenberg, *Where Have All the Voters Gone?* Cambridge: Harvard University Press, 2002; Robert Putnam ed., *Democracies in Flux*. Oxford: Oxford University Press, 2002; Russell Dalton and Martin Wattenberg, eds., *Parties without Partisans*. Oxford: Oxford University Press, 2000, ch. 3.

21. The question asked: "Here are some different forms of political and social action that people can take. Please indicate, for each one, whether you have done any of these things in the past year."

22. The 2002 European Social Survey and the 2005 U.S. Citizens, Involvement, and Democracy surveys also included a battery of different political activities that people might have done in the previous twelve months. Similar to the ISSP findings, fewer Americans vote in national elections, and Americans are less likely than Europeans to buy or avoid products for political reasons. For most other measures, however, Americans are more active than Europeans. For instance, 35 percent of Americans have signed a petition in the past two years, compared to 28 percent of Europeans; 23 percent of Americans have displayed campaign buttons or stickers during an election, compared to 9 percent of Europeans; and 21 percent of Americans have contributed money to a political cause, compared to 8 percent of Europeans. Similar cross-national patterns emerge from the Comparative Study of Electoral Systems project, Russell Dalton, "The myth of the disengaged American." In *Public Opinion Pros* (October 2005), also reprinted at www.cses.org.

23. Factor analyses identified two dimensions. The electoral dimension includes vote, discussing politics, and trying to convince others. The remaining items are strongly related to a second, non-electoral dimension. I then computed factor scores on both dimensions and compared national scores in Figure 8.5.

24. Mark Peffley and Robert Rohrschneider, "Democratization and political tolerance in seventeen countries: A multi-level model of democratic learning." *Political Research Quarterly* (2003) 56: 243–257.

25. Ibid.

26. Ibid.; also see Chapter 5.

27. Spain, for instance, does not follow the general pattern. First, both dimensions of citizenship are negatively related to tolerance in Spain. On further examination, I found that the general dimensions of citizenship are not configured in the same way among the Spanish sample, which may explain some of the divergence.

28. Alan Wolfe, *Does American Democracy Still Work?* New Haven: Yale University Press, 2006; Fareed Zakaria, *The Future of Freedom: Illiberal Democracy at Home and Abroad*. New York: Norton, 2003; Stephen Craig, *The Malevolent Leaders: Popular Discontent in America*. Boulder, CO: Westview Press, 1993; E. J. Dionne, *Why Americans Hate Politics*. New York: Simon & Schuster, 1991; John Hibbing and Elizabeth Theiss-Morse, *Congress as Public Enemy: Public Attitudes toward American Political Institutions*. New York: Cambridge University Press, 1995; Joseph Nye, Philip Zelikow, and David King, eds., *Why Americans Mistrust Government*. Cambridge, MA: Harvard University Press, 1997.

29. Associated Press, May 4, 1999.

30. Almond and Verba, *The Civic Culture;* also see Lipset, *The First New Nation*.

31. Russell Dalton, *Democratic Challenges, Democratic Choices*. Oxford: Oxford University Press, 2004.

32. Similarly, social rights are positively related to engaged citizenship (r=.26) and citizen duty (r=.17).

33. In separate analyses replicating those in Figure 7.2, citizen duty is more strongly related to trust in government (r=.17) than is engaged citizenship (r=.10). This implies that changing citizenship norms are increasing the percentage of critical citizens who are dissatisfied with government but more committed to democratic values.

34. Jean-Francois Revel provides a very sympathetic view of the American political culture from a European perspective, while also citing the critical European literature: *Anti-Americanism*. San Francisco: Encounter Books, 2000.

35. Stuart Weir and David Beetham, *Political Power and Democratic Control in Britain: The Democratic Audit of the United Kingdom.* London: Routledge, 2000.

CHAPTER 9

1. Karl Mannheim, *Freedom, Power and Democratic Planning,* quoted in T. Brennan, *Political Education and Democracy.* Cambridge: Cambridge University, 1981, 106.
2. Stephen Macedo et al., *Democracy at Risk: How Political Choices Undermine Citizen Participation, and What We Can Do about It.* Washington, DC: Brookings Institution Press, 2005; Fareed Zakaria, *The Future of Freedom: Illiberal Democracy at Home and Abroad.* New York: Norton, 2003; John Hibbing and Elizabeth Theiss-Morse, *Stealth Democracy: Americans' Beliefs about How Government Should Work.* New York: Cambridge University Press, 2002; Robert Putnam, *Bowling Alone: The Collapse and Renewal of American Community.* New York: Simon and Schuster, 2000.
3. Seymour Martin Lipset, *American Exceptionalism: A Double-Edged Sword.* New York: W.W. Norton, 1997: 267, offered a refreshingly balanced statement that summarizes our view: "The critics [of America] have exaggerated many of the problems in the quest to demonstrate decay. There is, however, no denying that the impression of a change in basic values exists, and to dismiss public perception [of crisis] as somehow wrong or misinformed is to deny the reality of individual experience.
4. Tom Brokaw, *The Greatest Generation.* New York: Random House, 1998; also see discussion in chapters 2 and 3.
5. I want to thank E.J. Dionne for helping me develop this description. He claims to prefer vinyl records of Frank Sinatra, but I see an iPod in his future.
6. Gabriel Almond, "The Civic Culture: Prehistory, Retrospect, and Prospect." Paper published by the Center for the Study of Democracy: http://repositories.cdlib.org/csd/96-01/.
7. Harry Eckstein, for example, discussed the concept of balanced disparities as one way to generate a balanced democratic culture. Harry Eckstein, *Division and Cohesion in Democracy.* Princeton: Princeton University Press, 1966.
8. Gabriel Almond and Sidney Verba, *The Civic Culture.* Princeton: Princeton University Press, 1963.
9. Putnam, *Bowling Alone.*
10. Francis Fukuyama, *The Great Disruption.* New York: Touchstone, 2000, 15.
11. For example, Robert Wuthnow, United States: "Bridging the privileged and marginalized?" In Robert Putnam, ed., *Democracies in Flux: The Evolution of Social Capital in Contemporary America.* Oxford: Oxford University Press, 2002; Macedo et al. *Democracy at Risk,* ch. 4.
12. Martin Wattenberg, *Is Voting for Young People?* New York: Longman, 2006.
13. This is based on analyses of the impact of distrust in government: Marc Hetherington, *Why Trust Matters: Declining Political Trust and the Demise of American Liberalism.* Princeton: Princeton University Press, 2005; Russell Dalton, *Democratic Challenges, Democratic Choices.* Oxford: Oxford University Press, 2004, ch. 9.
14. For example, Jonathan Cohn, "A lost political generation?" *New Prospect* (1992) 9; Ted Halstead, "A politics for Generation X." *The Atlantic Monthly* (August 1999).
15. Jean M. Twenge, *Generation Me.* New York: Free Press, 2006; also see William Damon, *The Moral Child.* New York: Free Press, 1996.
16. Cohn, "A lost political generation?": 30.
17. In contrast to Hillary Clinton's claim, the National Research Council has examined the empirical evidence and asked whether young people are working too much and too soon, so that it interferes with school and long-term career development: *Protecting Youth at Work.* Washington, DC: National Academy Press, 1998.
18. Ronald Inglehart, *Culture Shift in Advanced Industrial Society.* Princeton: Princeton University Press, 1990; Ronald Inglehart, *Modernization and Postmodernization.* Princeton: Princeton University Press, 1997.
19. For instance, one reviewer of this manuscript maintained that *Democracy at Risk* focused on institutional reforms to improve the democratic process and thus criticisms of its assumptions about youth and social change were unwarranted. However, in order to fix a problem it has to be correctly diagnosed in the first place. One of this book's basic arguments is that many analysts have gotten the diagnosis wrong, and so their proposed reforms are questionable.

20. Wattenberg, *Is Voting for Young People?*, ch. 7; Arend Lijphart, "Unequal participation: Democracy's unresolved dilemma," *American Political Science Review* 91 (1997): 1–14.

21. Alison Fields, "The youth challenge: Participating in democracy." Carnegie Corporation of New York, 2003.

22. For a discussion of the potential for Internet voting see Michael Alvarez et al., *Point, Click and Vote.* Washington, DC: Brookings, 2004.

23. Bruce Cain, Russell Dalton, and Susan Scarrow, eds., *Democracy Transformed?: Expanding Citizen Access in Advanced Industrial Democracies.* Oxford: Oxford University Press, 2003.

24. Cain, Dalton, and Scarrow, ch. 13; also Verba, Schlozman, and Brady, *Voice and Equality.*

25. The patterns over time are unclear. It appears that the decline in election turnout is greater among individuals with lower social status: Martin Wattenberg, *Where Have All the Voters Gone?* Cambridge: Harvard University Press, 2002. However, research does not show a growth in political inequality for other forms of political participation: Henry Brady, Henry, Kay Lehman Schlozman, Sidney Verba, and Laurel Elms. "Who bowls? The (un)changing stratification of participation." In Barbara Norrander and Clyde Wilcox, eds., *Understanding Public Opinion.* Washington, DC: CQ Press, 2002. Thus, the major patterns of inequality appear to be across different forms of action, rather than trends over time.

EPILOGUE

1. This description is drawn from Elizabeth Holmes, "Too young to vote, but old enough to caucus in Iowa," *Wall Street Journal* (October 10, 2007).

2. David Plouffe, "Enthusiasm and organization: A path to the nomination" (http://my.barackobama .com/page/community/post/dplouffe/CWT2).

3. David von Drehle, "Obama's youth vote triumph," *Time* (January 4, 2008). Skepticism about youth participation was a recurring theme in early reports of the primary campaign: Adam Nagourney, "Will Obama rock the youth vote?" *New York Times* (October 8, 2007); Andrew Romano, "The audacity of youth," *Newsweek* (October 9, 2007); Jill Lawrence, "Moved up Iowa caucuses could hinder youth vote," *USA Today* (November 11, 2007).

4. Many of the factors that explained Obama's appeal to the young, such as his opposition to the Iraq war and his emphasis on change in a year when most Americans thought the country was on the wrong track, also attracted older voters in the Democratic primaries. Here, however, we focus on the factors that explain Obama's disproportionate support among the young beyond his general success in the election.

5. Center for Information and Research on Civic Learning and Engagement (CIRCLE), "Revised estimates show higher turnout than expected: Iowa youth turnout rate more than triples" (January 4, 2007; www.civicyouth.org/PopUps/PR_08_Iowa_turnout_Jan4.pdf).

6. Pew Research Center, "Young voters in the 2008 presidential primaries" (February 11, 2008; http:// pewresearch.org/pubs/730/young-voters). There is evidence that exit polls may overestimate turnout by youth and some other groups, but this is less likely to change the patterns across elections. In addition, as research identified possible biases, the methodology of exit polls has been changed to improve their accuracy. See Michael McDonald, "A cross-validation of voter registration files and election survey demographics," *Public Opinion Quarterly* 71 (2007): 588–602.

7. The data include contests in Alabama, Arizona, Arkansas, California, Connecticut, Delaware, Georgia, Iowa, Illinois, Massachusetts, Missouri, Nevada, New Hampshire, New Jersey, New Mexico, New York, South Carolina, Tennessee, and Utah. In a few cases the 17–24-year-old group was not listed separately from the 25–29-year-olds; in these cases we filled in the same value for both groups.

8. See, for instance, Robert Putnam, "The rebirth of American civic life," *Boston Globe* (March 2, 2008).

9. YouTube's entertainment potential also benefited the Obama campaign. Obama girl's "I've got a crush on Obama" (and other Barelypolitical.com videos) stimulated interest in his campaign; the initial Obama girl video was viewed more than 8 million times by the end of the primary campaign. The will.i.am video "Yes we can" also recorded more than 8 million views by the end of the primaries, and his "We are the ones" video had more than 2 million views. It was not all entertainment. The "A More Perfect Union" speech on race had more than 1 million views on YouTube and another 4 million views on the Obama campaign Web site.

   In contrast, the most commonly viewed YouTube video on Hillary Clinton was the critical parody of Apple Computer's 1984 Super Bowl ad (5 million views by June 2008). The other heavily viewed Clinton YouTube videos were largely critical of the campaign.

10. Research finds that in-person contacting is a very effective way to mobilize young people. *Young Voter Mobilization Tactics.* Washington, DC: George Washington University Graduate School of Management, 2008; www.civicyouth.org/PopUps/Young_Voters_Guide.pdf.

11. Tim Dickinson, "The machinery of hope," *Rollingstone.com* (March 20, 2008).

12. By the end of May 2008 the Obama campaign had raised an unprecedented $287.5 million, largely through online donations (compared to $219 million for Clinton and $115 million for McCain). In February 2008, for instance, Obama's campaign raised a record-setting $55 million, $45 million of it over the Internet, without the candidate himself hosting a single fund-raiser. Joshua Green, "The amazing money machine," *Atlantic Monthly* (June 2008).

13. Dickinson, "The machinery of hope."

14. Alison Fields, *The Youth Challenge: Participating in Democracy.* Carnegie Corporation of New York, 2003, (http://www.carnegie.org/pdf/youthchallenge.pdf).

15. A UC Irvine student reminded me that Morgan Freeman also played the role of U.S. president in the movie *Deep Impact* and God in *Bruce Almighty.* Young Americans have grown up with a much different media portrayal of African Americans than their parents or grandparents did.

16. We expect that if Hillary Clinton had positioned herself as an agent of change and was running against the other candidates in the Democratic primaries, young engaged citizens might have voted disproportionately for her. But by running based on experience and the old politics, Clinton actively sought votes from older voters, the less-educated, and rural residents. Even young women leaned toward Obama in most primaries.

17. Many who criticized the lack of electoral participation by the young viewed it as an almost inevitable feature of a generation raised on television and an entertainment-oriented mass culture, and they were pessimistic about the potential for change without major institutional reforms such as compulsory voting. See Martin Wattenberg, *Is Voting for Young People?* 2nd ed. New York: Longman, 2007; Robert Putnam, *Bowling Alone.* New York: Simon and Schuster, 2000. The 2008 campaign showed that a different approach could engage young people. See Chapters 4 and 9; also see Fields, *The Youth Challenge*; and Jane Eisner, *Taking Back the Vote: Getting American Youth Involved in Our Democracy.* New York: Beacon Press, 2004.

18. Rock the Vote gave away a downloadable version of Sheryl Crow's new album to anyone who persuaded a friend to register to vote. When music groups got 150 of their fans to register to vote through a Myspace link, Rock the Vote hosted the band's songs on their Web site. The Ultimate College Bowl on Myspace had a contest between universities to sign up new voters; the campus with the most new voters won a concert by Death Cab for Cutie or Colin Meloy. Declareyourself.com partnered with MTV and registered nearly a million new voters for the 2008 election. The Obama campaign developed an app for the iPhone that used the stored phone numbers to produce a mini campaign phone bank, streamed news from the campaign Web site, and included a button to automatically donate to the campaign. In the weeks leading up to the election, the Obama campaign began running campaign ads in online computer games such as NASCAR 09, NHL 09, NBA Live 08, and Need for Speed. One of the most creative steps was Sarah Silverman's "The Great Schlep" campaign that encouraged young Jews to visit their grandparents in Florida and lobby them to vote for Obama.

19. CIRCLE, "Youth Turnout Rate Rises to at Least 52%" (November 7, 2008; www.civicyouth.org); Rockthevote, "Youth vote rivals largest in American history" (November 5, 2008; www.rockthevote.com). These estimates are based on exit polls statistics and initial estimates of turnout percentages. Past exit polls overestimated youth turnout, and so Figure 2 lists a 4 percent increase, which is at the low end of the current range of estimates. More precise data will come from the Current Population Surveys of the U.S. Census Bureau that will be available in spring 2009.

20. Edison Media Research conducted a national election estimate for the major television networks and on a subscription basis for newspapers. They combined traditional exit polls on election day with estimates of early voting patterns in each state. For three states they conducted election day interviews; the study had 17,836 respondents spread across all fifty states. I obtained these data from the published results on MSNBC.COM. I completed these analyses in early November 2008, and they provide a preliminary estimate of voting patterns.

21. John B. Judis and Ruy Teixeira, *The Emerging Democratic Majority.* New York: Scribner, 2002.

22. Mark Franklin et al., *Voter Turnout and the Dynamics of Electoral Competition in Established Democracies since 1945.* New York: Cambridge University Press, 2004.

23. Since 2000 we have learned how imperfect the voting system is in the United States. There are special problems for youth voters. Voter registration is often difficult if students live at college; some local

registrars of voting do not accept dormitory addresses as evidence of residence. On election day, new voter identification laws require documentation that is not generally available to students (such as a utility bill to prove residency). In 2000 and 2004 there were also cases where too few voting booths were allocated to precincts with a large student composition, which produced long lines if one wanted to vote. See Laura Fitzpatrick, "College students still face voting stumbling blocks," *Time* (October 14, 2008).

24. Russell Dalton, *Citizen Politics: Public Opinion and Political Parties in Advanced Industrial Democracies.* (Washington, DC: CQ Press, 2008, ch. 9).

25. Scott Keeter, Juliana Menasce Horowitz, and Alec Tyson, "Gen Dems: The party's advantage among young voters widens," Pew Center for People and the Press (April 28, 2008; http://pewresearch.org/pubs/813/gen-dems).

INDEX